T0383436

Optimizing Your Capacity to Care

A Systems Approach to Hospital and
Population Health Management

Optimizing Your Capacity to Care

A Systems Approach to Hospital and Population Health Management

Pierce Story, MPHM

Contributions by Joe Tye and Peter W. Wood

CRC Press
Taylor & Francis Group
Boca Raton   London   New York

CRC Press is an imprint of the
Taylor & Francis Group, an **informa** business

A PRODUCTIVITY PRESS BOOK

CRC Press
Taylor & Francis Group
6000 Broken Sound Parkway NW, Suite 300
Boca Raton, FL 33487-2742

© 2016 by Taylor & Francis Group, LLC
CRC Press is an imprint of Taylor & Francis Group, an Informa business

No claim to original U.S. Government works

Printed on acid-free paper
Version Date: 20160420

International Standard Book Number-13: 978-1-4665-9396-1 (Hardback)

Visit the Taylor & Francis Web site at
http://www.taylorandfrancis.com

and the CRC Press Web site at
http://www.crcpress.com

Contents

Preface: Kenji's Revelation

Since Kenji came to healthcare from an industrial engineering job at the local Toyota factory some seven years ago, much had changed. While he thought he could readily bring his Japan-instructed knowledge of Lean and continuous improvement from his beloved auto plant to his local hospital, the obstacles he faced made him rethink his approach and methodologies. He encountered staff and managers who not only had not heard of the performance improvement methodologies upon which he'd learned to rely, but resisted change every step of the way. Furthermore, he'd come to know that his hospital leadership and the physicians in the community were far less interested in workload optimization and dramatic improvements in efficiency than he was. Yes, they understood the need for quality improvement and could quote the hospital's motto from memory ("CARES," a nonsensical acronym that allegedly represented the goals of a better workplace and service to the community). But when push came to shove, he'd found that they had to focus their attention on keeping the doors open, and radical process change was just ... well, radical.

He'd also come to appreciate the extremes of variability and the extent of the interdependencies within hospital operations that were not present at his factory. There were no production lines here, no robotic precision, and no perfected takt times for each process. Work cells didn't seamlessly connect, as they might be three floors and two hallways away. He'd come to rely on tools that he thought he'd put permanently away after engineering school, like discrete-event and systems simulation and multilinear regression. He had come to understand that processes were done consistently only "sometimes, except when ...," and that gaining staff trust is as important as having data to make your point. And he'd come to appreciate the often enormous effort required to create process consistency, reduce variability, and instill staff with a deep understanding of interdependencies, waste, and patient-centeredness. Healthcare was just harder.

This had led him away from his beloved Lean as the end-all-be-all methodology. In fact, as he looked around the industry and chatted with colleagues, he realized that "lean" meant anything and everything related to process improvement, and often had little if anything to do with the approach, tools, and philosophy of its originators. Lean was just easier to say than "process and performance improvement." Furthermore, Lean hadn't done that well in healthcare, anyway. Though it was still the buzzword of the day, a quick glance at the CMS Hospital Compare website revealed that long-time and famously Lean hospitals did no better on key performance indicators than the average hospital. Their ED lengths of stay were the same as his, if not worse! So, if the best ones, those who had started "Lean Institutes" and lean training programs, weren't doing much better than the rest, what was the point? Thus he had opened his eyes quite a bit in recent years, and developed a whole new perspective.

Also fascinating for him as an engineer was seeing the direction that national healthcare "reform" was taking. While he completely understood the need for reform, it seemed to him that the current effort was less about improving the care of patients or lowering the cost than it was about shuffling who paid the bills. He was frustrated to see ACOs and Pay-for-Performance considered innovative ideas while the real constraints to improved metrics, access, and capacity were the fee-for-service reimbursement systems, age-old care and operational models, soul-crushing cultures, and outdated attitudes and relationships. Based on what the press was reporting, ACOs were themselves in need of lots of innovation. And the much-maligned insurance companies were charging customers more than ever while offering less coverage. It seemed as if "reform" was doing more to preserve and extend the current flawed system than to correct it.

Yet Kenji had refused to quit. Over the years, he'd continued to try to improve the systems within his own hospital's four walls, while realizing that his mother-in-law's illness and eventual passing away gave him ideas and inspiration to look outside his hospital to the community writ large for optimization opportunities and approaches. Thus he'd continued to build his internal POT, Performance Optimization Team. He'd decided that "performance improvement" seemed like such a limited goal and chose to use optimization instead. He also began to build "Care Circles" around patients with the help of his church and allies in his hospital's Case Management Department and Pastoral Services.

For the new Care Circles, patients were asked if they belonged to a church as they were registered for an inpatient stay or extensive surgery (with respect to privacy and the wishes of the patient, of course). Using an empty box in the registration field in their EMR software, registrars began regularly collecting this single but vital piece of data. If the patient's church had agreed to participate in the Care Circle program, they were contacted (with the written permission of patients) as their member-patients were admitted. This initiated a series of volunteer support services, both during and after patient discharge. These services included small tasks, such as the all-important ride home from the hospital, grocery store runs or walking the patient's dog; as well as more critical tasks such as monitoring the food intake, blood pressure, and weight of chronically ill patients once they were back at home. Though mostly non-clinical, these tasks proved to be invaluable to patients as they were discharged back into the community for care. Indeed, so passionate was Kenji about his idea that he was already expanding the initial efforts to other churches in his community, and had begun talks with the local Rotary Club about enlisting its membership.

He'd always known it was the "right thing to do." Indeed, he started it because his mother-in-law had so needed post-discharge, in-home help that neither he nor his wife had the time to do. While she had home-care nurses come by periodically, they were not going to help her keep watch on her sweet-tooth or make sure she got outside and walked each day. These, Kenji determined, were the tasks that anyone with a caring heart could manage. But Kenji never expected the ancillary results that the program had elicited.

Over the first 2 years of the program, the small number of Care Circles began to slowly impact length of stay (LOS) in the hospital. After some research and analytics, it turned out that his "Care Circle" patients had consistently lower LOS than other patients with like DRGs. After digging further, he found that patients in the Care Circles had fewer "excuses" for not going home than did the other patients.

Commonly reported constraints to discharge, such as the typical "Waiting for a ride from family," "Patient wanted to eat lunch before they left," "No one at home," etc., were simply not an issue for patients with a strong Care Circle around them. Rather, these patients were ready to go when their discharge day came, and often hounded their physicians and nurses to release them to go home early!

Furthermore, his Care Circle patients had nearly a zero rate of readmissions in the first 90 days. That's ninety … not thirty … NINETY! This, it was revealed through patient and physician interviews, was a result of the ongoing and person-to-person care that Care Circle patients received in addition to their normal post-discharge clinical care. Care Circle patients missed fewer follow-up appointments, maintained compliance with medications and physician directives more consistently, and were generally healthier than their non-Care Circle counterparts. This was a stunning, though unexpected, result of what was originally just good ol' fashioned charitable work of church-going folk.

And perhaps best of all, this was big news for his hospital leaders who [finally!!!] began to take notice of Kenji's work. After a presentation to the C-Suite of the hospital, he had been asked to present to the Medical Executive Committee and the Board of Directors on the potential for the Care Circle concept to expand and include internal, dedicated hospital resources to help manage a larger system of volunteers.

This, needless to say, impressed his superiors and co-workers, especially since his hospital had announced it was being purchased by the Varibigg Healthcare Corporation, a system of more than 75 facilities across the southeast. Varibigg was known for its cost–control measures, and Kenji hoped that Varibigg senior staff would see what his little group of systems engineers in his little hospital had done in recent years to improve care while controlling costs. Secretly, Kenji had thought about a position high-up at Varibigg, managing a large team of health-systems engineers and Care Circle coordinators in optimization efforts throughout the Varibigg family of hospitals. Even if a promotion wasn't in the offing, he'd hoped to at least make contact with more "advanced" counterparts in Varibigg hospitals elsewhere, so as to share and get new ideas for performance improvement.

Still, Kenji felt there was more that he needed to do to help his hospital reach a higher level of performance. He knew that they would need it as reimbursements continued to be cut and "reform," in whatever form it took, inched its way forward. He'd already worked in the ED, the OR, admissions and discharges. He'd done Value-Stream maps and simulations in nearly every major department in the facility. Using simulation and advanced analytical techniques, he'd demonstrated clearly the need for dramatic change to the surgical schedule, alterations to the way in which patients were admitted and discharged, and staffing patterns that would be based on patient demand and workload rather than nurse work-hour preferences or union rules and regulations. And, indeed, he and his team had made great progress. Nonetheless, he knew, and his simulation models had proven, that much more could be done.

But he still struggled with a few roadblocks. Because he was not a senior manager and did not have that level of authority, he could not force staff to change their ways. He could only cajole, beg, and occasionally bribe with offers of pizza or Krispy Kreme Donuts (he'd bought so many that he swore he knew precisely when the "Hot Now" sign would be turned on during any given day). He needed more of the staff to adopt bigger changes rather than being forced to accept them. While he was able to monitor them, they did OK, if not great. But, as soon as he moved on to the next project and the accountability waned, they occasionally lapsed into the old behavior. They needed to "own" the projects and the outcomes, just like he did.

Furthermore, physicians were often a pain in his keister. Though some were quite nice and cooperative, others remained in the ivory towers of old, convinced that somehow they were immune from the requirements of efficiency, effectiveness, and collaboration. They were stubbornly "old school," and resisted change seemingly for spite, even if it was clear that the proposed change would help them. In many cases, physicians hated the staff as much as the staff hated the physicians. And so, of course, the finger-pointing blame-game had started many years ago and continued unabated as a near art form of stubbornness and childishness. The docs, too, needed to "own" the changes. But since they were often less invested in the success of the hospital than the staff, they were less likely to truly "own" their performance improvement efforts. After all, if Kenji's hospital were to close, the docs would just migrate down the street to the competitor, or so they convinced themselves.

And don't even start him on the nurse union representatives (who seemed inherently and always opposed to anything new and different, even before hearing how it could help the nurses and their patients). They just didn't get how important efficiencies and workload optimization could be for staff satisfaction, retention, and culture. They were always too worried that Kenji was secretly trying to cut staff.

But perhaps most frustrating was the inability to get people to see his "big picture." Change was coming, whether the staff, managers, and physicians at his hospital or Varibigg realized it or not. And that change was going to be more or less painful, depending on how they embraced the need to optimize capacity now. Without serious, holistic efforts to change this facility, the changes coming might swamp them like a row boat in a tidal wave.

Though he had started them down the path toward capacity optimization, there were still a few elements of what he called "the basic blocking and tackling of capacity management" that they were not yet doing. Not even close! They still didn't manage admissions properly, and the ED still sometimes reacted as if every day's volume was somehow unforeseen. The unit managers seemed to think, "How on earth did all the patients come to need to be discharged today?" and "The ED always holds their admissions for shift-change," as if he hadn't shown them the admission patterns a hundred times. Of course, and sometimes rightfully, the staff would point at the physicians, both attending and consulting, and blame their general recalcitrance and ignorance for the plight they suffered each day.

Thus was Kenji's revelation. Kenji had decided that bringing all these changes together into a cohesive, integrated "capacity strategy" could not be mandated, even if his CEO or Varibigg were willing to take charge. No, these were changes that had to be internalized by every staff person, physician, and manager in the facility. Everyone had to own the patients they served, the facility they worked in, and the operational model that they supported. Everyone had to OWN it. All of it.

And his vision was one that scared a few people ... quite a few, in fact. His was a bold vision of entirely new operational models throughout the hospital. Why, he thought, should we continue to tune up the '62 Studebaker that was the ED patient care model? Why not light the fuse, blow it up, and build a 2016 Lexus that would perform better, faster, and more efficiently? What was the point of keeping the traditional impatient operational models, the "old" surgical schedule, and the "antique" relationships with external community resources? Why were we still trying to keep these clunkers on the road?

His role as a health systems engineer was, in part, to optimize the "Capacity to Care" of his hospital, so as to best serve his community as needed. This meant instilling a distinct and palpable sense of ownership by the caregivers, physicians, managers, executives, and all other workers at his facility such that true optimization of capacity could occur using bold new operational models. All those employed there would own each and every aspect of the hospital's function, from the front door to the loading dock.

Furthermore, his role entailed the continued expansion of the Care Circle concept into larger and larger areas of the community. More patients, physicians, and volunteers would gradually join in, helping aid patients in caring for themselves and taking charge of their own lives and bodies. While it would help his hospital with its metrics, the larger goal of patient wellness, cost reduction, and efficiency would be enhanced.

And through this, his newly envisioned role would begin to create an entirely new approach to patient health and wellness in the community writ large that not only cared for current and potential illness but encouraged, nay demanded, the ownership of the human body by its wearer. This ownership would drive out at least some of the excess of the system, and change the way people engaged with healthcare providers and facilities. It would, of course, take years to make this change, which would involve as many communal resources and contact points as he could muster. But it was the only way to holistically and completely impact the healthcare system.

Kenji leaned back in his leather chair, brought his mind back to the reality of his office, and slowly moved his eyes across his white-board-painted office walls. Only the single bookshelf interrupted the flow of the massive undertaking he'd inscribed in erasable marker on the walls of his office. Nearly every open space, even the back of his door, was painted with white-board paint. And now nearly every white space contained a piece of his bold vision for the future. And bold it was.

A glance at his watch told him the kids were home from school, and it would soon be dinnertime at home. As he put his feet on the desk and closed his eyes again, he thought of the first night he was introduced to the disaster of healthcare processes, that night nearly eight years ago when his son had to be taken to the ED of the hospital he now so desperately wanted to change. So many changes, so little time. But, he laughed to himself, time flies when you're having fun, and God had placed him in this spot for this job in this place. Good thing he was still young enough, and perhaps just naive enough, to pull it off.

Acknowledgments

First, as always, I gladly acknowledge a gracious and loving God who allows me to use the gifts He gave, as I am able and willing, for His glory and the betterment of my fellow man. While I hold no pretense that I have solved any of the world's problems herein, I hope that this effort will, somehow and in some way, serve God's purposes for my life and the lives of others.

I also joyfully acknowledge my beloved wife, Heather. Without her, my life would be dreadfully boring and empty. She is my ever-present source of the most positive thoughts, no matter what the situation, and is my inspiration, my strength, and my dearest friend. She is the reason this text exists, the reason it is edited at all, and, most importantly, the reason I look forward to each and every day.

Of course, I must always acknowledge my parents whose direction started me on the course of life and who supported me through even my worst mistakes. Also, my friends, near and distant, who offer support and confidence when times get rough, and critiques to force me to challenge my own thinking. Phil (alias PPS) and David (the best of Best Men!) and their lovely wives, Chuck and Thomas (dear friends, business colleagues, and Christian brothers), Andrew (the best darned boat captain ever!), and the many others who have touched my life in so many ways.

Of course, how could I begin to acknowledge those who have supported me without mentioning my dear colleague Victor? Without his Mensa-plus brain and Puritan-esque work ethic, these ideas would have remained nothing more than the scattered thoughts of a frustrated mind. Victor brought ideas to life, then nurtured them to be something better than they might have been in lesser hands. To him I am forever grateful.

I was also blessed to convince two of the industry's true visionaries, Joe Tye and Peter Wood, to pen chapters for this book, and I would be remiss if I did not mention them here. These passionate experts have written two of the most important components in the book without which neither the book nor the concepts purported herein would be of the highest possible value. They have added so much depth, breadth, and perspective to this effort that it simply would not be the same without their additions. You will likely find, as I have, that their concepts are the foundation which lies underneath the building blocks of a successful transformation of our healthcare system. They complete the work that I have begun herein, or perhaps more accurately, I try to complement theirs.

I would also like to acknowledge two great men who have gone on to be with the Lord, Drs. Joe Fortuna and Dave Eitel. Dr. Fortuna influenced me in many ways, and was the source of much of my learning on the machinations of the payment systems. He had an ongoing and strong faith in me (for some unknown reason) and continued to support me and push me forward. He was a great advocate for change in health-care, and worked tirelessly throughout his disease-shortened career to bring meaningful change to the system.

Likewise, Dr. Eitel was an engineer by thinking and a compassionate doctor by training. The blend made him a unique and special man who loved healthcare almost as much as he loved his family. A tireless champion, Dave worked hard to bring fresh ideas to the often staid thinking of our business until disease finally took him home.

These two men influenced me as much as they influenced the business and industry they served so selflessly and tirelessly. They were both, each in his own way, great contributors to the improvement of healthcare.

I also want to thank my detractors, whose insistence on the purity, sanctity, and exclusive value of their own regimented methodologies and approaches gave me inspiration to drive on, ask harder questions, be as objective as possible, and generate new ideas for the betterment of healthcare.

Not least, I would also like to thank Kristine, my contact at this publisher, who patiently waited and occasionally nudged, else this text might never have seen the light of day.

Thanks, all, for your help, prayers, and support.

Author

Pierce Story is the co-founder of Capacity Strategies, Inc., a firm dedicated to the optimization of the "Capacity to Care" in hospitals and communities. His unique expertise lies in "Dynamic Care Capacity Management" (a concept he has developed over the past 15 years); process and systems optimization; resource utilization; and the application of systems dynamics and process simulation to healthcare environments.

During his 25+ years healthcare career, Story has developed several innovative care and business models to improve health system operations and promote population health outcomes. His passion lies in creating holistic, systemic responses to key constraints facing healthcare, especially in low-income and at-risk communities. He has worked extensively in departmental and hospital-wide performance and capacity optimization as well as new facility planning throughout the care continuum, including work in emergency departments, surgical services, inpatient units, and community-based health clinics.

Story has written and lectured on capacity and system optimization, advocating for dynamic, healthcare-specific analytical, quality, and performance improvement tools and methodologies that add to traditional, manufacturing-based PI approaches. His other recent books, *Developing a Poly-Chronic Care Network* and *Dynamic Capacity Management for Healthcare*, detail innovative approaches to the optimization of the "Capacity to Care" throughout both hospitals and communities. Other publications include numerous articles on the use of discrete-event simulation in healthcare and a co-edited book, *Management Engineering for Effective Delivery*. He also trains hospital leaders on the principles of Capacity Management in annual courses held in Maine, South Carolina, and Tennessee.

Story earned his master's in health policy and management from the Edwin Muskie School of Public Policy in Portland, Maine, and is trained in both Six Sigma and Lean methodologies. He has served on the Leadership Council of the American Society for Quality's Healthcare Division, is a diplomate, past president, and former board member of the Society for Health Systems, and is actively engaged in the East Tennessee Health Executives Association.

Story lives with his beloved wife in Knoxville, Tennessee where he enjoys serving God in his local communities, plant collection and landscaping, and riding his vintage Harley-Davidson.

1 Introduction

Even as I write these pages, I remain convinced that I am not the sole owner of some secret formula or divine revelation on healthcare capacity optimization. That is, others think and have thought the same way. This is not a trivial matter, since the concepts herein are commonly seen as "advanced" or "highly sophisticated" by the clients I serve. Very few facilities are using anything like these concepts and approaches effectively or regularly, yet, there are certainly those in the industry who "get it." Indeed, nearly all healthcare professionals who hear and see what I am describing herein, in its entirety, will "get it," and usually rather quickly. This isn't rocket science, but it does require that you think about flight in a certain, unique way. This effort is, in part, meant to help people see healthcare operations and improvement in a new and very different way.

Mind you, there are still too few of us. But there is a rapidly growing group of people who understand the need for a holistic and dynamic approach to process and process improvement (PI), and, as I will call it herein, capacity optimization. I've met them, communed with them, and shared ideas, references, failures, and successes. And I know that their acceptance and support of these ideas means that they are valid and legitimate for the industry, since these people are themselves considered industry leaders. These are people of not only stature in the business but also of similar mindsets who have the tenacity and position to put ideas into practice, but not the calling to write.

Thus, the concepts purported in this book are in many ways similar to those that others, wiser and more experienced than I have developed, tested, and implemented over the years.

So, while there are ideas aplenty in the industry, mine are at least supported by people whom I respect, trust, teach, and learn from. I pen those ideas so that others may be able to glean pearls for use in their own efforts, and through subsequent dialog offer perspectives that will aid all of us. Indeed, many of life's great lessons are taught through the interactions with others rather than learned of our own experience. Sometimes, these interactions lead us to challenge our closely held beliefs, our ideas of how things "ought to be," our "old habits" and stasis, and the way we've done and thought about things for years, even decades. Accepting this challenge is difficult for many and that is why new ideas take so long to become accepted. Yet, each of us, no matter how lowly of status or high of position, has something to offer the world. Every nurse, every tech, every housekeeper, and physician has some pearl of wisdom to offer. This is why we must always and constantly share with and learn from others as we go through the trials and successes of life.

It is therefore our task to offer others the opportunity to share with us as we objectively receive, and simultaneously see past our personal inhibitions to share what we have with others. Keeping an open and objective mindset, and constantly challenging your own assumptions and solutions is perhaps the most difficult but most important element of learning, progress, and science.

I have personally witnessed rigidity of thought and practice among healthcare PI "experts." So rigid was one Lean consultant that she adamantly refused to create process maps using "swimlanes," even though the process we were attempting to map had many concurrently utilized resources in a complex interdependent system. Another was so "pure" in his Lean thinking that he refused to accept data analysis as a viable part of the project. "Lean," he stated adamantly, "is not about data ... it's about people, GEMBA, and waste. We don't need data to teach us anything ... all we have to do is ask the staff about what goes on." Yet another refused to consider the use of simulation when presented with the option, stating boldly "we can figure out everything we need to know from just walking the new processes," even though the ED she was trying to help improve hadn't been built yet. This degree of inflexibility is harmful to the system to be improved, as it signals repression of ideas, creativity, and enthusiasm. Even the best methodologies cannot tolerate such rigidity.

Thus, I contend that we must continue to challenge even the best and most dearly held notions, for just as only through fire is metal hardened and made useful, only through challenges do ideas become stronger. And it is by challenge that I not only learn, but teach and share. This "challenger" mentality has always been with me, I think ... just ask my beloved mother!

So, even if the concepts behind capacity optimization described herein are not the "generally accepted best practice," and are only known and loved by a few, they do in a very real sense challenge the status quo of PI methodologies, thoughts on staff and physician relationships and culture, the effective use of data, information technology (IT) systems, and information, and how we should generally manage the operations of our healthcare facilities. And I pray that this will be an important role for this book within the industry.

WHY THIS TOPIC?

Clearly, healthcare is in need of further optimization. If you've ever had a loved one in a local community hospital, you may know how frightening care can be, how insensitive nurses, physicians, and staff can seem, and how broken the operational systems are. Yes, these are complex systems. But their complexity is no excuse for their failings, and no reason to avoid the path to optimization.

And, yes, costs seem out of control and waste is abundant (I'll address these later in this book). Indeed, the goals of the healthcare system—the real goals, not necessarily those inscribed on the plaque in that lonely corner of the hospital lobby—are distorted by the very reimbursement systems, physician and nurse training programs, and hidden incentives that are supposed to support healthcare delivery.

And while much has been done, much has been written, and many solutions have been tried to improve performance, most healthcare systems have yet to tackle the most significant issues they face in a way that will ensure reasonable success and sustainability. Projects abound! Just recently, I heard of a hospital management team with 86 "priority initiatives," as if an organization could ever have 86 simultaneous priorities without being the size and scale of the federal government. Yet results are slow to come.* Backsliding is more common than sustained success. Mediocrity is accepted, since our goals are often either too limited or so unquantified that we don't know when success or failure has occurred.

Thus, if I am indeed to challenge, this book should press on the stasis and lack of progress in the world of what is known as "Healthcare Performance Improvement."

GOALS OF THIS BOOK

Given all that, I have a few simple goals in writing this book that are aligned with the aforementioned "whys." The first is to provide the industry fresh perspectives on new and/or improved operational models of hospitals and health systems. To achieve this, I will present what I have learned throughout decades of working in healthcare operations: that variability, interdependencies, deep data analytics, patient aggregation, physician alignment strategies, culture, etc., matter ... and matter a lot! In doing so, I hope to provide hospital and health system leaders with a solid knowledge of what I consider to be the essential tools, methodologies, and approaches necessary to successfully optimize the total "capacity to care," and allow them to begin moving, at whatever pace is chosen, toward a true population health model.

The second goal is to provide healthcare leaders and all those in quality and PI with a deeper understanding of that which the most common process improvement methodologies and approaches are NOT providing for the efforts to optimize performance. HINT: You'll need more than Lean in your toolbox!

Though common process improvement methodologies are useful, and offer many great ideas, concepts, and approaches, they lack just enough to keep them from being entirely effective in the dynamic world of healthcare. I cannot tell you how many people wrote and thanked me for penning one of my first works, *Dynamic Capacity Management for Healthcare*. It added to what Lean, Six Sigma, etc., were already doing and offered a very different perspective on performance optimization in the very dynamic environments of healthcare. Thus, herein, I want to continue to offer new tools, concepts, approaches, and methodologies for those who use Lean, Six Sigma, hybrids, etc., as well as those who have become disgruntled with the previous failures of the common methodologies and are therefore seeking something new and entirely different.

Third, to offer readers the basic "blocking and tackling" of capacity optimization. In even what I consider the best-managed facilities, the basics are not being done, or done consistently. Indeed, from what I have seen, every facility could do more to optimize capacity ... much more! This is rather shocking, given how many decades we've been working on process improvement! Yet, it often seems as if we've just started thinking about becoming efficient. This is likely due to myriad factors, from an inappropriate use of manufacturing tools and techniques, to recalcitrant staff, to misaligned incentives for hospitals and physicians, and lack of tangible vision. Therefore, I want to be sure that industry leaders know well the basics,

---

* The "infamous" healthcare systems that claim greatness in performance improvement methodology implementation have spent years, sometimes over a decade, to get where they are. And where they are is, if you peel back the onion skin, not much better than the rest of healthcare.

the "blocking and tackling" of capacity optimization, so that they can quickly get on their way to better performance. This book is meant to help them achieve this relatively simple goal.

Please note that if your hospital/health system is not consistently doing the basic "blocking and tackling" of capacity optimization described herein, don't even think about hiring that multimillion-dollar Lean-consulting firm to back a busload of $3500-per-day recent MBA graduates up to the loading dock and unleash them to do value stream maps. At best, they'll tell you about the same thing that any health systems engineer worth her salt will tell you, which by my experience is about 1/8 to 1/4 of the information you'll get from reading this book. Neither the "big" Lean firms nor the expensive boutique Lean and Lean Six Sigma firms will offer you the kind of improvement opportunities you'll get herein, no matter how much you pay them. Hold off until you are doing the basics. Otherwise, you're wasting your money.

However, the even-better news is that after you implement the basics, you still won't likely need that busload of expensive recent grads. If you are doing these important things, your staff will learn to see things very differently and be able to use that new vision to create new ideas and improvements. Thus, you will find that they are able to create the kinds of changes you will need to continue advancing toward true and full-capacity optimization. The basics can get you as much as 80% of the way ... the new vision of your staff and physicians will show you the rest of the way.

Fourth, I want to ensure that hospitals that undertake capacity optimization understand that it is a holistic effort, encompassing everything from IT to physician relationships to culture change. You can no more optimize your capacity using stone tablets and pixie dust than you can with a toxic nursing culture, siloed clinical departments, or adversarial physician relationships. This approach is intentionally complex and multifaceted. It has to be that way because there is no other way to achieve capacity optimization. Each element left out of the puzzle leaves not just one gap but potentially several as the interdependencies of the system negatively interact.

Yet, I also want to stress that through a holistic approach, you will actually make your efforts easier. By seeing your system as a system, and then addressing all the elements listed herein, you touch upon all the major constraints to optimization simultaneously. One leads to the next and the next, as the interdependencies guide you to the next step in the change effort. And having the system in mind as you make the change means that you will avoid the traps of narrow change implementation: limited value and constrained results. *Note that I use a 100-Day implementation program, creating game-changing leaps in performance rather than small, incremental changes. While stunning to some, my approach has been proven repeatedly.*

Fifth, I want to demonstrate the financial, communal, and personal/human resource benefits of capacity optimization. This is not just about better financial performance. Yes, you will get that, in spades. But capacity optimization is bigger than that. It is also about both the community you serve and the staff you deploy. It is about helping the members of your community own their individual bodies, and helping the staff own their work and patients. It is about changing the way your patients see themselves, those around them, the community they live in, and the healthcare system that they use. It is about changing the way staff see their roles, the patients they care for, and the community they serve, and changing their view to look at care provision as something far more than a means to a paycheck.

It can also be about suicide. Not in the literal sense, of course. Rather, it is about being willing to remake your facilities (i.e., your hospital and all the ancillary services and facilities that are associated with it) into something they currently are not in order to better serve your community. Thus, it is about lighting the fuse that might well lead to blowing up your care delivery models, such as thinking more about keeping patients out of your facilities rather than in them. It is also about changing the culture of your staff and physicians to one of "ownership" rather than "accountability" such that they don't need your supervision any more. That is, working yourself out of a job!

Finally, I most certainly want to provide you a way forward into the future of healthcare delivery. As many suspect, dramatic changes are coming, including at least alterations to the reimbursement systems, quality expectations, and care models. If you wait for the government to provide you with direction, you'll be the last guy in town to modernize, and probably the first to be targeted for takeover or, worse, closure.

Fortunately, the tenets of capacity optimization are inherently aligned with the future of care delivery and reimbursement modification. By addressing the basics of capacity optimization, you'll ensure that you are fully prepared for whatever the market throws at you because your facility(s) will be run as efficiently and effectively as possible, with the inherent ability to flex capacity up or down as needed, throughout your clinical footprint. Your community will be engaged such that capitated and bundled payments can be readily accepted. You will have a cooperative relationship with your key physicians and their processes that ensure that patients are treated well, efficiently, and effectively. You, staff, and physicians will "own" your facility, not just work there, and their old "accountability" will be internalized into "ownership" by the passion they have for the work they do and the community they serve.

Does this seem to be "pie in the sky?" Dreamy? Lala land? Well then, with all due respect, I know by that thought that you are not yet doing all the basics of capacity optimization. In fact, how ridiculous the previous paragraph seems to you indicates how far you've come in your journey toward capacity optimization. If you are further along, it doesn't seem so ethereal. Starting or continuing on the journey will help you and your facility(s) see the potential that lies within that might be hidden by old systems and operational models, habits, and culture.

A CAVEAT TO THE CLAIM OF "HOLISTIC"

Yes, there is a limit to the breadth of this book. Thus, there are gaps that experts in certain fields may see. They wonder if I have captured all the elements of a truly holistic approach to healthcare capacity. They may question the validity of a capacity management approach that does not include much if any detail on their specific area of interest, and might therefore find the entire concept flawed.

However, these readers must understand that there are limits to a book of this scope and scale. And while I attempt to bring forth an option for a "community care" model (the "Care Circle Network" [CCN]), this book by no means can touch every circumstance and possible scenario. Rather, it is meant to provide: (a) an approach, a framework, and specific "to-do's" to achieve capacity optimization, particularly within the hospital and (b) a communal approach to caring for patients outside the hospital that allows for the flexibility to include other factors and specific patient subpopulations. Thus, simply because a specific hospital department or community subpopulation isn't explicitly covered does not mean that they are forgotten or ignored. To the contrary, the inclusion of all areas of the hospital and most subpopulations within the community care models described here is both possible and recommended. I simply cannot cover all of them in detail herein.

One gap that will be clear to those who know their side of the business is mental health. You won't read much about mental health in this book, despite its growing importance to the wellness of our populations.* This is not because I think the subject will be trivial or inconsequential, nor because I think it will be solved on its own, nor because I feel that it should be part of a separate health system. To the contrary, mental health is and likely always will be part of the healthcare system, if for no other reason than many healthcare patients, particularly those with chronic diseases, are also mental health patients. Indeed, according to some studies, the advent of diabetes can increase the likelihood of clinical depression by a significant percentage.

Rather, the gap is due to the inherent limitations of the topic and scale of this book. Indeed, there is an entire book on capacity optimization of the mental health systems waiting to be written! I will therefore freely state that mental health is not represented deeply herein. Yet, I will also strongly state that mental health should be considered as part of a communal approach to wellness. Capacity for the mental health patient population, growing as it is, needs to be part of the discussion of the capacity to care of any and all communities and population health models. This is as true of rural areas as it is of urban areas, perhaps more so.

Other "gaps" are due to the fact that there are only so many hospital processes, departments, and operations I can cover in the breadth of a single book. We will not typically touch on the details of processes within departments such as sterile processing, Cath Lab, Lab, and other ancillary departments. Naturally, as part of a true capacity optimization and management approach, process changes that alter the up- and downstream patterns and "outputs" of these systems relative to the performance of other areas of the hospital (e.g., as Lab turnaround time impacts wait times in the ED or inpatient units) need to be evaluated and managed within the context of system PI efforts, so as to avoid the negative impacts of the interdependencies within and between these areas.

Thus, when I use the term "holistic" and "capacity optimization" know that there are unspoken portions of the healthcare system that are entirely necessary and critically important, but which are not stressed herein. They are and should be part of your capacity management efforts, even if they are not specifically part of the capacity management strategies or community care models mentioned in this book.

---

* Indeed, worldwide, it is estimated that some 700 million people suffer from some form of mental illness.

Finally, as regards limitations to this book, we will only briefly discuss the role of IT innovations and systems. Suffice it to say that the world of IT continues to innovate at a rapid pace. Whether or not these innovations truly aid in capacity optimization will be up to the judgment of the user.

I hope you will find this book to be an enjoyable, educational, and perhaps enlightening, or at least a confirmation that there are others out there who think that same way you do.

2 Healthcare Cost
An Overview of the Issues

A FRANK CONVERSATION ABOUT THE COST
OF THE U.S. HEALTHCARE SYSTEM

The insertion of cost into our discussion is important due to the goals of this book as they relate to population health management (PHM) and the goals of capacity management as a support mechanism to PHM. For if we haven't discussed the cost of the healthcare system, and therefore the return on investment ("ROI") of any changes we might make to our capacity optimization levels, we might not properly understand what we hope to gain from a better managed and more optimized system capacity. Indeed, if optimized capacity does nothing more than make us feel better about our healthcare system, then we have not accomplished two of our primary goals … cost reduction and the general support of PHM as part of capacity optimization.

There are several things that make our healthcare system here in the United States so relatively expensive, despite having what some describe as the best healthcare system in the world. These include

- Healthcare resources that are the most expensive in the world
- Financial incentives within the system as perverse as one could possibly make them
- Wasteful spending on everything from defensive medicine to clinically unnecessary tests and surgeries
- We don't own our bodies, our healthcare, or our healthcare system
- Our expectations for care delivery are often ridiculously high

Let's start with the resource cost issue. Back when the debates on "Obamacare," a.k.a. the Patient Protection and Affordable Care Act (PPACA), a.k.a. the Affordable Care Act, were going on, I recall being amazed and frustrated with the acceptance of the blanket statement that our healthcare system was (and is) the most expensive in the world. Worse was where the blame was laid. The Left commonly laid the blame at the feet of the for-profit insurers and their allegedly well-heeled and overcompensated executives (who, by the way, happen to be among the biggest financial benefactors of the bill's implementation). Also to blame were pharmaceutical manufacturers who seemed to charge exorbitant amounts of money for their patented products, as well as medical device manufacturers and hospitals. Occasionally, someone in the debate might bring up physicians, but only rarely, and usually within the context of a discussion on the ever-pending yet ever-delayed cuts to Medicare reimbursement rates (the so-called "Doctor Fix") or wasteful, defensive spending. But no one ever truly evaluated the cost of the system from a cost-accounting standpoint. If they had, we might have had a very different system.

That's because the cost of our healthcare resources is stunning when put into its proper context. First, any good CEO or health systems engineer knows that at least 65%, and a more commonly estimated 70%–80%, of the cost-of-care delivery is tied up in human resources. The nurses, techs, aides, physicians, and other clinical and non-clinical resources make up the vast majority of the cost-of-care delivery. All you need to do is consider the ongoing human resource cost within a hospital or clinic against the cost of construction (less than 3%), supplies and drugs, and simply running the business (maintenance, upgrades, technology, equipment, etc.). Human resources, regardless of how effectively or efficiently they might be used, make up a huge percentage of the total of cost-of-care delivery. Of course, every healthcare system faces these same issues. But the relative cost of the U.S. resources is what makes our system relatively expensive.

For a clear example of the differences in resource costs between the United States and its developed counterparts, let's look at nursing. On the basis of international wage data* (albeit somewhat aged), a U.S. nurse salary is roughly 70% higher than that of a French nurse, 50% higher than a Canadian or German nurse, and about ten times that of a Thai nurse's. And that's just salary! That doesn't include benefits, bonuses, or overtime pay. These additional payouts would very likely dramatically increase the variance between pay scales of the U.S. and non-U.S. workers to well over 100%. Indeed, unionized California nurses can make over $200,000 per year by managing their overtime pay—as much or more than some U.S. physicians.

Similarly, U.S. "general physicians" (as the database refers to them, most likely referencing the U.S. equivalent of a general practitioner) make some 30% more than similar physicians in the United Kingdom, but 300% more than the French, 250% more than the Italians, 60% more than the Japanese, and almost 900% more than a Czech physician. Again, these figures don't include the benefits and bonuses that can come to employed physicians, nor the payments that come to some specialists from medical manufacturers and pharmaceutical companies. Importantly, data on the relative cost of specialists is lacking; yet, we know how well neurologists, cardiologists, and other surgical specialists are paid for their work. It would not be unreasonable to assume that the same percentages or even greater international disparities in pay applied to these specialists as well.

Furthermore and importantly, patient-to-nurse ratios are typically higher in OECD (Organization for Economic Co-operation and Development) countries than in the United States, where states such as California and New York have mandated union-supported ratios in hospitals. While in France, the inpatient ratios of patients to nurses are sometimes eight or ten to one, here, it can be mandated to as low as four to one. This further adds to the cost-of-resource differentials between nations.

---

* http://www.worldsalaries.org/. Data here are relatively old but offer a good comparison of international wages. Assuming that the wages of non-U.S. healthcare workers have not dramatically increased, and knowing that the wages of U.S. healthcare workers have gone up, not down, it is likely that these comparisons would hold relatively true if more current data were available.

Thus, even if we used the same patient-to-provider ratios (which we don't), if 70%–80% of the basic operational cost of the U.S. healthcare system (staff) is at least 50% higher than the basic operational costs of the rest of the industrialized world, it would be difficult for the U.S. system to come anywhere near the costs of those other nations. Indeed, without drastically reducing either staff pay or the number of caregivers, it is literally impossible to match the costs of the OEDC countries. Thus, given these relatively high costs and the large percentage of total cost made up by human resources, it is not at all surprising that our system is far more expensive relative to the gross domestic product (GDP) or any other measure/metric one chooses. Thus, those who rail against the cost of insurance company executive pay focus on only a tiny percentage of overall care costs and are missing the costliest elephant in the room.

Most importantly, if these numbers accurately reflect the current state of healthcare spending, dramatically reducing the total cost will be difficult at best. This is even more true since the United States faces future resource constraints in nurses, physicians, and other clinical resources (e.g., techs), making it unlikely that healthcare will break the laws of economics and reduce the cost of these vital and high-demand resources.

WASTE

We often think of the cost of waste, "defensive medicine," and unnecessary procedures as costing hundreds of billions of dollars.[*] Some estimate the amount of waste to be as high as 20% of total health expenditures.[†] Then there are operational inefficiencies in poor processes, staffing inefficiencies, and a general lack of control over expenditures. And that is true … waste and inefficiency are rampant in healthcare. Yet, every healthcare system has some waste. The U.S. system is even more expensive than other nations because the underlying, operational cost associated with these wasteful expenditures, from excess labs due to defensive medicine to unnecessary referrals for inappropriate tests, still often resides with human, mostly clinical resources. It takes human resources to run those excess tests, count those excess meds, accommodate those unnecessary visits, and generally do all that wasteful work. Thus, the aforementioned resource cost issue exacerbates the relative cost of the waste that exists, making our waste more expensive than everyone else's waste.

PERVERSION

Making matters worse are the perverse incentives built into the U.S. healthcare system. For example, physicians have been caught conducting unnecessary procedures

---

[*] Kelley, R. 2009. Where can $700 billion in waste be cut annually from the U.S. healthcare system? Thomson Reuters. http://www.factsforhealthcare.com/whitepaper/HealthcareWaste.pdf and Kelley, B. and Fabius, R. 2010. A path to eliminating $3.6 trillion in wasteful healthcare spending, Thomson Reuters. http://thomsonreuters.com/content/healthcare/pdf/white_papers/path_eliminating_36_trillion.

[†] Berwick, D. M. and Hackbarth, A. D. 2012. Eliminating waste in U.S. health care. *Journal of the American Medical Association* 307(14): E1–E4.

on patients who otherwise might need only physical therapy or non-invasive treatments in order to obtain the fees associated with surgeries. Some physicians will turn away patients not because they do not need care but because their insurers, particularly government programs such as Medicaid, pay relatively less than others. And hospital leaders get upset when their EDs and ORs are not full rather than celebrating the general well-being of the communities they serve. In other words, the providers of healthcare do what the reimbursement systems pay them to do, which leads to perverse incentives that emphasize "work more make more" rather than proper and effective care provision and PHM. Small wonder our systems are difficult to change … it's hard to take away the candy jar!

And sadly, the U.S. government has been the main culprit in the ongoing struggle with proper incentives. Each effort, from Stark laws to the Diagnostic-Related Group (DRG) to the current PPACA legislation, has its own unique set of improper incentives. Furthermore, the United States continues to skirt around the primary issue in the reimbursement and incentivization mess: fee-for-service (FFS) reimbursements.

The good news is that more and more health systems are coming to realize that "capitation" will soon replace the unsustainable FFS system. While Health Maintenance Organizations (HMOs) and even their recreated cousins, the ACOs, are maligned as ineffective business models, the shift away from FFS to a set fee per covered life is starting. This will help drive out some of the costs of the system, even if the resources we need continue to go up in price.

THE 80–15–5 AND THE POPULATION'S VIEW

One reasonable approach is to divide the population by an 80%–15%–5% split, largely based on the use of resources as defined by the cost-of-care delivery. That is, the top 20% spends most of the healthcare in dollars, with the top 5% consuming roughly half of all healthcare spent, and the top 20% accounting for nearly 80%.[*] This split makes sense from several perspectives, including resource allocations, management of the cost-of-care delivery, and the management of finances, insurance, and expenditures. With this in mind, let's look at the cost of the provision of care for these categories of our citizens and what it will mean to our PHM and capacity optimization discussions.

Sadly, most of us don't "own" our health. And, let's face it, being unhealthy is a lot easier, tastes better, and requires less time and effort than being healthy. Taking care of one's body is even more difficult as one ages, or after a weight spurt puts us heading toward obesity, or after a disease such as cancer has struck a blow. Simply put, if healthiness were easy, everyone would do it. But it is not, and we have come to accept our bodies as mere carriers of our lusts and bad decisions rather than treating them with the respect that afforded a God-given creation.

Furthermore, people do stupid things. Alcohol and drug abuse are becoming more prevalent rather than less, and new drugs continue to flood the market (e.g., synthetic marijuana) as people seek higher highs. We binge on the buffet at the local

---

[*] http://kff.org/health-costs/issue-brief/health-care-costs-a-primer/.

KFC or pizza joint, drink excessive amounts of alcohol, and refuse opportunities to walk even one flight of stairs. Smoking rates in the population are stuck at around 22% after years of decline even as otherwise intelligent and knowledgeable teenagers continue to take up one of the most addictive habits known (a fact upon which governments rely for a most ironic, ever-renewing source of tax revenues).

Thus, people make very poor life choices and get very sick from them. And until you can completely control people's life choices, you can bet that many, if not most, will make bad ones. Don't blame the candy makers, the cigarette companies, or the distillers of beer and liquor ... they are responding to the demands of the marketplace. When one closes another opens. Prohibition of the 1920s, prostitution restrictions, and the black market for untaxed cigarettes demonstrates that people will readily work around legal restrictions and constraints to obtain the products and services they want, regardless of how destructive those desires might be.

Whether this comes from a "You only live once" attitude, general complacency, a cultural emphasis on sexuality, sensuality, drugs and alcohol, or a lack of proper education, the attitudes of our citizens are not conducive to optimal health. And as long as we refuse individual health ownership and determine that we either do not want or will not accept responsibility for our bodies and everything about them, we will forever have an overly expensive healthcare system.

This relates to the issue of PHM because if the goal is "the promotion of the optimal health and well-being of individuals and the population writ large ... via appropriate expenditures," then we must decide to what extent we can control the costs of the system. If costs are out of our reach, and if we can do little if anything to reduce them or control their growth, then we give up on a significant goal of healthcare reform. And, as we have seen, controlling costs requires that we make dramatic decisions about the way providers are paid, the cost of those providers, and the prevalent attitudes about health within the citizenry.

Health ownership, then, is a critical concept to the financial, social, and spiritual benefits of PHM. Yet, we have successfully driven personal responsibility as far as possible away from the cost of the provision of health (as measured by the actual cost of insurance). Insurance largely picks up the tab when our lifestyle, diet, and personal care choices create disease, injury, pregnancy, and poor health outcomes. This is exacerbated by the subsidies that support many Americans' health insurance bills and removes them from the need to even know, let alone do anything about, the cost of care. We are made to believe that our bodies should be equalized when it comes to the cost of care, regardless of whether our diseases and functional limitations are self-inflicted or genetically dictated. Whether our smoking causes our cancer or not, our politicians have removed any personal responsibility from our decision making and certainly from the repercussions of our decisions. Thus, in many cases, our choices are supported by a system that is being made forever forgiving and thus even less and less demanding. And, as we have seen, these outcomes further drive up the cost of care as poor choices put greater demands on the system and thus drive demand for resources and system costs. Thus, ownership is hampered by a lack of need for personal responsibility relative to the actual cost-of-care provision, maintenance, and management. Nothing in Obamacare changes this, and indeed some parts of the legislation make this reality far worse.

RELATIVE HEALTH

Remember, however, that health is relative to the individual. I no more want to adopt a total vegan diet than I want to be obese. Yet, Americans' diets and habits are "OK" to some, "detrimental" to others, and "unacceptable" to still others depending on one's perspective. And the "science" doesn't always help us here. What is now considered bad might have once been considered good due to the ever-changing definition of "proper" diet and exercise. Meat and potatoes, once considered staples in the American diet, are now considered "bad" for us to varying degrees. Or not! We've gone from low-fat to low-carbs to low-glycemic index recommendations from "the experts." Still, there are some common-sense approaches to diet and exercise that defy contradiction. Yet even with the consistency in the research on common-sense measures such as caloric intake, many families still make a regular habit of "fast food." Stereotypically, you rarely see skinny people regularly dining at Popeye's or KFC (my personal favorite) or the local rib joint.

Then there's exercise. Your stereotypical "good ol' boy" isn't one for the treadmill or laps at the pool at the Y on a Saturday afternoon. It seems that those who need it most don't do it enough, those who don't seem to need it are addicted to it. Not only that, the "science" behind the need for exercise seems to change. Running was once the way to go, then came the bad knees and hips in long-term runners. Cycling is an option, yet it takes its own toll on the joints. Now we hear that too much exercise can be as bad as none!

Still, even with the confusion on the perfect exercise routines and diets, poor choices are endemic to a population. And those choices can lead to some very bad outcomes and higher costs. And since ownership isn't driven by responsibility for sharing the cost of care, it is difficult to drive better habits into those for whom health means very little, or for whom health is simply defined differently. In the end, health is a relative measure. Try as we might to educate, cajole, incent, and command, health will be as important to the individual as that individual makes it, and will be defined only relative to his own value systems, environment, sense of self-value and self-image, and personality.

This has been proven in recent efforts to create better population health via insurance coverage. Comparative studies show that we can offer health insurance coverage to even the poorest of our population, yet their relative health (as measured by standard metrics of health management) doesn't change. Research on the impact of state funding of health insurance has demonstrated that coverage for those poor who had no access to health insurance does not necessarily equal greater utilization of care resources, and generally does not lead to an improvement in health outcomes. Indeed, research shows that states that expanded insurance coverage to those who had no insurance saw no impact in overall health metrics among that population. Essentially, insurance does not translate into better health, even though utilization of health services might increase.[*] Thus, health "insurance" only works if one takes health "ownership."

---

[*] http://www.povertyactionlab.org/publication/insuring-uninsured.

We are now seeing that, even with "universal coverage" available, people make choices to avoid paying for healthcare insurance and coverage against disease and accidents. Despite the ongoing risks associated with life and living, only roughly 11 million of the some 44 million uninsured in the United States have bothered to sign up for insurance made available by state and federal insurance exchanges, a.k.a. "Obamacare." And millions of those already had health insurance but were forced off their plans and into the new system when the law took effect, making the impact on the uninsured far-less dramatic than originally hoped. And of those, some 85% are subsidized, meaning that they likely would have chosen to remain uninsured were it not for government assistance. And even then, early results from 2015 show that only 65%–75% of those newly insured were signing up for a second year of insurance.* So, we see that even the threat of fines and taxes and the offering of substantial incentives and subsidies cannot force or entice the uninsured to jump into the system. That leaves tens of millions without effective coverage, meaning that the system remains as fundamentally flawed as ever, but with a $1-trillion price tag added on.

Thus, only personal responsibility and the ownership of one's health will drive the population toward a higher "plane" of population health and the ability to consistently manage it. This cannot be mandated like a seat-belt law, or restrictions on the sale of alcohol to minors. And clearly we cannot "incent" our citizens either. Ownership must come from within the individual, and this requires a shift in culture that will be decades in the making. As that shift is being made, perhaps parallel to the shift away from FFS, we can begin to truly address the cost and life-quality issues that PHM promises.

END OF LIFE

Of course, no discussion of cost and quality of health and life would be complete without touching on the end of life (EOL) and EOL care. It is known that EOL is a large part of the typical America's total healthcare "spend." And yes, it all requires human resources in various places in the system, from the intensive care unit (ICU) to the nursing home to the hospice center. We'll cover this in greater detail as we get into the concept of the CCN and how the reorganization of the care system can be enabled. Suffice it to say for now that this is indeed a significant portion of our total spending. Fortunately, it can be managed by education and simple decisions about personal preferences.

SUMMARY

Thus, if we are to impact cost in a meaningful way, we must be willing to revamp care models to reduce the concentration of caregivers relative to the number of

---

* https://www.cms.gov/Newsroom/MediaReleaseDatabase/Fact-sheets/2015-Fact-sheets-items/2015-09-08.html.

patients/citizens, while seeking ways to reduce unnecessary care and thus reduce waste, and instill a sense of health ownership in the population. And it all seems to start with the latter, for without it, we likely cannot attain the others.

PHM is the promotion of the optimal health and well-being of individuals and the population writ large to the extent possible, necessary, and desired via appropriate systems, resources, care models, and expenditures; a collaborative, inclusive effort to help that population care for itself; and the promotion of attitudes of health ownership within individuals and the community that will lead to the optimization of health outcomes. All these will impact cost in the end. The goal, then, of capacity optimization is to create a system that supports, enables, and maintains PHM by creating the necessary operational models, resource pool, systems, and infrastructure that will create the opportunity for the realization of the PHM definition we have created here, and in doing so will impact cost and other key metrics.

3 Introduction to the Section on Workplace Culture

This book is meant to cover myriad subjects as part of a holistic approach to true capacity optimization. I contend that without addressing *all* the components of your "capacity to care," from the departments in your hospital to the interdependencies between them to the relationships you have with the wealth of communal resources, you will never reach true optimization, and never offer your community the care you could. Of course, the breadth of this topic is enormous and thus requires some segmentation. I have therefore broken the book down into three main sections, each reflecting important categories of your optimization effort.

As you embark or continue on your own optimization journey, you will inevitably need to address each of these major categories. If your hospital's internal operational models are such that optimization has been nearly reached, it may be time to look into your community to begin to more appropriately tap the many care resources available and fully integrate them into your care model. Likewise, if you have struggled to get anywhere near optimization in your hospital, you may need to step back and address the culture that makes up the "Invisible Architecture" (as Joe Tye calls it) that may be keeping you from attaining your goals.

The three major categories of this book are, in order of appearance, workplace culture, hospital capacity optimization, and your community of care. Culture is an often-forgotten element in the optimization puzzle. Yet, without an accepting, positive, energized culture, your efforts toward optimization will surely be limited, at best, and fail miserably at worst. Culture, especially in healthcare, is perhaps the dominant detractor to true capacity optimization. Why? Largely because traditional accountability, wherein a boss or shop foreman can drive workers to be productive under a threat of firing or other punishment, simply doesn't work with highly educated resources such as nurses and doctors. Try telling your busiest orthopedists to do as you ask or be fired! Yeah, right! Yet, bad culture is as endemic in healthcare as germs, and can be as deadly. Thus the culture section comes first. If you don't have a healthy, positive, and passionate culture, you really needn't read any further until you do. Once you do, you might be quite surprised by how easily the rest of the optimization effort goes!

Next is the hospital capacity optimization section. This of course includes the optimization of your "internal" hospital capacity and your ability to care for as many patients as possible with a given amount of time and resources. This section is critical for the future of your delivery system, since failure to achieve optimization here will mean difficulty surviving the future changes to reimbursement and patient demands. You simply *must* optimize your internal capacity in order to survive in the future. In this section, you will be given a detailed description of each element of the "Blocking and Tackling of Hospital Capacity Management," along with keys to proper data analytics and strategic operational models. By just doing the basic "Blocking and Tackling," you will get 80% or more of the way to true capacity optimization within your hospital.

Yet, this is perhaps one of the most difficult concepts for leaders to grasp. I am constantly amazed by the number of allegedly well-trained and experienced CEOs who still want to "fix surgery," or "start with the ED," or "start with some lean projects" rather than tackle the problem as a systemic problem. The very idea of creating a holistic solution to what is a holistic problem seems to be so daunting to many hospital leaders that they immediately retreat to the easy, quick, and nearly entirely ineffective solutions. But if a hospital wants to optimize capacity, it must do so holistically, with all major system components linked together and driving toward the ultimate solution.

The last section is the community of care. It is the most forward thinking of the sections, and requires the greatest change in mindsets. While there are a host of available resources in any given community, most of them remain disconnected, even shunned, by hospital leaders. Yet, without fully integrating the entire community of care into a cohesive care organization, you will leave many resources untapped and thereby reduce your chances for full optimization. With all the current talk of the use of technologies, people, and organizations within our communities, the vast majority of hospitals see their community of care as either an unnecessary hassle or even a detractor from their goals (e.g., by reducing admissions and ED visits that bring revenues).

Yet, any smart CEO will realize that involving their community of care is tantamount to future success. There will come a day when capitation or some form thereof will rule the reimbursement world, and a good CEO will be fully prepared by proactively tapping their communal care resources.

All three sections make up the holistic approach to the capacity optimization. Each section is difficult in its own way, and each is critical to success. All three must be part of the effort if true and full optimization is to be achieved. And only when you have mastered all three will you be able to say that you have optimized your capacity to care.

So, let's get started with the first element … culture.

4 Making the Transition from a Culture of Accountability to a Culture of Ownership by Joe Tye

I first met Joe many years ago at a conference where he was speaking. I stood in the back of a standing-room-only crowd and listened intently to Joe reveal his principles and ideals. I, like many in the audience, was immediately hooked. I took one of the books he was graciously giving away and devoured it on the plane ride back home after the conference. That book, which so deeply touched my life and my thinking, and has touched many lives in healthcare, was *The Florence Prescription*. Joe has hit the cultural nail squarely on the head.

Joe continues to publish books and articles. He is by far the industry's leading expert in healthcare culture change, and his work with his clients is truly transformative and utterly amazing. Joe's blogs are published daily, through which he shares stories of his clients who make great transformations of their hospital cultures, and tips on how to make change happen in your life and the lives of those around you. Joe is, if nothing else, a true giver of knowledge.

I am honored to call Joe a friend and colleague, and was truly thrilled when he agreed to write a chapter for this book. I felt that such a chapter was absolutely necessary for this particular book because without a positive culture your efforts to optimize your capacity via new operational models will be difficult at best, impossible at worst. Culture eats everything for lunch!

If you have a negative culture anywhere in your facility, my advice would be to (1) go ahead and read the rest of this book, (2) put the book on the shelf with a solid knowledge of what needs to be done and the path you need to take to get there, (3) *go fix your culture*, then and only then (4) come back and start on the optimization of your capacity to care. It is just that important!

Many, many thanks to Joe for his contribution to this effort. Without his chapter, this book would have been left with a gaping hole in its holistic approach.

INTRODUCTION

The management buzzword of the 1990s and early part of this century was "empowerment." Over the past 10 years or so that buzzword has gradually been replaced by "accountability." It's almost as if people are saying that they tried the empowerment thing and it didn't work, so know we have to hold people accountable by looking over their shoulders, motivating them with rewards and punishments. Think of the metaphors we use for accountability—cracking the whip and holding someone's feet to the fire! Is it any wonder that people intrinsically resist being told that they are going to be held accountable!

No one ever changes the oil in a rental car. They return it with a full gas tank because that's in the contract—they are accountable for it. But they don't wash and wax the car and they don't check the oil because there is no pride of ownership. When you move from a culture of mere accountability to a culture of ownership, you create a sustainable source of competitive advantage for both recruiting and retaining great people and for earning long-term patient loyalty.

Accountability is, of course, essential—especially when people's lives are at stake—but it's not enough, not in today's turbulent and hypercompetitive world. You cannot hold people accountable for the things that really matter. Caring, compassion, pride, passion, and enthusiasm—those qualities must come from within. Accountability is extrinsic motivation—having your feet held to the fire by someone else. Ownership is intrinsic motivation—walking across hot coals because you believe in something. Not only can you not hold people accountable for the things that really matter, but also an excessive focus on accountability has a real downside. We've repeatedly seen how trying to hold people more accountable achieves a short-term pop in results that quickly deteriorate into another "program of the month" that came and went.

There are two fundamental problems with an excessive focus on accountability. First, it sends a subtle but unmistakable message that people cannot be trusted to hold themselves accountable. Second, it's exhausting for managers; it takes a lot of energy to hold people's feet to the fire, to keep checking up on them. Eventually people on both sides of that equation wear down and you backslide. People can be held accountable for parroting the customer service script and wearing the happy face pin, but not for saying the words like they really mean them and not wearing the happy face pin upside down. You can hold people accountable for saluting but not for caring.

THE JOURNEY FROM ACCOUNTABILITY TO OWNERSHIP

A Culture of Ownership Is Not Created By Economic Interest, It Springs from Emotional Commitment

Organizations need to hold people accountable for fulfilling the terms of their job descriptions, and for not behaving in ways that are inconsistent with the values and mission of that organization. But in today's turbulent and hypercompetitive world, that's not enough to remain competitive, much less to make the now-proverbial jump from good to great. Great organizations are characterized by people holding themselves and each other accountable for their attitudes and behaviors as well as their performance because they have pride of ownership. Any time you hear someone say "that's not my job," see someone ignore a customer or walk by a patient room where the call light is on, or not stoop down to pick up a piece of paper on the floor, that person is just renting a spot on the organization chart. They're not taking ownership for the work itself. They are not thinking like owners, they are thinking like renters.

Accountability is doing what *you are supposed to do* because someone else expects it of you; accountability springs from the extrinsic motivation of reward and punishment. The *Merriam-Webster Dictionary* definition of accountability is: "Subject to having to report, explain or justify; being answerable, responsible." Any organization that seeks to promote accountability according to this definition is virtually guaranteed to have a workplace where people do only what is in their job description and never take initiative or go above-and-beyond what they are being held accountable for.

When you break the word "accountable" down you get ac-count-able: able to be counted. But total quality management (TQM) guru W. Edwards Deming—the man who said that what gets measured gets done and encouraged clients to measure almost everything—also said that the most important number in your organization cannot be counted. How does one count pride or measure enthusiasm? You can certainly see these things in people's attitudes and behaviors in the best of organizations, but they cannot be counted or measured.

Accountability is essential in organizations: managers need to be accountable for achieving performance and financial goals; salespeople must be held accountable for achieving sales goals; nurses must be held accountable for giving their patients the right medications; military officers must be held accountable for maintaining proper discipline in their units; teachers must be held accountable for assuring that their students are learning. Accountability is essential, but it is not sufficient. It is just the baseline, the price of entry.

Ownership is doing *what needs to be done* because you expect it of yourself; ownership springs from the intrinsic motivation of pride and engagement. The *Merriam-Webster Dictionary* definition of ownership is: "The state, relation, or fact of being an owner," which in turn is defined as "to have power or mastery over." Fostering a culture where every employee is encouraged to think like an owner and to have mastery over their work will inevitably outperform an accountability driven organization in every dimension that really matters including employee engagement, productivity, customer service, recruiting and retention success, and profitability.

United Airlines has a culture of accountability, Southwest Airlines has a culture of ownership, Walmart has a culture of accountability, Costco has a culture of ownership, Hertz has a culture of accountability, and Enterprise has a culture of ownership. In each case, the culture of ownership is winning the competitive battle.

In Values Coach consulting engagements we often hear people say something to the effect that "we don't hold each other accountable." But when we press the issue, they're usually not really talking about accountability—they're talking about ownership; they are really saying that people don't take ownership for their work, their results, and their relationships. So it's important to distinguish those things for which people can be held accountable by holding their feet to the fire, and those things for which they cannot be held accountable but which must be accomplished through personal ownership.

You Can Hold People Accountable for	But Not for
Complying with rules	Living values
Showing up on time	Being emotionally present
Discipline	Loyalty
Saying the right words	Asking the right questions
Meeting budgets	Thinking entrepreneurially
Meeting deadlines	Working with passion
Results	Dreams
Competence	Caring
What they say at work	What they say at home
Appearance	Pride
Treating people with respect	Honoring people's dignity
Saluting	Laughing
Their job description	Their life decisions
Keeping their feet to the fire	Putting their hearts into the work

CULTURE EATS STRATEGY FOR LUNCH

You've probably heard the aphorism "culture eats strategy for lunch," originally coined by Peter Drucker. Of course, culture and strategy interact, and in the ideal case are mutually reinforcing, but it's a rare organization that has a culture plan as robust as its strategic plan. An organization with both a great culture and effective operating strategies will be most successful, but the healthcare leader who focuses on strategy without also working to create a strong culture does so at the peril of the organization. As David Maister argues in his book *Strategy and the Fat Smoker*, we all know what the strategies are (quit smoking and lose weight, give great service, and be highly productive). The problem is that we lack inspiration and resolve to implement the strategies, and these are qualities of culture. Let's start by looking at some of reasons why culture trumps strategy and why your organization should therefore have a cultural blueprint.

1. *People are loyal to culture, not strategies:* Southwest Airlines has the highest loyalty in the airline industry, but its people are not loyal to the company because of such strategies as fuel price hedging, free bags, and first-come first-served seating. Rather, they are loyal to a culture that honors individuality, fellowship, and having fun. With experts predicting the likelihood of serious shortages of healthcare professionals in the years to come, hospital leaders should begin now working on fostering a culture of ownership that attracts the best people and earns their loyalty.
2. *Culture provides resilience in tough times:* When Starbucks ran into serious trouble several years ago, founder Howard Schultz returned to take the helm as CEO. In a remarkable turnaround effort that is still ongoing, they implemented numerous great strategies. But what saved the company during its darkest days was not strategic brilliance, rather it was cultural resilience. As Schultz wrote in a *Harvard Business Review* article (July–August, 2010): "The only assets we have as a company [are] our values, our culture

and guiding principles, and the reservoir of trust with our people." It's quite clear that the healthcare environment will get a lot more challenging in the years to come; the most successful organizations will couple creative business strategies with resilient ownership cultures that buffer them against the uncertainty and anxiety of a turbulent and hypercompetitive world.

3. *Culture is more efficient than strategy:* Another example from Southwest Airlines: during fuel shortages caused by the first Gulf War in 1991, Southwest's employees voluntarily donated money from their paychecks to help the company purchase fuel. The company could have achieved the same end with a strategy of mandatory pay reductions, but that strategy would have come at a much greater cost. Watch the reaction of a typical nurse who has been told that he or she must "do more with less" and you'll probably see a gag reflex. At the hypersuccessful online shoe store Zappos, though, "do more with less" is one of the company's 10 core values. This value has been engrained into a uniquely positive culture, and Zappos employees take pride in finding ways to honor it.

4. *Culture creates competitive differentiation:* In the Pacific Northwest, Les Schwab dominates the retail tire industry. They sell the same tires you can buy at any other tire store, but they're the only tire store where a technician runs out to your car to greet you the minute you pull into the parking lot. Texas Roadhouse is America's fastest-growing steakhouse chain; employees proudly wear T-shirts proclaiming that they "heart" their jobs, and on every shift they stage a pep rally (called the alley rally) in the center of the restaurant. Many a hospital has been disappointed when a "customer service" program consisting of giving people a script and a happy face pin has failed to achieve the desired result of increasing patient satisfaction (in fact, poorly implemented, this strategy will actually reduce patient satisfaction and employee engagement). Patients don't remember what was said (the script) nearly as much as they recall the spirit in which it was said, and more than anything that spirit is influenced by the culture of the organization.

5. *A great culture can galvanize a counterintuitive business strategy:* In his book *Delivering Happiness*, Zappos CEO Tony Hsieh says that people in the company's call center do not have quotas or time limits when taking calls. This is in stark contrast to most call-center operations where productivity is monitored to the microsecond. Hsieh says the record length of a single call is more than 7 hours: this is a company selling shoes, but some people call them for psychotherapy! In fact, over the past year I've told thousands of people in my speaking audiences about how a Zappos call-center employee named Mary Ann (when's the last time you remembered the name of the person answering your call to a call center?) handled my call in such a way that I actually didn't want the conversation to end. That is the sort of advertising money cannot buy and strategy will not earn.

6. *Culture humanizes strategy:* Hospitals across the country are adopting Lean process improvement strategies. This is a good thing, but if there is not simultaneous work on fostering cultural commitment it's likely to

be perceived as simply speeding up the assembly line, creating employee resistance and increased risk of failure. At Virginia Mason Medical Center, which has pioneered Lean in healthcare, the Lean strategy has been coupled with a no-layoff policy. Jamie Orlikoff—who sits on the medical center board—says they have learned that you should not try to fix cultural problems with structural solutions, and have thus coupled the Lean strategy with a culture that honors employee job security. They have, in effect, coupled Lean management with "lean on me" management.

7. *Cultural miscues can be more damaging than strategic miscues:* When Dave Carroll, lead singer of an obscure band called Sons of Maxwell from Halifax, Nova Scotia, asked United Airlines to reimburse him for damage done to his Taylor guitar during a flight, he got the runaround. When he threatened to write a song about them if they didn't pay for repairs, they ignored him—to their subsequent regret. To date, more than 20 million people have viewed his video "United Breaks Guitars" and its two sequels—and he's written a business book with the same title. Not only that, the Taylor guitar company made their own video on how to pack a guitar so United won't break it. This is a classic case of self-inflicted public relations disaster. If United had the sort of customer-centric culture for which companies like Nordstrom (or, for that matter, Virgin Airlines) are known, this multimillion-dollar PR black eye would never have happened.

8. *Strategy can be copied but culture cannot:* At one time or another, every major airline has attempted to copy strategies implemented by Southwest Airlines (some of which Southwest copied from others). These copycat efforts have had marginal success at best, largely because they were imposed upon a culture that was not receptive. A competitor can copy your strategies for promoting a women's health program, and can recruit away your best OB nurses, but they cannot copy or steal your culture. And if you get culture right, your best people won't want to leave anyway.

9. *When strategy and culture collide, culture will win:* When Robert Nardelli took the helm at Home Depot, he implemented an array of cost-cutting strategies. These strategies increased sales, profits, and stock price, but at the cost of trashing the employee-centered culture that had been nurtured by company founders. Nardelli was eventually fired, but his failure to honor the Home Depot culture when pushing through his strategies inflicted wounds that will take a long time to heal. By contrast, when Louis Gerstner led the turnaround effort at IBM, he honored the culture that had been created by Thomas Watson senior and junior. In his book *Who Says Elephants Can't Dance?* Gerstner wrote that he learned "culture isn't just one aspect of the game, it *is* the game" (emphasis in original).

In *American Icon: Alan Mulally and the Fight to Save Ford Motor Company*, Bryce Hoffman wrote: "The biggest and most important difference between Mulally and his predecessors is that he attacked the root of the problem: Ford's corporate culture. He took a sledgehammer to the silos that had divided the company into warring fiefdoms for generations. He forced everyone to stare reality in the face without flinching or turning away. It was not easy, nor instantaneous, but in the middle of a truly existential crisis, Ford's executives finally stopped making decisions based on what was best for their own careers and started trying to figure out what was best for the company as a whole."

Contrast the efforts of Mulally and his team to change the culture at Ford with what happened at GM over the same time period. They did not use their time in bankruptcy protection to dismantle the sort of siloed culture that had existed at Ford. Rather a caustic culture was, according to the Valukas report into the safety scandal that resulted in the largest ever automobile recall, responsible for a situation where nobody accepted responsibility for fixing the problem. It was a culture where "the GM salute" (arms crossed and fingers pointed outwards at other people) reflected a culture where no one took ownership.

FOSTERING A MORE POSITIVE HEALTHCARE CULTURE

When Midland Memorial Hospital in West Texas opened a gorgeous new facility with all state-of-the-art private patient rooms, they expected patient satisfaction to skyrocket. Surprisingly, it did no such thing: it actually declined. They soon realized that by opening the beautiful new building, they had raised patient expectations dramatically but had done nothing to change the attitudes and behaviors of people working there, so patients got the same old treatment. The new building made the gap between patients' expectations and the reality of their experience wider than it was before.

With help from our team at Values Coach they began working on a Cultural Blueprint for the Invisible Architecture™ of their organization. When it comes to the things that really matter, including employee engagement and patient satisfaction, Invisible Architecture is more important than the visible architecture of bricks and mortar. In a very real sense, it is the soul of your organization. When helping clients create a Cultural Blueprint for their Invisible Architecture, we use a construction metaphor in which the foundation is core values, the superstructure is organizational culture, and the interior finish is workplace attitude. As with visible architecture, in a well-designed organization there is a seamless interconnection between the foundation, the superstructure, and the interior finish.

THE FOUNDATION OF CORE VALUES

A hospital's statement of core values should define who you are, what you stand for, and what you won't stand for. Many hospital values statements suffer from two serious weaknesses: (1) they are written in boilerplate language that does nothing to inspire pride and commitment on the part of people who are expected to live those values and (2) they do nothing to differentiate that organization from every other hospital claiming to care about excellence, compassion, and quality. And while values statements that lend themselves to a memorable acronym can be effective, it's usually obvious when words have been force-fit into something like I CARE (the letters will almost predictably stand for integrity, compassion, accountability, respect, and excellence).

When we worked with Memorial Hospital of Converse County in Douglas, Wyoming, they had a statement of values spelling out the acronym CARE, but nobody—including people with the word "chief" in their job titles—knew what the letters stood for. At one leadership retreat, we divided people into small groups and gave them just 3 minutes to define the values that inspired them as individuals. It was fascinating! In a 3-minute exercise, these groups came up with values statements that were more inspiring and meaningful than the plaque that had been tacked on the wall for nobody knew how long. Over the next year, MHCC engaged employees, providers, board members, volunteers, and others in a dialogue about values. They went from the insipid acronym CARE to a robust statement with seven core values, each defined by a statement of philosophy and reinforced by five to six statements of behavioral expectation, as shown in Figure 4.1.

Midland Memorial Hospital has never had a formal statement of values, so we conducted focus group sessions with employees, physicians, board members, and others. Through that process, it became very clear that three core values drive the organization: Pioneer Spirit, Caring Heart, and Healing Mission. The hospital's leadership team is now working to define specific values-based cultural norms and behavioral expectations for each of the three. Because they want something that every employee can embrace and be proud of, they've also asked me to write a fictionalized account of the history and future plans of the hospital in which its values, culture, and behavioral expectations are illustrated by the characters in an engaging story.

THE SUPERSTRUCTURE OF ORGANIZATIONAL CULTURE

One of the exercises we conduct in leadership retreats is asking participants to define their culture in just six words. Paradoxically, the stronger an organization's culture is, the easier it is to succinctly define. At Southwest Airlines, for example, they define their culture in a six-word motto (counting the hyphen): Servant's Heart, Warrior Spirit, Fun-Loving Attitude. At Cypress Semiconductor, they call themselves The Marine Corp of Silicon Valley. When your culture is so clear and distinct that you can define it in just six words, you almost never make hiring mistakes, your people are clear about the organization's behavioral expectations, and customers always know what to expect.

It's a rare hospital that's that clear about its culture. Rather, you see a fragmented culture that's more like a patchwork quilt. The culture in Nursing is different than that in Lab, Pharmacy, Housekeeping, Administration, or the Business Office, and within Nursing, there are different cultures in med-surg, operating rooms, emergency department, and newborn nursery. There's a different culture on day shift and night shift, and yet another on weekends. At one hospital leadership retreat, responses to the six-word culture definition exercise ranged from "We love patients and each other" to "This place sucks then you quit."

We have put a great deal of thought into what six words would define a culture of ownership in a healthcare organization and it's this: *Emotionally Positive, Self Empowered, Fully Engaged.* One of the resources at The Florence Challenge website (www.TheFlorenceChallenge.com) is a Certificate of Commitment to these three

"Invisible Architecture"

Memorial Hospital of Converse County is more than a place, it is a culture, built upon our seven essential values. These values, as described by America's Values Coach, Joe Tye, are our organization's Invisible architecture, the unseen support of our hospital's culture. They are what define us, molding the behavioral standards we choose most important as an organization.

Integrity

We hold ourselves accountable to the highest ethical and performance standards, demonstrating honesty, professionalism and sincerity. Therefore ...

- I will always speak honestly & tactfully
- I will talk with, and not about, others
- I will do what I say and say what I do
- I will treat everyone with dignity
- I will own and work to correct my mistakes

Respect

We believe respect for one's self and for others is the foundation of honor and the basis of integrity. Such respect is essential for nurturing the innovative spirit of our hospital. Therefore ...

- I will seek to make all people feel valued & appreciated
- I will be professional, courteous, honest & thoughtful in all my interactions
- I will protect confidentiality – knowing my audience
- I will protect others privacy – knocking before entering

Ownership

We believe in taking ownership for ones responsibilities and goals. As owners we recognize it is our responsibility to do what is right for our patients, our hospital and our coworkers. We understand each of us plays a critical role in fulfilling our mission. Therefore ...

- I will not say, "It's not my job" or "we are short-staffed"
- I am available to assist, encourage and help others
- I will be a good steward of all resources
- I will take responsibility for my actions and behavior
- I will think "team," sharing successes & failures together

Patient-Centered

We provide care that is respectful of and responsive to individual patient preferences, needs, and values. We will remember that people are our reason for our being here, not an interruption of our work. Therefore ...

- I will actively "see" and "listen to" others
- I will rush to meet their needs, exceeding their expectations
- I will genuinely care for others as I want to be treated
- I will respect others dignity and privacy
- When we fail to meet expectations, I will acknowledge, apologize, and make amends

Compassion

We recognize every person as a whole human being with different needs that must be met through listening, empathizing and nurturing. Therefore ...

- I will be hospitable, anticipating others needs
- I will listen attentively and act on what I hear
- I will strive to relieve fears and anxieties
- I will advocate for my patients and co-workers
- I will use AIDET:
  Acknowledge, Introduce, Duration, Explanation, Thank you

Competency

We are dedicated to employing, training, and providing staff with the appropriate tools needed to respond to the unique needs of our patients, our coworkers, and our community. Therefore ...

- I will make sure that I am well-trained in all aspects of my job
- If I do not know what to do or how to do something I will ask
- I will always practice safety, and use best practices with confidence
- I will seek to continually improve my job skills and people skills
- I will provide private, constructive feedback for inappropriate behaviors
- When interviewing, I will strive to hire only the best

Joy

We believe employees who enjoy their role within the organization and their relationships with one another create a healthy environment for all. We look for both fun and humor, when appropriate, in our daily work. Therefore ...

- I will make an honest effort to always be positive
- I will look for the best in people and situations
- I will smile while greeting everyone – whether in person or on the phone
- I will seek to see the positive in stressful situations
- I will seek to lift the spirits of all around me

MEMORIAL HOSPITAL
of Converse County
Advanced Medicine. Hometown Care.

FIGURE 4.1   The values statement of Memorial Hospital of Converse County.

FIGURE 4.2   The Florence Challenge Certificate of Commitment.

qualities (Figure 4.2). When everyone in a department or nursing unit signs and publicly posts these certificates (often with their pictures next to the signature) it serves as both a daily reminder to employees and a notice to patients and visitors of the expectations they have placed upon themselves. Many hospitals, including those mentioned in this article, launch their values and culture initiatives by sharing the book *The Florence Prescription* with some or all of their employees.

One of the most powerful ways of crafting culture is the combination of simple rituals coupled with success stories from those practices. For example, at Midland Memorial Hospital, all managers have been encouraged to lead their staff in reading each day's promise from The Self-Empowerment Pledge™, and a growing number of employees are wearing wristbands for each day's promise. The pledge is included in Figure 4.3, along with a picture of the daily reading of each day's promise that occurs at Star Valley Medical Center in Afton, Wyoming. As people have begun to take these seven promises to heart, they're starting to share impressive stories about achieving goals, redefining priorities, and in at least one case even breaking a long-standing drug addiction.

INTERIOR FINISH OF WORKPLACE ATTITUDE

One of the most important lessons I've learned in my 20 years with Values Coach is this: culture does not change unless and until people change. That's why we

(a)

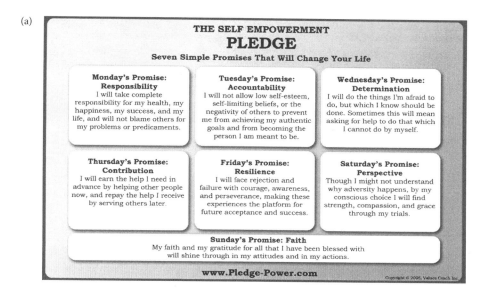

THE SELF EMPOWERMENT
PLEDGE
Seven Simple Promises That Will Change Your Life

**Monday's Promise:
Responsibility**
I will take complete responsibility for my health, my happiness, my success, and my life, and will not blame others for my problems or predicaments.

**Tuesday's Promise:
Accountability**
I will not allow low self-esteem, self-limiting beliefs, or the negativity of others to prevent me from achieving my authentic goals and from becoming the person I am meant to be.

**Wednesday's Promise:
Determination**
I will do the things I'm afraid to do, but which I know should be done. Sometimes this will mean asking for help to do that which I cannot do by myself.

**Thursday's Promise:
Contribution**
I will earn the help I need in advance by helping other people now, and repay the help I receive by serving others later.

**Friday's Promise:
Resilience**
I will face rejection and failure with courage, awareness, and perseverance, making these experiences the platform for future acceptance and success.

**Saturday's Promise:
Perspective**
Though I might not understand why adversity happens, by my conscious choice I will find strength, compassion, and grace through my trials.

Sunday's Promise: Faith
My faith and my gratitude for all that I have been blessed with will shine through in my attitudes and in my actions.

www.Pledge-Power.com

Copyright © 2006, Values Coach Inc.

(b)

FIGURE 4.3   The Self-Empowerment Pledge and the daily promise at Star Valley Medical Center.

always begin a values and culture initiative with a Culture Assessment Survey for all employees. This is an excellent way of encouraging managers to remove the rose-colored glasses we often wear when assessing our own cultures, and the results are almost always less than we would hope for. The good news is that holding up this cultural mirror often provides the spark of motivation that is needed for people to pay attention to, and work to change, negative attitudes and behaviors.

Following are some of the questions we typically include in this Culture Assessment Survey (rated on a five-point scale with responses from "Strongly Agree" to "Strongly Disagree"). We have never seen a hospital with an aggregate score higher than 4.0, and it's not uncommon for some questions (especially that related to positive attitudes and respectful behavior) to have an average score of well below 3.0.

- Our people are creative, productive, and enthusiastic about work and their own personal and professional development.
- Our people are fully engaged in their work and committed to the mission of our organization.
- Our people know the values of this organization, and are committed to assuring that those values are reflected in the way that they do the work they do.
- Our people reflect positive attitudes, treat others with respect, and refrain from complaining, gossiping, or pointing fingers.
- Our people effectively manage change and are advocates for progress.
- Our people feel a great sense of pride in being a member of our team.

Another question asks people to estimate what percent of total paid hours in their organization are wasted on complaining, gossiping, and other forms of toxic emotional negativity. At Midland Memorial Hospital, the initial survey suggested that about 12% of all paid hours were so wasted. As bad as that sounds, it is not at all atypical of hospital survey results. The second survey conducted 4 months into the Values and Culture Initiative suggested that total has been cut in half, resulting in more than $7 million in wage and salary expense being directed into more productive activities. And this does not account for the positive impact of greatly enhanced patient satisfaction and more positive community image that have been direct results of these attitude and behavior changes on the part of individuals.

One of the most powerful tools we use to raise awareness of toxic emotional negativity in the workplace is The Pickle Challenge™. This is based upon the simple promise included in Figure 4.4. Midland Memorial Hospital has embraced this by having pickle jar-decorating contests, a fund-raising initiative in which people are fined a quarter for each complaint and the money is donated to their Catastrophic Employee Assistance Program, and other activities. In their recent accreditation survey, surveyors commented upon how impressed they were with the impact The Pickle Challenge has had on the overall organizational culture.

RESULTS

As you might imagine, we have seen results ranging from minimal sustained impact to profound cultural transformation. At Fillmore County Hospital in Geneva, Nebraska, CEO Paul Utemark said, "I got a whole new team and didn't have to change any of the people." At Star Valley Medical Center in Afton, Wyoming, CEO Charlie Button says their work on values and culture was the key factor in that organization being designated one of the Top Twenty critical access hospitals in America by the National Rural Health Association.

(a)

I've Taken The Pickle* Pledge.™

"I will turn every complaint into either a blessing or a constructive suggestion."

By taking *The Pickle Pledge*, I am promising myself that I will no longer waste my time and energy on blaming, complaining, and gossiping, nor will I commiserate with those who steal my energy with their blaming, complaining, and gossiping.

* So-called because chronic complainers look like they were born with a dill pickle stuck in their mouths.

Copyright © 2008, Values Coach Inc.

(b)

FIGURE 4.4 The Pickle Challenge and Midland Memorial Hospital pickle jar-decorating contest.

The HR department at Midland Memorial Hospital sends an unmistakable message to employees that they are taking The Pickle Challenge and The Self-Empowerment Pledge very seriously.

At Midland Memorial Hospital, there have been dramatic improvements as they launched their Values and Culture Initiative this past spring (the first survey was conducted in February and training began in April). As shown in Figure 4.5, the proportion of employees disagreeing with the statement that they treat others with respect and refrain from toxic emotional negativity was more than cut in half, and the proportion of employees agreeing with that statement has nearly doubled.

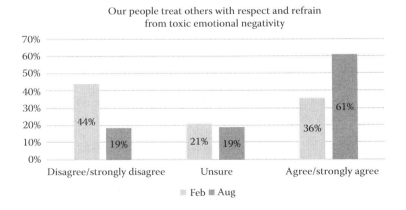

FIGURE 4.5   Changes in survey responses over a 4-month period.

Similar changes were seen in other questions relating to pride in the organization, being engaged in the work, and effectively managing change. It is no coincidence that as the initiative started, patient satisfaction scores have trended strongly upward and are now at all-time highs.

KEY LESSONS FOR FOSTERING A CULTURE OF OWNERSHIP

In working with hundreds of organizations over the past 20 years, we've learned some important lessons about effective culture change. These are the most important:

Lesson #1: Senior leadership must be visibly committed, but this often takes the form of high-leverage symbolic actions. At Midland Memorial Hospital, for example, CEO Russell Meyers references The Pickle Challenge and The Self- Empowerment Pledge in his Monday staff emails, and members of the executive team wear wristbands for the seven daily promises of The Self-Empowerment Pledge.

Lesson #2: Middle management must be engaged and not allowed to opt out. In our experience, this is the single-best predictor of a successful values and culture initiative. When the middle management team is solidly behind the effort, we're surfing a powerful wave; when even a few convey the message to their people that they've opted out of what they consider to be a ridiculous waste of time, we end up swimming against a very strong countercurrent.

Lesson #3: The Human Resources department must be completely and visibly behind fostering a culture of ownership, and in particular support managers who need to discipline or terminate employees whose attitudes and behaviors sabotage that culture. One of the primary excuses we hear from middle managers as to why they can't hold people accountable for toxic negative attitudes is that they would not be supported by HR. That excuse should be preempted by a clear understanding of the expectations of middle managers and of HR in dealing with cultural misfits.

Lesson #4: Define specific actions that people can take to show commitment to your values and cultural expectations, but be clear about the personal benefit since, as the late Zig Ziglar reminded us, everyone listens to the same radio station—WIIFM, What's In It For Me? When sharing The Pickle Challenge and The Self-Empowerment Pledge, we always stress how living these promises not only contributes to organizational excellence, but also helps individual employees to more effectively achieve their own personal and professional goals.

Lesson #5: Resistance is inevitable from people who, for whatever reason, have a vested interest in preventing positive culture change. If the leadership team perseveres in the face of this resistance, some of the most negative employees will eventually get on board and become real Spark Plugs, while those who don't will become marginalized and eventually leave or be asked to leave. If the leadership team does not persevere, though, they end up contributing to the self-fulfilling prophecy of just another program of the month.

Lesson #6: Integrate the principles of your Invisible Architecture into policies and procedures, recruiting and retention activities, new employee orientation, performance appraisal, and continuing education activities.

Lesson #7: Engage the medical staff in a serious manner. Physicians can have a disproportionately positive impact on a values and culture initiative when they are visibly engaged and supportive, but they can also undermine the effort by siding with the cynics who want it to fail. It is a rare organization that engages the medical staff in culture matters; in my 20 years of conducting leadership retreats for hospitals, I have almost never seen more than a token physician or two (if that) in the room.

Lesson #8: Don't be afraid to ask people to assess progress. There is no such thing as "survey fatigue." People only get fatigued by filling out surveys that are not acted upon. Take off the rose-colored glasses and don't try to excuse or explain away unacceptable results.

Lesson #9: Continue building your momentum. At Midland Memorial Hospital, for example, the next phase will be training a core group of employees to become Certified Values Coach Trainers who in turn will share our course on The Twelve Core Action Values with the rest of the organization during 2015.

Lesson #10: Encourage employees to engage their families. In our experience some of the most highly engaged employees for fostering a culture of ownership—the people we call "Spark Plugs"—are those who are sharing The Pickle Pledge, The Self-Empowerment Pledge, and the other techniques they learn at work with spouses and children at home. For that reason, whenever we conduct a Values Initiative we include special sessions open to employee family members.

CONCLUSION

It's often said that culture eats strategy for lunch, but it would be more accurate to say that the greatest source of competitive advantage is strategy that is supported by an Invisible Architecture of core values that are enthusiastically embraced, a positive organizational culture, and workplace attitudes that optimize a spirit of ownership. Every organization has a strategic plan. You should also have a culture plan that defines your expectations for the organization's Invisible Architecture.

Joe Tye is the founder and head coach of Values Coach Inc. that provides consulting, training, and coaching on values-based life and leadership skills and ownership culture for healthcare clients. He is the author of 12 books including The Florence Prescription: From Accountability to Ownership *and* All Hands on Deck: 8 Essential Lessons for Building a Culture of Ownership.

Invisible Architecture, The Pickle Challenge, and The Self- Empowerment Pledge are trademarks of Values Coach Inc.

5 Terminology of This Book

To best allow for an understanding of the concepts, operational models, and ideas herein, it is necessary to familiarize you with some of the terms I'll be using throughout this book. Please refer to these as needed as you continue your exploration of healthcare capacity optimization.

CARE CIRCLE NETWORKS

The Care Circle Network© (CCN) is "care collaboration on steroids" and a huge leap forward in the evolution of care and business models. Originally put forth in the book, *Developing a Polychronic Care Network* by this author, CCNs were designed to address the limited human and financial resources available in our healthcare system, the growing care needs of an increasingly aging population, and the opportunities for care resources that lie in the latent capacity within our communities.

CCNs open up vast new potential for simultaneous cost control, capacity expansion, community and physician integration, and outcomes quality management within ACOs, patient-centered medical homes (PCMHs), and traditional FFS models. Importantly, CCNs add greatly to the capacity of care managers and patient navigators in the care of capitated populations. CCNs are being implemented around the United States, and are based on the following structure.

Using existing web-based collaboration platforms and the oversight and guidance of a patient's physicians, the CCN "engineers" the integration of commonly available but rarely utilized communal resources directly into care and assistance roles for patients with specific needs. These familiar resources, such as friends and family, volunteers from churches and civic groups, residents and clinical students, retirees and soccer moms, etc., are appropriately trained and then integrated into "Care Circles" around patients to perform assigned tasks within the physicians' care plans. This could not heretofore be achieved due to the limitations of communication and lack of accountability now afforded by the CCN model.

The CCN is supported by a "light" management infrastructure that takes the hassles and workload of resource management off the physicians' practice, allowing clinicians to focus on patient care and care plan oversight. With this, physicians collaborate and communicate, but do not deal with the "day-to-day" resource management, resulting in an expansion of their "capacity to care" without additional workload or administrative costs and burdens.

DOWNSTREAM

In this book, the term refers to the direction of influence or impact *after* the process, activity, or operation in question. So, in the case of the ED, discharge is "downstream" from arrival, and the arrival patterns influence processes "downstream" from the patient arrival, such as physician assessment, testing, and disposition. Most commonly, I will use this term to refer to the influences of the interdependencies of a larger system.

DYNAMIC CAPACITY ANALYSIS, MATCHING, AND MANAGEMENT

Originally developed by this author many years ago, dynamic capacity analysis, matching, and management (DCAMM) was meant to be an alternative to the relatively "static" analytical and process improvement methodologies healthcare adopted from manufacturing industries. Those methodologies, which include Lean and to a certain extent Six Sigma (SS) and the overlapping of the two, do not account well for the variability and complex interdependencies that make our hospitals, clinics, and healthcare systems inherently difficult to run. Indeed, these methodologies are thereby "static" in their approaches, meaning that they are set and structured regardless of the changes in the demand on the system.

Alternatively, DCAMM is based on the notion that healthcare systems are inherently "dynamic," changing every hour of every day as patient demand and care capacity ebb and flow. In order to respond adequately to the dynamic ebbs and flows in demand, our care capacity must also be dynamic, matching the variable demand in order to most effectively and efficiently meet it. Hence, dynamic demand must be met with dynamic capacity if the entire system is to be fully optimized for performance, resource allocations, and costs.

Here in this book, you will see the term "Capacity Management" used alternatively with DCAMM. In this context, they will be used interchangeably unless otherwise noted.

INTERDEPENDENCIES

This term herein simply refers to the interplay between departments, areas, or processes and operations as they function and the causal relationships and impacts of one to another. So, for instance, the ED flow is interdependent with the inpatient flow in that the two impact one another. While there is some dependency between the ED and inpatient side, there are also significant causal relationships between the two. Therefore, please allow for a broad and loose use of the term in this book, knowing that interdependencies refers more to the relationships between two departments, areas, or processes and operations than actual dependencies.

HEALTH OWNERSHIP

Health ownership is simply a more intense level of relationship with one's body, care, and caregivers. It is more intense than the more common "user" relationship that most people have with their bodies and caregivers, by which our bodies are used in any manner which is most pleasing, regardless of the complications these choices, actions, and activities may have. The casual "users" seek enjoyment rather than proper maintenance and management, even when the short- and/or long-term negative risks and impacts of actions and activities are known and predictable. When something goes awry and illness, injury or disease strikes, these casual "users" may or may not follow doctor's orders, change behaviors, and make an effort to improve their health status. Indeed, they might be viewed as having an attitude closer to that of a renter than an owner ... one who isn't truly committed to and responsible for that which they have at their disposal.

Ownership is also more intense than the kind of patient engagement many caregivers seek to obtain as part of new cost-savings programs. Patient engagement, as a recent industry buzzword, is meant to reflect a more inclusive healthcare system that interacts with patients more heavily to promote the kind of activities and decisions that would allow for better short- and long-term outcomes. Ownership, by contrast, is more intense, focused, and self-initiated. The owner seeks out better care, invests time and attention to health and wellness information and learning, eliminates bad habits voluntarily, and works to maintain their God-given bodies. While both are good goals, the latter will be much more effective if it is attained.

Importantly, owners within a larger population encourage others to own their bodies as well. They promote the wellness, healthy lifestyles, and positive approaches to health among those around them, and aid those who cannot help themselves. They are as invested in their community as they are in themselves, as the health and wellness of their community has a direct bearing on their own costs and availability of care and insurance. Thus, while they actively seek to prevent illness, when it erupts, they actively seek the best and most cost-effective solutions.

Health ownership is a key component in the overall strategies of population health management and the control of costs, resources, and capacity in the broader healthcare system. Without it, our capacity will necessarily need to be larger than it might be.

OUTLIER

Refers to something that lies outside the main body or group that it is a part of, such as an ED LOS that lasts 36 hours; a patient whose weight and history of smoking puts him at risk for a standard surgery; or an individual process time that takes four times longer than the typical process time.

UPSTREAM

In this book, the term refers to the direction of influence or impact *before* the process, activity, or operation in question. So, in the case of the ED, arrival is "upstream" from discharge and the discharge patterns influence processes "upstream" from the discharge process, such as physician assessment, testing, and disposition. Most commonly, I will use this term to refer to the influences of the interdependencies of a larger system.

HOUR OF DAY, DAY OF WEEK, WEEK OF MONTH, AND SEASON OF YEAR

This complex acronym is often broken down into its components in this book, as follows:

HOD: hour of day
DOW: day of week
WOM: week of month
SOY: season of year

THE FIVE PILLARS OF HEALTHCARE CAPACITY OPTIMIZATION

Common to the discussion of healthcare change is the Institute for Healthcare Improvement's (IHI) well-known and often quoted "Triple Aim." These aims are

- Improve the health of the population
- Enhance the patient experience of care (including quality, access, and reliability)
- Reduce, or at least control, the per capita cost of care[*]

This is also reflected in the new "three aims" of the Center for Medicare and Medicaid Services (CMS), which Dr. Don Berwick brought with him when he moved over from IHI to lead CMS. These aims lit a fire in healthcare that has yet to be extinguished, and should forever be remembered as a "tipping point" (to quote Maxwell) in the history of the evolution of healthcare delivery. By bringing the Triple Aim to CMS, Dr. Berwick made the famed work of the IHI national in scope and fundamental to the future of healthcare delivery in the United States and elsewhere.

Yet I firmly believe that the concept of the three elements of the Triple Aim encompasses much more than just those commonly listed (because they are most often listed without proper definition and footnoting). Indeed, the detailed description of the three aims adds many ancillary yet important aims to the shorter list of stated objectives. While the three aims are certainly laudable and important goals, I believe there are other, equally important, considerations for the system that deserve explicit mention. In fact, by influencing a few additional factors simultaneously, and implementing new care systems such as the CCN, we can optimize the impact of all of the elements and ancillaries of the Triple Aim and move our society toward true health ownership.

This is particularly important as it relates to capacity management and a community-wide, community-engaging approach to capacity optimization. The elements that I considered when developing these principles and concepts many years ago relate directly to the healthcare needs of the patient, community, resources, and the entire system. Simply put, as capacity management herein is a broader approach, we necessarily need a larger set of pillars if we are to adequately goal set and monitor our performance. These include the obviously important and succinctly stated elements of the Triple Aim, such as cost, as well as the unspoken ancillaries such as access and quality. If achieved, the Five Pillars will result in the attainment of the first and perhaps most important of the three IHI aims, population health. Thus, at risk of adding yet more confusing nomenclature to the many healthcare discussions, I will add the "Five Pillars" of capacity management. I will speak of these throughout the remainder of this book, and define each element in the section below.

Understand that, in the end, the goals of all those trying to improve the delivery of healthcare are likely very similar if not identical. Therefore, it would not be surprising if the concept of the Five Pillars only lasted you until the end of the reading of this book. As long as you, the reader, understand how capacity management

---

[*] Details on the Triple Aim initiative(s) can be found at www.ihi.org.

concepts, implementation tools, and methodologies impact the Pillars, the Triple Aim, and similar groups of optimization metrics, you will have received the correct message. Remember, too, that the Five Pillars should apply to the entire community of care and the optimization of your entire capacity to care, not just your hospital, clinic, nursing home, or any other institution.

If for no other reason than distinction of the scope of the solutions, the Five Pillars are herein set apart from other healthcare nomenclature. As the scope, scale, and foci seem to be much broader and holistic than those of other solutions, the new care models described in this book need their own goals and objectives that align with its potential. The Five Pillars support and are supported by concepts like the infamous Triple Aim, and thus the latter is in no way meant to be downplayed or made any less significant. But for true capacity optimization and the movement toward health ownership, the Five Pillars better speak to the full capability to forever change the delivery system.

The Five Pillars are the optimization of

- Quality and outcomes
- Access
- Capacity
- Cost reduction
- Participant gratification

Let's describe and define these in greater detail as they relate to the broader, community-wide approach of this book.

Quality and outcomes is at the top of the list, though not because it is a more important goal than the others. All are equally important, as failure to achieve any one will inevitably and negatively impact the others. Quality is secondarily included in the IHI Triple Aim, but only as part of the second aim, "patient experience," and only if you read the fine print. I feel that quality and outcomes are important enough to warrant their own category, as many of the patients in CCNs (such as polychronics) will need the highest possible quality of care in order to see positive results in the remaining four Pillar metrics. Furthermore, quality and clinical outcomes, as increasingly important focal areas for payors and providers alike, should warrant a special category to be considered on equal footing with cost reduction.

Quality is commonly and generically known as a degree of excellence, or some superiority in kind. Quality can be both an outcome and an indicator of outcome measures like organizational effectiveness.* The latter indicators are most commonly relative measures, as quality can be either subjective or quantitative, and is often determined through comparative standards to other, lesser samples. Quality in healthcare can mean everything from the patient experience ("How good did I feel after the procedure?") to lack of adverse results ("Zero surgical infections during a given timeframe") to a clinical measurement ("Diastolic function," or "Percentage of patients receiving tPA within 3 hours of the onset of a non-hemorrhagic stroke").

---

* Winn, B. and Cameron, K. 1998. *Organizational Quality: An Examination of the Malcolm Baldrige National Quality Framework*. Springer Publishing, New York.

Quality can also refer to a measurement of the functions and processes that support clinical operations, such as cleanliness of operating rooms/theaters.

Quality related to clinical outcomes is a combination of the above. The term "quality outcomes" often reflects a combination of patient experience, clinical indicators, and standards of care. When discussing quality and outcomes, it is therefore important to settle on those clinical measures for which standards will be set, such as degree of post-rehab knee flexure for non-revision total knee replacement surgeries, while employing flexibility in the measurement of non-clinical indicators such as patient satisfaction. The measurement of outcomes can thereby be "amended" as needed to reflect the patient's experience and desires ("I can at least walk now even though I can't bend my knee as much as the doctor would like."), while using stricter clinical guidelines among caregivers ("Zero tolerance for central line infections"). This can make quality outcomes a "squishy" measurement, for which a completely rigid set of standards cannot be made. Care must be taken to quantitatively account for the variances, so as to effectively study and compare quality outcomes within and outside a given care system.

Yet, high-quality care is an obvious goal, as the alternatives (poor-to-moderate quality) will mean negative impacts on our other metrics, including patient satisfaction, cost (e.g., readmissions for the same procedure), and capacity (rework always reduces total capacity). Without an attention to and desire for the highest possible quality and outcomes, the other metrics of the Pillars will not be fully optimized.

Access is also mentioned as an ancillary to the second aim. Access will be critical in the coming years as an aging and increasingly chronically diseased population requires more and more resources, which in turn are increasingly financially constrained and relatively fewer in number. Yet access will have many more meanings in the future. Access will include access to clinical information, such as care processes and interventions; patient-specific information, such as web-based patient "portals"; care resources, whether they be physicians, clinics, social workers, or EDs; and access to physical space, such as a hospital bed or pharmacy. Access will vary by geography, with varying forms and types available based on the one's relative proximity to other people and facilities and resources.

All forms of access must be optimized relative to one another in order to maximize the effectiveness of the entire care system. As access can occur in an increasing number of ways and locations, e.g., the Internet, direct care provider contact, "minute clinics," virtual monitoring, etc., the possibilities for increasing access will multiply, assuming patients have the ability to take advantage of the many new access points. Access points may and should expand to include both "real" and virtual locations, the latter of which can both transmit clinical data and accept educational materials and clinical advice. Therefore, when we consider access in any new care system design, we should consider the availability of multiple potential points of access within a broader and more complex care network.

Capacity is perhaps the most important but most overlooked of the Pillars. Indeed, it is neither directly nor indirectly referenced within the Triple Aim, yet it encompasses all the key elements required for care provision, such as resources and labor, physical space and facilities, access points (as mentioned above), and processing capability, some of which are in short supply. Capacity refers to the general and total capability of the system to provide care, as well as that of the capabilities of individual components and resources within the system. Capacity is, then, the sum total of the capacities of all the components of the entire care system, regardless of their form or format. So, capacity encompasses clinical resources and their ability to care for and manage a certain number of patients or citizens within a population, as well as the clinical physical plant, such as the number of ED beds within a given geographic region, and all the current and latent care resources available throughout our communities.

Capacity is critical as we will see in the other chapters of this book, certain clinical human resources will be in increasingly short supply as their numbers dwindle relative to the increasing demand. Supply of these clinical human resources simply may not be able to keep up with the growing demand of retirees and the elderly. Therefore the system's total care capacity may be relatively reduced. (This is, of course, a relative measurement. As the actual number of physicians, nurses, etc., is due to increase, the actual, numerical capacity of the system will go up. However, as the demand will outstrip this new capacity, the relative capability to care for the population will decrease.)

Capacity is also reflected in processing capability. If there are not enough spaces in the hospital or clinic, additional clinical resources will not help. Likewise, if we create a system in which the processing of patients and information is difficult, tedious, or onerous, then the care capacity of the system is inevitably reduced. Thus, capacity can and should include reference to the processing capability and technology infrastructure required to effectively treat and manage patients. Without the right infrastructure and processes in place, the capacity of the system might be greatly reduced.

Thus, when we refer to "capacity" in this book you should think holistically about its meaning and how the various forms of capacity are included in its definition.

Cost. The capacity optimization models described herein are specifically focused on cost reduction. Cost is also one of the three IHI Triple Aims. Indeed, the original impetus of the "Dynamic Capacity Management" work many years ago was dramatic cost reduction to "save the system" from itself. Cost is an obvious consideration for any healthcare reform proposal. Without dramatically reducing total provision cost, any healthcare reform will fail to support our national economy because sustainable economic growth and high employment will be hampered as healthcare consumes too many financial resources, draining important capital away from the rest of the economy. Furthermore, the inefficient use of resources that drives costs also drives more resources to healthcare and away from more productive facets of the economy. Thus, like the Triple Aim and similar objectives, the Five Pillars include a distinct cost reduction element. Fortunately, cost reduction is a key attribute for the care systems proposed in this book.

Participant gratification. Although patient satisfaction is important, it is not enough in the new world of care delivery. In order for the care systems to function properly, and in order for health ownership to instill itself within our society, *all* participants must receive something of an emotional and psychological benefit. And I believe that the "something" should be more than simple "satisfaction." There needs to be a sense of "participant gratification" that can only come from doing something significantly "good," either for yourself or someone else. Gratification, at least by my definition, is a deeper and more significant sensation than mere satisfaction, and more appropriately applies to an environment that promotes personal responsibility (specifically in the form of health ownership), community engagement, and long-term system change. That's why I replace the over-used term "satisfaction" score with a term that implies a "higher level" and more broadly applied sensation.

Indeed, the concept of "patient satisfaction," in and of itself, and by definition, is too limited for me. First off, though patients matter, so do the healthcare workers in whom we invest and in whom our patients trust. More importantly, it has even been suggested that the focus of "patient satisfaction" is wrong. According to some, the focus should instead be on "physician satisfaction," because with physician satisfaction comes the best inpatient care and outcomes focus, and patient satisfaction as a by-product. However, even this

- Leaves out the other clinical resources commonly associated with care provision. Think of the fussy Rad Tech who grumbles impatiently through an exam.
- Fails to account for the myriad other non-clinical resources that can add to or take away from a patient's satisfaction. Think of that billing clerk with that nasty, "I'm entitled" attitude.
- Fails to account for the satisfaction of parents, friends, and certainly the host of communal resources into which we might tap. Without their gratification, none of this is possible!

Alternatively, gratification can and should be felt by the patient and all others in the system, from communal resources to physicians to office and hospital staff. Furthermore, the sense of gratification should come to all participants from the "higher good," that is being achieved through effective capacity management, the benefits developed for patients and the community, and the patients' sense of accomplishment through self-help and communal support.

6 Introduction to Section on Hospital Capacity Optimization

Now that you have, or are developing, a positive, caring, and inclusive culture at your facility and have reviewed the terms we will be using, you can now move quickly and effectively toward the optimization of your hospital's capacity to care and (in the next section) the integration of your communal resources into the care of your patients.

In order to optimize your hospital's total "capacity to care," you must look at your system as a system. That is, *not* as a group of individual departments and entities that can be managed separately and "fixed" in isolation. We've "been there, failed at that!" Rather, you must see the interdependencies of your various departments and understand, predict, and properly manage those interdependencies and their respective variability in order to squeeze out capacity and get the most out of your resources, physical plant, and revenues.

Understanding the interdependencies of your capacity is relatively easy. Indeed, you'll see a descriptive visual representation of those interdependencies below and in the text to follow (Figure 6.1). Managing them, however, takes a very different mind-set than most CEOs and hospital leaders have. Sadly, most of our leaders still want to "fix the ED" or "start with the OR" or "start small and work our way up." We have seen for decades that these band-aid approaches will give some, often only tempo-rary relief, but do not speedily create an environment in which leaps in performance can be had. Indeed, just look back at ED and OR conferences from many years past to see that the same issues being discussed ten or more years ago are the same issues discussed today. Length of stay, "boarding," etc., remain dominant issues. But if our methodologies were sound, we'd at least have different issues to discuss, having solved the previous ones.

Thus in this section, I propose a very different way of examining and addressing the common problems facing hospitals (and clinics and other care environments). The methodology was originally known as "Dynamic Capacity Analysis, Matching, and Management," or "DCAMM." This is now used interchangeably with "Capacity Optimization" in this book, since the latter just flows a little easier. The concept is simple: our healthcare systems are "dynamic" … that is, they change every hour of every day. Thus our solutions must be dynamic since a "static" solution will fail to keep up with the inherent changes in the system and work only to the extent that the circumstances best match its specific parameters. Rather, our dynamic sys-tems require dynamic solutions that use data to predict variability and morph as the parameters change within and outside the system. Managing systems dynamically

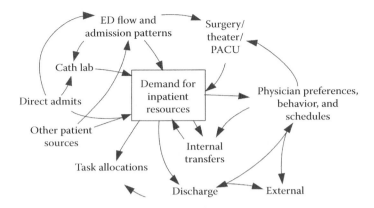

FIGURE 6.1   A visual representation of the interdependencies of hospital-wide capacity.

will allow us to squeeze more capacity from those systems and prevent more bottle-necks, constraints, and performance lags.

In this section, we will use a variety of means to help you understand and use "dynamic analytics" to attain optimized capacity. The ultimate goal is a holistic and dynamic approach to our very dynamic care environments that will yield the kind of performance that we all seek. To get there, you will need to put aside your tendency to "start small," start in this or that department, or "work in baby steps." You need to move your mind to a bigger vision of optimization and capacity and see how the various pieces and components fit together into a dynamic whole. Only then will you be able to grasp and implement real and meaningful leaps in performance.

7 Dynamic Capacity Management
An Approach to Capacity Optimization

Recall that the systems we are trying to develop are meant to care for the population at the lowest-possible societal costs while instilling a sense of personal health ownership. But we must accept the fact that the U.S. system will inherently be more expensive than that of other "peer" countries, in large part due to our relatively higher resource costs. Nonetheless, our costs must still be as low as we can make them given the constraints to effective cost control with which we are faced. Furthermore, we must pledge to use our limited and available resources as efficiently and effectively as possible so as to extend the maximum possible capacity to the healthcare needs of our communities.

HEALTHCARE *IS* DIFFERENT

To do so, we must realize that our care systems are indeed unique relative to all other industries. Unlike most manufacturing environments, healthcare is inherently "dynamic," changing every hour of every day. Just ask the manager of an ED, a surgical center, a neonatal unit, or an outpatient clinic. Patients and their disease states, demand patterns, volumes, etc., all vary to some degree over time and are certainly less than perfectly predictable (though as we'll see later, patterns exist even in the chaos of a busy ED). As I stated in the original book on this subject, "Hospitals are more like battlefields than Toyota production lines."[*] Meaning that while a Toyota factory worker knows at the beginning of each shift what work he will be doing, on what car type, and in what capacity, a nurse or physician can rarely predict exactly what their clinical interactions will be like throughout the day.

This dynamism creates special requirements for the optimization of the functionality of our healthcare systems. It requires a different way of thinking. Because the demand for care of and from our communities is dynamic, changing every hour of every day, seasonally, and throughout the year, so too must our capacity be dynamic if we are to meet that demand with the properly aligned and optimally provided resources. Thus capacity must dynamically match demand.

---

[*] Story, P. 2011. *Dynamic Capacity Management for Healthcare: Advanced Methods and Tools for Optimization*. CRC Press, New York, NY, p. xvii.

VARIABILITY AND INTERDEPENDENCIES

Two concepts are critical to the understanding of dynamic systems such as healthcare. The first is variability. Variability is a key factor in making our systems dynamic and requiring a dynamic approach to optimization. Therefore, variability must be understood, quantified, predicted, and matched to the extent possible. If it is not, we will either have too much capacity (excess resource costs, excess inventory, or too many rooms) or too little (scarce and/or overextended resources, long wait times, delayed care, and increased morbidity and mortality).

To understand the impact of variability on system performance, consider if you will, a system in which there is limited variability, much like a manufacturing production line of, say, automobile parts. The arrival of each piece of work (in the form of an unfinished automobile part) is predictable. The work to be done on each part is also largely predictable, as in most stereotypical production lines. Each worker has a specific set of tasks to do on each part that passes by. These tasks take a predictable amount of time. Then the now-more-finished part moves down the production line to the next worker and set of tasks. Here, there is little worry that a bolus of parts will show up at the front of the line. Even if there were such a bolus (perhaps when a supply truck makes a weekly drop-off), automobile parts won't complain or get angry and leave and go to another factory, much less die, if they wait for a while until they begin their trek down the production line. And, as the length of each set of tasks along the way is relatively predictable, the total time of production can be known. Importantly, the parts that make the trek down the line are all known entities, each like the other. When they finish the production process, they should all look, feel, and perform the same as the others.

See the differences already? Does that sound like your emergency department or outpatient clinic? Of course not! Healthcare is different in so many ways because of the inherent variation in nearly everything within it, from the patient types that arrive to the care processes they go through to the clinical outcomes they exhibit after a care episode.

Let's also look at the deception of the average, because we so routinely use averages to gauge the performance of just about everything in healthcare. Think about *average* length of stay, *average* volumes, *average* number of tests, *average* number of visits per physician, etc. Yet, averages can be very deceiving to the processes they are meant to describe because, due to their nature, averages don't fully describe process variability. Indeed, averages can give you a very false sense of the performance of your system or process. This can be shown using a simple spreadsheet and a calculation of averages. Table 7.1 shows three sets of numbers, added and averaged horizontally. Examine the rows in Table 7.1.

The sets of numbers all have the same average, six, shown in the rightmost column, but have vastly different highs and lows. This is a simplistic yet revealing example of the impact of variability on the decisions made with averages. So, for instance, if this data represented the number of patients admitted to an inpatient unit on Tuesday afternoons, nurses would find the situation created by data Set 1 much less chaotic and much more predictable than that of data Set 3. As the range of data in Set 1 is very "tight," between five and seven admissions, each day would be

TABLE 7.1

Deception of the Average as Shown in Three Series of Numbers with the Same Overall Average

										Average
Set 1	5	6	7	5	6	7	5	6	7	6
Set 2	3	6	9	3	6	9	9	6	3	6
Set 3	11	1	11	1	1	1	11	11	10	6

expected to be largely like the last and the next. It will feel less chaotic than the range of data Set 3, which goes anywhere from one admission to 11. Imagine trying to work in the world of Set 3, where the range around the average is very high. Indeed, think about trying to staff for the data Set 3 situation versus the others!

Now, think about the last process or value stream map you created for your department, unit, or healthcare process. Did it evolve as your volumes, patient types, or patient-specific demands changed over time, or was it the same for each and every circumstance, situation, and occurrence? Most commonly, it was the latter "static" map. Of course, that "stasis" in your process map may have been quite appropriate for the tasks the map was meant to replicate. Indeed, at a low-level, highly granular process level, variation might be either minimal or inconsequential or both. Take, for instance, the triage process in a low-volume ED that might remain static regardless of the volume of arriving patients, or the registration process upon arrival for day surgery. However, if the process or value stream map for an entire ED fails to change as flu season arrives, staffing patterns change, or the volume ebbs and flows, it might not be functionally correct 100% of the time. In other words, under certain scenarios and conditions, the process breaks down. Thus, you will commonly hear staff describe the "Yeah, but …" scenario when mapping a department-wide flow as they remember scenarios in which external or internal factors changed and required the process to change and/or caused the process to break down. Therefore, if at least some of our work environments are dynamic enough to warrant it, our work and processes must vary to the extent necessary to maintain whatever optimization we have attained. This dynamism could come in the form of changes to the staffing, processes, or other responses depending on the nature of the variations of the system.

Thus, you may indeed need a "dynamic" map (and yes, there is such a thing!), one that allows for the accommodation of varying processes, systems, and demand through dynamic adjustments to capacity. Or, you may need multiple maps of the same process depending on the extent of the changes required to accommodate the variation. That is, your process may need to flex significantly as the circumstances in which you are performing work flex. Of course, process mapping can be critical to the understanding and quantification of processes, and is commonly a starting point for most process analysis, by whatever name. But, due to the dynamic nature of some operations and processes, it may be difficult to find a single, universal approach to the process that will work in each and every situation, making it difficult to have a single and universally applicable process map.

Variation comes into play in several ways within our systems. Think about the variability of process times (e.g., the time required to perform a total joint replacement or, at a smaller scale, the time required for ED triage); volumes by HOD and DOW; patient types; and disease states and comorbidities. Indeed, variation hits complex systems in many ways simultaneously, making the systems much more difficult to optimize by impacting everything from the need for human resources to the need for equipment and physical plant to the cost of the provision of care. *Indeed, it is said that variation kills efficiency in the same way that culture kills strategy!*

Variation, then, is a key element in the reason for the need for a dynamic approach to optimization. Without accounting for variation, you will never optimize your complex systems.

INTERDEPENDENCIES

The other key element that makes our healthcare systems so dynamic is the "interdependencies" among departments, areas, processes, and operations. Interdependencies arise as one department, area, process, or operation influences the ones upstream or downstream from it. In complex systems, these interdependencies can become quite daunting as the variability in each element plays on and against the others in the system.

Were our systems free of variability, the interdependencies of the system would be of little issue. Think again of the automobile parts factory wherein there is a series of processes linked together by a conveyor-driven production line. As long as the required process time for each worker's tasks with each part is relatively predictable, one can predict when the next part will arrive downstream and when another should be expected from upstream. Yes, the processes are interdependent in that one process leads to and is impacted by the next. But this impact is essentially non-existent and unnoticeable since, because there is little variability, there is little to cause delays or constraints in the entire system. Only when one or more of the processes along the way varies significantly does the system become more difficult to understand and predict. So, for instance, if a worker's tasks on a part are variable each time, sometimes taking much longer and sometimes much less, predicting the downstream arrival of that worker's part to the next worker becomes much more difficult or even impossible. Think here of the time required for an ED physician's disposition decision on all the patients he or she sees in a given day, or the recovery times of patients with heavy sedation. And when all the processes in the system vary, predicting the total processing time for a given part becomes very difficult. This is much closer to the situation we face in healthcare.

Figure 7.1 graphically shows the complex interdependencies of hospital-wide interactions.

It shows, for example, that the demand that comes into and out of the ED into the inpatient units competes with the demand that comes from the OR and direct admissions. Because the downstream demand changes as volumes, acuities, and patient needs change (they are ALL variable!), the interdependencies among and between these areas change throughout the day, week, and year.

Likewise, there are interdependencies between the hospital and external resources and entities such as nursing homes, long-term acute care (LTAC), and home health.

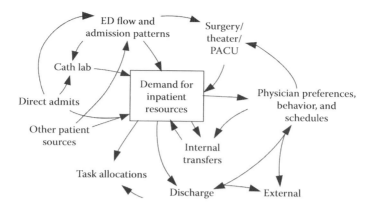

FIGURE 7.1   A visual representation of the interdependencies of hospital-wide capacity.

If, for instance, a given nursing home refuses to take admissions after 1600 on Friday and throughout the weekend, the hospital's "upstream" systems can become constrained, leaving patients languishing in their inpatient units until Monday afternoon, with high costs and unnecessary stress on hospital financial resources and staff while they wait for an appropriate level of care.

Interdependencies influence workload, workflow, staff and physical plant requirements, and the ability to move patients efficiently and effectively throughout their systemic journey. Constraints in one area yield constraints in others. Worse yet, great improvements in one area often yield up- or downstream bottlenecks in another, leaving the system no better or even worse off than before. This is why failing to recognize interdependencies is a crucial flaw in many process improvement methodologies where a "process focus" leaves the system still lagging in performance. As an analogy, we play "Whack-A-Mole" with our constraints. That is, we chase the bottlenecks and constraints around the system only to find another elsewhere within the system that needs to be addressed. Mapping and understanding the impact of these interdependencies, and the variability with them all, is critical to systemic optimization. And unfortunately, this is not something most process improvement methodologies teach or use.

Interdependencies Writ Large

On an even broader scale, we see the systemic interdependencies that influence health in our communities. As a nation, we are beginning to discover what I have been preaching for at least a decade … that we are not addressing the interdependencies of the many social, economic, physical, environmental, and spiritual factors of health and well-being. That is, we are focused on fiddling with care provision rather than on altering the entirety of the care system to be more localized, personalized, broad in scope, effective, and efficient. We will see this in the subsequent chapters of this book related to the community of care and the improved management of communal resources.

SUMMARY OF VARIABILITY AND INTERDEPENDENCIES

Thus, these two factors, variability and interdependencies, have created the need for new analytical methodologies and approaches in the complex world of healthcare capacity optimization. I herein propose that the concept of dynamic capacity management is an additive solution for this pressing problem. Let's now delve into the relevance of this dynamism to our goal of system-wide capacity management.

DEMAND PATTERNS AND THE RELEVANCE OF RANGES

As mentioned earlier, these seemingly chaotic systems are not impossible to grasp and control, though they may often seem to be. Even within the most-seemingly chaotic of systems, there are normally patterns within the variability and, thus, patterns within the interdependencies that can be detected and used for system management. These patterns are critical for assessing, understanding, predicting, and working within complex systems. This is particularly true in critical areas of hospital operations, such as the ED, which we'll focus on here.

Think of the arrivals of patients into an ED (a classic source of "demand" for care). Figure 7.2 shows an example of the arrivals-per-hour pattern taken from data of an ED over the course of several weeks.

Figure 7.2 shows the average volume of patients arriving per hour (shown as the bars in the chart), as well as the most common volume range around the average (shown as lines called "High" and "Low"). Though volumes will always vary from ED to ED, this arrival *pattern* is likely not dissimilar to that of your ED, with increasing volumes in the late morning, continuing until early evening, and dropping off only during late-evening hours. The patterns are similar if we break out DOW though, again, the volumes will likely vary between the busiest and less-busy days.

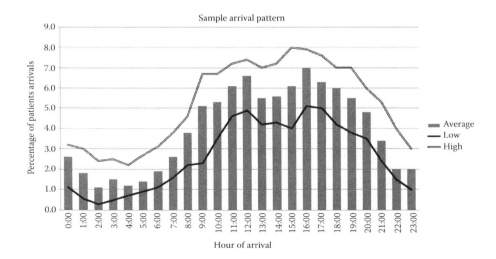

FIGURE 7.2 Sample arrival patterns of patients into an ED.

However, note that the lower the volume, the more randomized arrivals will be. So, for instance, the arrival patterns of patients into critical access hospital EDs is far less "patternable" than that of a busy urban hospital. The daily volumes are such that patterns are harder to detect, as there may simply be more time between individual arrivals. So, rather than detecting patterns by, say, the hour, one would likely look for and detect patterns in larger time segments, such as 3- to 6-hour blocks. Likewise, arrivals of cath lab patients into a relatively small and low-volume cath lab would be patterned on longer time slots than those of very busy cath labs. But regardless of the size and volume of your department, if your demand is unscheduled, you can very likely find meaningful demand patterns if you look at the data properly.

That said, refer back to Figure 7.2 and its three-data series, the average and the high and low ranges around the average. It is these latter ranges that are in fact far more important and useful to us as we study demand, for if I know the most common range—that is, the range of volumes I have seen historically within a given period—we can predict that the range will hold true in the future. This is far easier and, frankly, far more important to the optimization of our operational models than predicting a single number (most commonly, the average).

THE RELEVANCE OF RANGES

For instance, even with the best of historical data, I could not accurately and consistently predict the exact volume your ED will see tomorrow between the hours of 1000 and 1200. If you were guessing at tomorrow's volume, you might instinctively guess the average volume for those hours. But, you would commonly be incorrect to some degree, as the average only represents one value out of the entire range of possible values in the historical data set. Alternatively, you might predict the mode (the most common value) in the data set for those hours. Yet, even the most common data point might only occur 20% of the time, depending on the degree of variation in the system. Thus you would have an eight-in-ten chance of being wrong.

However, that same historical data will very likely show you the most common range around the average volume, which means that you can readily and confidently predict the range of the volumes tomorrow during those hours. This range of values is that which most commonly occurs throughout the data period, forming a relatively "tight" band around the average. If you select this range of values, you may be wrong on occasion, but if historical patterns hold true, you should be correct more times than not. This is simply based on the fact that you are choosing a broader set of possible behaviors rather than just a single possibility. You will simply be correct more often. But this range is important to us for reasons other than accuracy bragging rights.

First, these ranges show that my otherwise largely unpredictable world can become relatively predictable and certain. I can now routinely predict a range of demand/arrivals, giving me more certainty about the environments in which I work, which lends well to a more positive and less chaotic work environment. In our client analytics, we commonly use a range of between 60% and 80% of historical occurrences to predict future behaviors. Predicting behavior that will occur upwards of 80% of the time offers a much more complete understanding of the world in which

52 Optimizing Your Capacity to Care

you work, and can aid in more flexible and effective solutions design. Thus a deeper understanding of demand ranges offers our clients a much better understanding of the overall requirements for servicing their communal demand.

Second, the most common ranges allow you to study the system's ability to handle various demand scenarios. Simple historical "detective work" can show what occurs when various volumes arrive into the ED per hour, and to what extent a higher- or lower-than-average volume impacts the overall historical performance. So, I can detect what volumes put the ED over some "tipping point" and cause its performance to degrade. I can also study the "downstream" behaviors of interdependent departments and areas to gauge their ability to manage the output of the ED at various levels of activity. This might include radiology, lab, transportation, or inpatient units.

Third, the ranges allow me to distinguish what is normal and abnormal demand on a given day in a given season. So, for instance, a normal summer Tuesday might see a total ED volume of between 135 and 160 patients based on historical data. Occasionally, of course, there will be "one of those days" when the volumes are either higher or lower than the common range. But being able to discern the most common days from these "outlier" days helps to distinguish when and at what levels I might need to alter the system's capacity.

Before we move on, it is worthwhile to point out that ED volumes are not the only application for the concept of patterning. We commonly use this concept with clients to analyze demand for surgery, admissions, direct admission arrivals, discharges, and other important milestones and processes along the patient's care continuum. Indeed, we will often apply these same patterning concepts to the "capacity side" of the equation, as they too must necessarily vary over time.

Now that we can distinguish the normal from the outlier, let's talk a little about the latter.

OUTLIERS

In systems with high variability and complex interdependencies, there are often "outliers." That is, those relatively rare occurrences that lie outside the main body or group that it is a part of, such as an ED LOS that lasts 36 hours; a patient whose obesity and history of smoking puts her at risk for an otherwise standard surgical procedure; or an individual process time that takes four times longer than the typical process time. Outliers, because they are extremes, have a much more dramatic impact than small, more normal variations. Indeed, outliers are what tend to drive our systems to break down, resulting in longer-than-normal LOS, delivery times, wait times, etc. And outliers are commonly what staff remember most often when you ask about working conditions or other attributes of the systems in which they work.

In this book, I will refer to outliers in a number of ways. Here in this chapter, I will use the term to describe the instances of variable volumes, process times, and other quantifiable system attributes that are outside normal behavioral patterns and their impacts on the interdependencies of the systems. Here and elsewhere, I will refer to outliers in the overall population of patients, such as "poly-chronics" (patients with multiple chronic diseases). As we move into community care models later in this book, Chapter 16 will detail groupings and categorizations of patients that aid in distinguishing various levels of care requirements, resources, and costs of care provision. This includes 5% of the population (outliers) who use and cost the most and the 80% who use and cost the least. Thus outliers can refer to extremes in data, processes, populations, costs, and other variants.

In a given process, outliers have a tendency to be randomized in their appearance into the process or area they impact. Think of "bus crash day" in the ED, or a surge of flu patients … largely if not totally unpredictable. This makes them all the more troublesome as they don't follow any of the normal, readily detectable patterns of occurrence. While there are, no doubt, statisticians who could even help ascertain these patterns, for practical purposes we will assume them to be random in their appearance, and most definitely severe in their impact(s) on system performance.

Outliers may need to be managed differently from the more normal variations in our systems. Whether the overweight smoking diabetic surgery patient or the abnormal volume of mental health patients arriving into the ED, processes and operational models may need to flex to fit the situation. This is of course another reason for the need for a dynamic nature in our capacity management approach.

RELEVANCE TO CAPACITY MANAGEMENT

Obviously the dynamism of our systems requires a different approach than is common among the typical "industrial" process improvement methodologies. Theirs are made for the relatively static worlds of production lines, wherein a part arrives every X minutes and is moved on down the line precisely Y minutes later. Theirs are relatively simple environments in which there is relatively minimal variability, and certainly few if any "outliers." Hospitals are, on the other hand, all about the variation, interdependencies, and outliers that impact performance. Beyond this, there is great variation in the demand within the community writ large … in our clinics, nursing homes, and physician offices. This yields greater degrees of dynamism within our systems and a greater need for dynamic analytics and optimization efforts. Of course, understanding the dynamism in demand may seem daunting. Yet, there is still one side of the demand–capacity continuum that we have not addressed.

MAKING CAPACITY DYNAMIC

We have established that demand is dynamic, changing throughout the system every hour of every day of every season. We have also established that variability and interdependencies combine to create this dynamism that so plagues our performance optimization efforts. And, finally, I hope you are convinced that healthcare needs its own performance optimization methodology if we are ever to truly reach optimal performance. That is, if we are ever to properly match demand with available capacity, we need something very different from what we have used in the past. But before we align the stars, we need to examine the "yang" of demand's "yin," capacity.

Capacity can be broadly defined as the care needed to meet the demand generated. Capacity can come in the form of physical plant (offices, hospitals, and clinics), human resources (techs, nurses, and physicians), and operational models that enable the necessary care to be done. Capacity, like demand, is dynamic, whether by intentional or unintentional design. We would like for capacity to be flexible enough to meet the ever-changing patterns of demand, while understanding that some outliers (e.g., extreme demand into an ED) are sometimes just unpredictable enough as to make immediate capacity matching nearly impossible. Thus, we would like to be able to intentionally alter capacity to dynamically match the incoming demand.

However, we currently flex our capacity in ways that do not reflect the demand in the system. This ineffective use of capacity can look like inpatient nurse shifts that do not accurately reflect workload from admissions and discharges throughout the day; lab and radiology-staffing patterns that do not reflect the number of tests and exams ordered; or community resources that close on weekends just as they are most needed by the community. These errors in capacity management are normally not intended to purposefully inconvenience patients and other up- and downstream care providers, but are rather relics of past operational models that are no longer effective. Furthermore, these errors may be reflections of siloed workload and workflow preferences, built without regard to systemic impacts or without system knowledge of the interdependencies of systemic operations.

Thus, in order to dynamically, accurately, and effectively manage capacity we need to do two things: (1) understand the demand patterns and their outliers for which capacity is to be made available and (2) understand the actual capacity that each element of the system adds, so as to appropriately increment and decrement capacity as necessary.

The first has been described in detail previously in this chapter. The second requires a deep study of the resources, processes, and operational models to assess how much capacity is available using various combinations of the elements of capacity at the various levels of demand. So, at a process level, if I add a tech to ED triage, how much additional capacity do I get? At a department level, if I add a neurosurgeon to the surgical schedule, what capacity does that add to the community and the hospital's total "capacity to care?" At a hospital level, if I build a new emergency department, am I augmenting total communal capacity or am I just stealing patients away from another facility, which doesn't truly add to the community's "capacity to care" but rather merely shifts the location of care provision? And at a community level, how many primary care physicians are needed to manage the care of my community's "poly-chronics?" Some of these are easy to answer, others not. Regardless of your locus, you need to consider the demand that you are facing, when it arrives and in what forms, and the best forms of capacity to match it.

In doing so, you likely need to toss out traditional models, staffing patterns, resources, and care locations to make way for new community care and operational models. Thus, your ED may be split into several sub-EDs, each seeing different kinds of patients. Your human resources may find themselves in disparate locations doing new and very different tasks as the community becomes more aware of its care needs and takes on the health ownership described earlier in this book. You may incorporate tele-health as well as the myriad communal resources available to augment your own "capacity to care" and enable a healthier populace. And you may align with many or even all of the providers (defined very broadly!) in your community even before population health payment models begin to take shape.

Start with the process level, in most cases. Here, you can study the individual processes' capacity to handle demand, keeping in mind the up- and downstream capacity and requirements as you consider changes. This automatically leads to a broader examination of the larger system, whether that be at a small scale (e.g., a single department) or a larger scale (e.g., an entire hospital). Continue to examine the demand patterns and the impacts of outliers on the capacity requirements, and determine where, what, and how much capacity is required at each stage/process/level. Continue this as you look into the larger-systems questions where you examine your entire catchment area or community and the capacity required to effectively meet the variable demand it generates. To this add an analysis of the various communal resources within your community, from churches to civic clubs to schools to volunteers to assess how, where, when, and to what extent you might align with and deploy them. This could yield an examination of the total capacity offered by all the hospitals, clinics, physician offices, and all communal resources in your community and a determination of where, when, and by how much capacity is lagging or excessive.

Thus your new methodology would take into account the aforementioned dynamism in both demand and capacity and the variety of capacity-enabling options available to you and your community. This becomes the analysis, matching, and management of the full "Demand–Capacity Continuum," which is the goal of this section.

DCAMM AND OTHER PI METHODOLOGIES

However, your current process/PI methodologies are likely not up to this task, as they may lack critical analytical approaches and capabilities that will enable your success. As you may only have a cursory knowledge of the more popular "industrial" PI methodologies, and even less knowledge of their possible integration with DCAMM, let's take a quick look to see what a truly dynamic approach might add to your existing or future approaches to optimization.

Six Sigma, once hailed by a few large hospital systems as the "final solution," has largely fallen by the wayside in healthcare. I don't see too many purely Six Sigma shops, or pure Six Sigma consultants in healthcare. This is largely because Six Sigma got a bad name for itself with the scale and scope of projects (which were by definition and requirement large scale) and the demands for large amounts of data (which at the time was not as available as it is now), whereas other methodologies were less rigorous, analytical, and complex. A few of the good parts of Six Sigma that were retained were some minor analytical applications such as control charts and basic analytics. As Lean came onto the scene, Six Sigma was quickly either abandoned or melded into the former.

Lean began to invade healthcare several decades ago, with very mixed results. Lean was first successful because, frankly, anything was better than nothing, and the bottom was a great place from which to start. Lean required no complex analytics, no rigorous methodologies, or large-scale projects. Indeed, Lean was quite good at very small, incremental improvement efforts. Chipping away at a problem (e.g., fixing ED triage) seemed better than tackling the entire problem head on (e.g., hospital-wide flow), even though this has been shown to be problematic as well. This approach was meant to give confidence to staff and local managers by allowing "quick wins."

Lean, as practiced in manufacturing, did initially come with some relatively rigorous methodologies. Indeed, a few high-end consulting firms still stick with at least some of the original Lean approaches and methods. But, as it was adopted into healthcare, it quickly morphed away from this rigor and has now become, in most circles, little more than a process improvement effort called Lean for the sake of the need for a name. Some have made themselves rather famous as Lean shops, though their efforts to make significant progress has often taken a decade or more. Indeed, "Lean transformations" are sold as multiyear, multimillion-dollar projects that purport to evolve the entire system and all its workers into a Lean-thinking organization. The actual long-term successes of these "transformations" are few, though the consultants purporting success are many.

Unfortunately, these days Lean has few real standards. Therefore Lean means just about any process improvement work in healthcare. There is no governing body controlling what is and is not called "Lean," nor are there universal education standards, nor standard tools, techniques, or methods. Indeed, if you ask five CEOs of hospitals with ongoing Lean programs what Lean is all about, you might get five very different answers. Some will say "waste reduction," others will say "process improvement," and still others might say "rapid improvement and VSMs." That's because Lean in healthcare long ago lost its true core as less regimented and more "fluid" followers adopted, adapted, molded, and borrowed from the original works by Lean authors and thinkers and melded it with what might actually work. Small wonder, really. Process improvement was invented well before the 1940s when what we know today as Lean budded onto the scene, and healthcare needed something more than what had been adopted from manufacturing. What were once value stream maps are now just ordinary process maps, sometimes in highly modified forms such as "swimlane" maps. Lean has some great ideas, such as focusing on the six to eight categories of wastes (muda), getting your work areas organized (5S), managing inventory (Kanban), management involvement in PI (Gemba), and deeply understanding the process flows (VSMs). Yet, much of this is either lost or purposefully left out to avoid creating complexity and confusion among healthcare staff.

LEAN SIX SIGMA AND WHAT IT MISSES

What has emerged is becoming increasingly successful. Until recently, some 70% of Lean projects in healthcare ultimately failed, and its reputation as a PI methodology has already been abandoned in favor of a "blended" approach that borrows from many and hybridizes new approaches. It is not surprising, then, that Lean was melded with Six Sigma (which added a data and analytical bent to Lean's hands-on, dataless focus) in healthcare. Now, like Lean itself, Lean Six Sigma (LSS) can roughly be defined as process improvement with some data thrown in for measurement and management.

Despite some of the good it brings, LSS still lacks a great deal. Lean tends to be very "process oriented," meaning that Lean projects called Kaizen Events, Rapid Improvement Events, etc. (see, we can't even agree on a name for improvement experiments!) tend to be focused on small parts of the system rather than on the system itself. Indeed, Lean has failed so miserably in the past in part because it failed to address the very systemic dynamism that we are discussing in this book. Lean doesn't "do" hospital-wide optimization all at once because its methodologies are made for improving processes, not systems. This is why hospital- and system-wide change can take decades under the Lean approach.

Also, typically, Lean tends to be very "non-data" oriented. Even when mixed with Six Sigma, Lean relies on observation, singular value streams of limited scope, and commonly fails to account for complex interdependencies and variation. Indeed, one infamous healthcare Lean author once told me, "We don't need data. Hospitals don't have it anyway." The impact of this failure can be felt throughout the implementation efforts. Variation, for instance, is assumed to "wash out" to the average, giving Lean consultants an easy excuse to avoid complex analysis and deal at the highest levels of the process. Yet, as implementation is tried and variation hits the process (e.g., summer changes to flu season in winter), the process breaks down, staff become frustrated, and revert quickly to the "old ways" that they know best (which, frankly, might be the appropriate response if studied within the context of the environment). As you now know, this leads to a failure to take into account the impact of outlier-level variation on system performance. And this in turn can yield some very errant solutions!

Don't take all this the wrong way ... LSS is not bad! It isn't great, and will never get healthcare where it truly needs to be ... but it isn't all bad! Indeed, there is much that the melding of some of the Lean tools, approaches, and Six Sigma analytical methodologies can bring to a more dynamic approach to system optimization. But LSS alone will never solve for healthcare's truly dynamic systems. Healthcare, as I've stated for over a decade now, needs its own process improvement approach to systemic capacity optimization.

That approach is what this book is all about.

SUMMARY

As we have seen, as you have experienced throughout your healthcare career, your communal demand varies, sometimes significantly, by HOD, DOW, WOM, and SOY.[*] Furthermore, if you have examined your capacity at all, you know that your capacity also varies as resources come on and off shift, units and floors open and close, physicians are added to or leave your OR, and competitors add physical plants. The ability to match capacity with this dynamic demand is a critical component of the optimization of your capacity to care. Without dynamically matching demand with capacity, you will forever have either too much or too little capacity, yielding everything from long wait times for service to physical limits to serving your community to excessive resource costs and higher-than-necessary total cost of care.

Examining your capacity will require you to toss out old operational and care models in favor of new ways, places, and resources to care for patients in the community,

---

[*] HOD—hour of day; DOW—day of week; WOM—week of month; and SOY—season of year.

inclusive of many that you have never considered or haven't tried to integrate in the past. Once you have a solid understanding of the demand, its variation and outliers, and fully understand all the available capacity in your community, then and only then can you begin to effectively manage the "Demand–Capacity Continuum" on a large, community-wide scale.

8 The Blocking and Tackling of Hospital Capacity Management
An Overview

The impetus for the following chapters came from my learnings from my history in performance optimization in healthcare, and a deep understanding of the needs for system optimization. In so many of the facilities in which our company works, we continue to see a dearth of what we would consider to be the "basics" of capacity management. Whether in the OR, ED, or inpatient units, hospitals are simply not doing what we call the "Blocking and Tackling" of capacity management.

Furthermore and importantly, few, if any, have truly tapped into their "community of care" and embraced all the resources that community has to offer. The vast majority only focus on those external resources and relationships that can impact revenues or perhaps reduce some direct costs associated with a specific program (e.g., bundled payments).

The term "Blocking and Tackling" comes from the old Green Bay Packers football team and its legendary coach, Vince Lombardi. The Packers, it is said, won games because they did two things better than their opponents: blocking and tackling. In a famous quote, Lombardi states: "Some people try to find things in this game that don't exist, but football is only two things—blocking and tackling." Thus, the Packers had players like Jerry Kramer on the offensive line and Ray Nitchzke on defense who were the best in their respective positions at football basics (blocking and tackling). As a result, they didn't have to rely solely on their skilled players like the quarterback, wide receiver, or kicker to always make big plays to win games. The games were won "in the trenches," as game broadcasters would always remind us.

The phrase has been adopted to refer to anything fundamental to achievement, whether in school (e.g., reading), business (e.g., integrity), or life generally (e.g., a positive outlook). I use the term here in a similar fashion, referring to the fundamentals of capacity management without which hospitals cannot achieve higher levels of performance. Obviously, the need for dramatic change is great and growing rapidly. But without doing the basics, the Blocking and Tackling of Capacity Management, hospitals cannot possibly achieve the great leaps toward optimization that will be so germane to the future of healthcare delivery.

Most are neither difficult nor expensive. None are impossible. Yet all require solid and strong management, visionary leadership, and collaboration from all parties in the system. All require changes to be made in most systems, and all require a positive culture and a proactive, engaged workforce (see Joe Tye's chapter in this book).

Of course, the former drives the latter; so, both must be in place, or else one can squash the other.

Implementing the Blocking and Tackling of Capacity Management will mean becoming well prepared for any possible future delivery and reimbursement models. Properly implementing these elements will get your facility eighty-plus percent of the way to full capacity optimization, and do so without great expense, time, and frustration.

Most importantly, by giving you these relatively few, simple elements here in this book, I am giving you the means by which to make great leaps toward optimization *without the need for million-dollar consultants and crazy–expensive software!* Indeed, I see the million-dollar Lean consulting firms offering *far less* than what I am including here for under $100!

So, as you read through the next few chapters, keep the goals of optimization in mind. Remember what you've already learned about culture (from Joe Tye), and the essentials of DCAMM, interdependencies, and the dynamism of our complex healthcare systems. Remember, too, that we will at some point move to a population health operational and reimbursement model, and health ownership is a key goal for those models. This alone should give you the impetus to examine your current levels of optimization and the use of the elements of the Blocking and Tackling of Capacity Management listed in the chapters to follow. Look for your gaps, and work quickly to fill them. *Only* once you have done this, should you consider calling in the expensive consultants to help you get the next 10%–20% of the way to optimization. My hope is that you will have figured out what you need to do by the time you implement the essentials listed herein.

9 Blocking and Tackling of Capacity Management in the Emergency Department

Why are we still discussing this? Is the optimization of ED performance really that difficult? Is moving patients through an ED really that hard? Is the systemic optimization of the hospital so elusive that we must continue to beat our proverbial heads against brick walls of constraints and bad process? One would think so! In reviewing some rather old journals and conference notes that date back to the early 1990s, I saw much the same topics that we see in today's journals and conferences. These include solutions for ED throughput, solving ED length of stay, improving patient flow through ED redesign, and Lean for ED flow. In reviewing the presentations from a 2014 "patient flow" conference, I found largely the same topics, concepts, and ideas as I'd seen a decade ago at a very similar conference.

Perhaps we've just received bad advice from the "gurus" of the business. Without naming names, I know plenty of "Lean" consultants, "management engineering" experts, and "patient flow" technology providers whose advise is, in my humble opinion, not only bad but frankly counterproductive. They still haven't quite grasped the need to look at the system as a system, and choose instead to pick and choose individual, sometimes overly small, projects in what they depict as a "long march" towards better productivity and patient care. What they are actually doing is playing "Whack-A-Mole" with the EDs issues and constraints. As they solve for, say, triage throughput, they push a bottleneck downstream to physician productivity where the gains die on the hill of inpatient placement constraints.

I recently ran across a classic example of such a disservice. A well-paid and very well-known Lean consultant had been hired to "fix" the ED. This particular ED had horrible problems with inpatient placement constraints, and post-disposition lengths of stay averaging 3–5 hours! So what did this Lean expert choose to attack? The front end, of course! By his methodologies, starting at the front and working his way back into the ED would gradually help solve all the problems this ED faced, and thus, through myriad value stream mapping sessions and kaizen events, lead the ED to a better place. Frankly, I fear this hospital is spending a lot of money for nothing!

I also recently ran into a very frustrated CEO who had spent literally millions of dollars hiring one of the "big name" firms to fix, once and for all, his EDs issues and constraints. The "big name" firm had its regimented approach from which deviation was not allowed. To borrow a phrase, they had their story and they were sticking to it!

In typical consulting firm fashion, they (figuratively) backed up a bus to the front door and off-loaded a battalion of recent graduates and recent MBAs with clipboards and 6 weeks of healthcare training. Needless to say, they knew what the problems were before anyone set foot in the place, and they had their prescription already filled out based on the prescriptions from their other engagements. It was as rote and as basic as it could be. And it didn't work.

As a last example, I ran into yet another Lean consultant who, to his credit, was well-versed in Japanese terminology but knew little or nothing about healthcare. "I don't need to know healthcare … I know Lean," he proudly proclaimed! In his mind, and frankly in the minds of every other Lean consultant I've encountered, Lean is so universally applicable that it works in every situation, in any market, and with any operational model. Sadly, in chatting about his projects, he confused the ED and OR and couldn't begin to describe the nuances of the interdependencies in hospital-wide flow. "No worries!" he said. "We'll just value-stream the whole thing and get to the bottom of it quickly. Lean works … it just does." Needless to say, this consultant banked his ridiculous fees yet the hospital failed to see any long-term results from his efforts, and put the blame squarely on the physicians and nurses rather than the methodology or approach he had pulled from his limited knowledge.

Indeed, an examination of the data in CMS' Hospital Compare database reveals some unpleasant truths. Take a look at the self-proclaimed leaders in the most common PI methodologies, particularly Lean, and you'll find that their key ED performance metrics are no different, and sometimes worse, than just about any average hospital. Indeed, they fare mediocre at best on Admit LOS, wait times for admission after disposition, discharge LOS, and Door-to-Provider time. Even hospital systems that teach other hospitals Lean do no better than most average facilities of comparable volume and size. How could this be, given the multi-year history of Lean in these facilities? How could they be hitting the same LOS walls as everyone else? I don't mean to be unreasonably harsh, but shouldn't we ask why these systems, in particular, so steeped as they are in industrial PI methodologies, fare no better than any others?

A recent meta-study reveals similarly damning results. Forty-seven hospitals used Lean methodologies for 2 years to improve ED performance. Out of those EDs, 13 saw NO improvement in key metrics over the 2-year period. Of the 35 others, the average reduction in discharge LOS was a mere 25 minutes. That's it!?! In most hospitals, that's barely a 10% impact … in 2 years!

Certainly, we cannot say that we haven't given the ED its due focus. Indeed, the ED is often the first area addressed by external and internal consultants and senior managers. Clearly, then, something is amiss. For all the millions spent on external consulting, books and training, and internal staff oversight and overtime, where are the awesome results that mean the most to patients, like length of stay, wait time for admission, and door-to-doc times?

Perhaps the issue is that Lean and the other methodologies don't focus on these metrics, rather focusing on waste reduction, elimination of excess inventory, reduction is staff travel times, and other forms of waste. These are certainly all laudable goals. And yet the key metrics by which EDs are typically judged aren't moving beyond a certain inflection point.

This could only be due to two reasons:

- We have truly reached the limit of ED performance improvement.
- Lean and others alone are not adept at dramatically moving these particular needles.

I tend to believe the latter. And that is what this chapter is all about.

Thus, for starters, hospitals might be simply getting the wrong answers from the consultants they hire and the educational conferences they attend. That is not to say that Lean projects don't work. Indeed, they can! While I have seen many failures, I have also seen many successes where Lean ideas and tools (e.g., value stream maps, walking the process, and looking constantly for waste in the flow) help to solve big problems. Just the idea of waste elimination is often inspiration enough for staff to begin engaging in the performance improvement effort. Lean can be a great process improvement methodology if applied in the right way to the right environment.

The issues come when the solutions developed for one process or area butt up against the failings of the up- or downstream processes or areas. Then, the wheels of improvement in the former begin to fall off. And this is why so many senior managers have become so disenchanted with Lean as a methodology … not because it is bad per se and in and of itself, but rather because it missed enough key elements of performance optimization that its failure rate is overly high. Indeed, it is said that some 70% of Lean healthcare projects fail in the end, especially in the long run. This explains why in some of the largest and most successful hospital systems, the term "Lean" is not allowed to be used!

These gaps in success are in part due to what also seems to be missing in these approaches … a "systems" view. That is, a view of the system as a dynamic, interdependent system that needs to be analyzed and fixed as such. Obviously, Lean has been tried, as has Six Sigma and other process improvement methodologies. While good for certain process improvements, these methodologies continue to show their lack of ability to create widespread systemic change due to the inherent inability to look system wide at the complexities of system operations.

What I therefore purport herein (and in previous works) is not the elimination of Lean, Six Sigma, or other methodologies but rather an addition to them. Healthcare *is* different! So we might as well accept the fact that, as I have stated numerous times before, "Hospitals are more like battlefields than Toyota production lines." Thus we need to treat healthcare differently, address issues and constraints differently, and solve for problems in a very different way. We can certainly borrow and keep elements of Lean, Six Sigma, and other methodologies that make sense (e.g., Gemba, statistical analysis) but add critical components that will allow for a more robust, sustainable, and effective solution.

With this in mind, let's look at the ED, perhaps the most studied department in the hospital, and the one with the most to gain from patient flow optimization. In my efforts to do so, I will focus on those systemic issues that most commonly impact ED operations. Thus I will not deal with each and every process and function in the department … that is a book in and of itself. Rather we will discuss those key operational elements that are impacted and constrained by the up- and downstream operations to which they are connected. We'll start at the "front end" of the ED process through to the "back door" and into the community, and discuss key important concepts that make up the blocking and tackling of ED operations. Our discussions will include not only ED operations but those of other departments, supporting services, and the community writ large. The latter, as we will discover, is perhaps the most important element in the future of your ED's delivery system.

BREAKING DOWN THE ARRIVAL DATA

ARRIVAL PATTERNS

We don't get to schedule admissions into our EDs. If we did, we might find it easier to function. However, we can no more control ED arrivals than we can control the traffic on the freeway that creates the accidents that lead to our ambulance arrivals, or the children whose activities lead to broken limbs and sprained ankles. But that doesn't mean that we are at the mercy of ever-variable and unpredictable arrivals. Rather, we can study and learn to predict them with stunning accuracy.

A colleague, Dr. Kirk Jensen[*] (who runs one of the best ED and hospitalist physician staffing firms in the country) once presented a slide of some 50 hospital ED arrival patterns layered one atop the other. The line chart, similar to that shown in Figure 9.1, showed nearly mirrored arrival patterns of patients across a 24-hour period. Starting with midnight on the far left, we see a steep decrease in arrivals as the volumes drop in the wee small hours of the morning. Beginning at about 0700, they begin to perk up. By 1100, arrivals per hour are on a steep upward climb that continues and peaks between 1200 and 1400. Commonly, these volumes remain

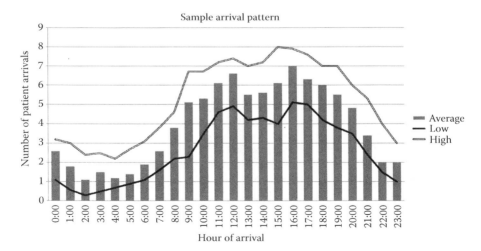

FIGURE 9.1   Sample of an ED arrival pattern.

[*] Dr. Kirk Jensen is the chief medical officer of BestPractices, Inc. www.best-practices.com.

steady throughout the afternoon, and begin to drop only in the late afternoon and early evening. By 2200, the volumes have fallen into a relatively low but steady state, slowly declining until the very early morning of the next day.

As this pattern is consistent from hospital to hospital, day to day, and week to week, your hospital is very likely to have a similar pattern. It may not precisely match these patterns, and obviously your volumes will vary. But our work has shown that this pattern is frighteningly similar between facilities. And if there is a pattern to the arrivals, you have something by which you can predict future arrivals. And this predictive capability is quite important for your efforts to improve performance.

Of course, Figure 9.1 only shows the gross average, high, and low over a long period of time. This, as you now know, is not sufficient for the full study of performance. For instance, when we typically look at average arrivals per day, or average inpatient admissions, we fail to break down those numbers by DOW, much less than by HOD. So, we immediately lose the nuance of the variation and instead take the gross average, which will rarely actually happen on any given day. Similarly, those who use queuing models often rely on the same, average number since queuing models are not themselves dynamic enough to manage any better inputs.

Instead, we need to know the variability within the patterns that we see, else we'll fail to understand the degree to which the norm is violated and even what the norm really is. So we need to break these data down into subcomponents to better understand their value for management. Let's see how we can break down our arrival patterns to give us more information about how our systems operate.

PATIENT TYPE

First break down the arrivals by patient type. This could be grouped by ICD-9 categories or other generalized groupings so as to discern what types of patients arrive when. Are all types scattered throughout the data? Or do certain patient types present during certain hours of certain days. At a hospital in a wealthy retiree area of Florida, the data clearly showed a unique arrival pattern of chest and upper GI pain patients on Monday mornings. Other areas have shown similar patterns of chief complaints.

"FREQUENT FLIERS"

Do you know when your "frequent fliers" and drug seekers tend to arrive? If you haven't studied your data closely, you may be missing opportunities to effectively intervene in their care and health management through appropriate solutions and effective staffing patterns. Knowledge of the habits and patterns of your "frequent fliers" can be critical to your efforts to control costs, manage staffing, and optimize your overall capacity. As you will see shortly, there are also opportunities to intervene with these patients to prevent unnecessary ED visits in the future.

In a study I completed on the arrival patterns of mental health patients into a large urban medical center, the data proved hospital management's conventional wisdom to be completely wrong. This particular facility had a very nice, modern, and well-staffed mental health center attached to it. It was open during typical "business hours" (0800–1730) and took mostly scheduled patients, but allowed for some walk-in appointments. The hospital assumed that the ED's mental health frequent fliers (some of whom visited the ED over 100 times in a single year) were thus more prone to arrive after hours when the local mental health center closed, since access was so close and easy during the day. However, the data showed that these patients arrived to the ED during "business hours" when the mental health clinic was open and seeing new patients. In fact, their arrival patterns dropped after hours rather than grew, similar to that of other patients.

This examination was critical to helping the hospital address this high-need, high-cost population. Further study revealed the hours during which these ED mental health frequent fliers (and indeed all mental health patients) were likely to arrive. ED staffing was altered to include mental health providers (staffed through the adjacent mental health center) while more open slots for walk-in appointments were provided at the mental health center.

Never let your assumptions get in the way of good data analysis! You may find that your hospital is simply different from most others and thus requires a unique set of solutions.

LOW-VOLUME PATIENT TYPES

These might include your mental health patients, traumas, or chest pain patients depending on the community in which you live and the demographics you serve. Depending on the volumes of a given patient subcategory, arrival and downstream demand patterns may be more, or less, easily discerned. Remember, though, that the lower the volumes, the more "random" the arrivals will seem within the day and week. For example, arrival patterns of mental health patients may follow a pattern of daily total volume (e.g., four per day during weekdays, six per day, and 80% of weekend days). But the actual pattern of arrival *by hour of day* is far less discernable. As there are so few, it is difficult to assume a consistent arrival every 6 hours, or that one patient arrives during the 1300–1400 hours each day. More likely, their arrivals are nearly randomized throughout the afternoon and evening. Therefore, depending on the volumes and the patterns gathered from your data, you will need to adjust the expectations for the analysis you are able to obtain. This also requires you to change the way in which you use the data for decision making. For these lower-volume arrivals, it is best to gauge any patterns which can be discerned which could help you control the flow and resource allocations, regardless of the time frames. So, for those low-volume mental health patients, it might be appropriate to use blocks of 4–5 hours, during which a patient is expected to arrive. This will aid you in using resources more wisely, allowing for the expectation of a given number of arrivals within a given time frame. This in turn helps you better anticipate what seems to be randomized work. This may also help you determine any historical patterns of outlier arrivals, or those patients arriving with some degree of consistency within a typical time range but in higher percentages of unexpected volumes.

Acuity

You will also want to study your arrival patterns by acuity, for this can show you when to open and close your fast track and low-acuity areas, how to staff them, and how to staff both the "front end" and registration. Of course, likewise, it can show you how you need to staff the "main" side, and what resources are needed when. As you work through the staffing of fast tracks and other "split flow" areas, you must keep the arrival patterns in mind in order to properly align processes and staffing (your "capacity") to match the incoming "demand" of the community vis-a-vis arrival patterns.

We often hear trauma nurses complain of the "boluses" of trauma arrivals. They never seem to fit a pattern, and come in bunches rather than spread out over a period of time. Yet, while trauma arrivals will likely be more randomized except in the most busy EDs, you may want to see if there are any "gross patterns" to the data that might show the likelihood of arrival within a given 3–4-hour period. Though seemingly worthless, this answer will give you some insights into the likelihood of several traumas within a given period, and the occurrence of "outlier" intervals in which the patterns simply do not hold true, either on the high or low ends of volume.

Acuity arrival patterns will likely demonstrate when and in what form staffing needs to be provided, and during what hours your inpatient demand increases and decreases. As we'll see later, you can use this information to everyone's advantage.

DOW and Seasonality

Although the pattern in Figure 9.1 holds fairly consistently across EDs, both volumes and arrivals will vary by DOW. It is important to understand all of the above breakouts by DOW and HOD. These are commonly missed by process improvement consultants and projects, yet this level of detail is required if you are to get to a state of much higher optimization. For instance, EDs commonly see heavier volume on Mondays than Fridays. This would logically require at least a different staffing pattern if not different process flows and placement algorithms, depending on the degree of the differences. Without discerning the sometimes subtle differences by DOW, you may miss opportunities to reduce cost, improve staff satisfaction, and maintain better performance standards. Furthermore, by breaking out DOW and admitted patient arrivals, you'll be able to work more closely with the inpatient units and help them to help you by predicting their own internal workflows and workloads.

Then there is the seasonality of these patterns to be taken into account. Seasonality in both the ED and the OR can have a significant impact on total demand. Furthermore, there is the evolution of the community demand which inevitably takes place, as well as marketplace changes such as the increasing use of "minute clinics" and urgent care centers. Lastly, there may be ongoing efforts to improve ED flow within and downstream from the ED. These variations and changes to the patterns of upstream and subsequent downstream demand are enough to cause significant disruption (both for good and bad) in demand patterns and downstream flow, and therefore must be considered as they are related to the function of the ED and total system capacity.

ADMITS AND DISCHARGES

I saved this for last as it is the most relevant to our discussions herein. You must split the arrival data into admissions and discharges and examine their respective arrival patterns. These patterns may look very similar. Indeed, they are likely to replicate that shown in Figure 9.1. But by examining the specificity of the arrival patterns of your admitted patients, you can start to generate ideas on how to better solve for the downstream admission delays. After all, if you can predict when they show up on your doorstep, you can better predict when the care needs to begin in earnest, when your portion of their care will be completed, and when downstream resources (those outside the ED, such as transportation and inpatient beds) are likely to be needed. We'll get more into these downstream solutions shortly. For now, be sure to examine these two arrival patterns closely, so as to be able to discern the HOD and DOW patterns that will aid you in improving performance, staffing, and throughput.

RELEVANCE FOR STAFFING AND FLOW

As mentioned above, arrival patterns can show you much about your workload and workflow, and thus your need for staffing throughout the ED and beyond. Examination of when patients arrive, which patients arrive, and their ultimate destination (e.g., an inpatient bed or home) offers you the opportunity to "staff to demand." This is still a surprisingly unfamiliar concept in many hospitals, or is sometimes ignored or rejected by staff and nurse unions which prefer static staffing models. Yet the ability to manage the workload (via staffing and process) according to the demand generated by the arrival and ongoing presence of patients is a key element in the optimization of healthcare costs. Because so much of a hospital's budget (60% or more) is made up of staff, the ability to control staff costs is paramount to financial viability.

By using arrival patterns as the first indication of workload demand, we can control how staff is allocated, where, and in what roles. Furthermore, as new admitted patients arrive, the ED can help the inpatient units predict their short-term staffing needs, workload, and workflow.

Thus, the examination of arrival patterns, by HOD, DOW, patient type, and downstream destination, is the key to the performance and cost management of the system.

BLOCKING AND TACKLING OF ED CAPACITY

Now that you understand your arrival patterns and volumes of patients you'll be dealing with, we can begin to change the operational model to better and more efficiently process these patients through the ED and the hospital. Let's take a look at some of the basics of blocking and tackling of ED capacity management.

ED B & T: EYEBALL DISPOSITION

This is one of the key "blocking and tackling" elements that remains untapped. If you are running an ED wherein inpatient bed access delays are blocking up your flow, and in which your ED to inpatient transfer processes are broken, there is simply no excuse for avoiding this relatively simple process step. It is perhaps one of the most critical factors in the successful movement of patients from the ED to inpatient units, and represents the best opportunity to predict and schedule admissions. Therefore, if you are doing nothing else to improve ED to inpatient flow, you should be doing this.

I recommended this in an earlier book many years ago. Essentially, it is a way to use the experience and knowledge of the clinical staff to expedite the flow of information downstream which in turn expedites the flow of patients to the inpatient units.

Eyeball disposition allows for the true meaning of "triage" (i.e., the definition from the French word, meaning "to pick" or "to sort") and a more-focused purpose of the ED staff: to disposition patients to their proper caretakers. Skilled nursing staff and/or physicians assess the patient in the "front-end" processes (e.g., triage and registration), as early in the patient visit as is possible, allowing for an immediate understanding of the probable disposition of the presenting patient. If the patient is suspected of needing admission, notification is immediately sent to the probable unit(s) of admission, such that expectations can be set and preparations made. Time limits and expectations on the disposition process should be set forth and strictly followed. For instance, if it commonly takes 2.5 hours to complete the required workup on a back-pain patient, then the expectation should be that the floor will receive the patient in no more than 3 hours (allowing for some variability). A scheduled admission time could even be set up such that transport and inpatient nurse assistance can be scheduled for the admission event. At the very least, the unit nurses and unit director will know of the impending arrival of the patient, and when that patient is to be expected. (There is more detail on the post-eyeball disposition processes later in this chapter.)

This eliminates much of the mystery around admissions. Allowing for preparation time encourages staff and physicians to communicate and schedule events in the admission process, such as nurse-to-nurse reporting and physician-to-physician communication. The more that these events can be melded into the process, the more they can actually be scheduled into an otherwise randomized series of process steps. Thus, pushing the admission/disposition decision as far upstream in the ED flow as possible will allow for much more freedom, flexibility, and proactive work.

It has been well documented that physicians and many experienced nurses can accurately assess a patient as an admission within seconds of laying eyes upon them. Studies have shown that ED physicians can accurately disposition a patient as either an admission or discharge 95% of the time within 30 seconds of the first evaluation. Experienced triage nurses get it right over 80% of the time, and even relatively inexperienced triage nurses are better than 50% correct. If true, then, why do we wait for hours for lab results, specialist and hospitalist opinions, and radiology reads to make a "final" disposition decision? We may not know precisely the diagnosis and treatment plan, but really … what is an ED for? Diagnosis and treatment planning, or "Disposition?" In the formal sense of a true ED, it is the latter. If taken to a logical conclusion, the purpose of an ED physician then is to stabilize the highly acute patient, achieve initial diagnostics, and disposition the patient. In the case of the admission, this means placing the patient in the care of inpatient staff on an inpatient unit who can then spend the time and attention necessary to see the patient through to a healthier status. So, again, why do we wait hours before "officially" admitting a patient, knowing full well within the first minute that our patient is "going upstairs?" There are several reasons why this delay has been allowed.

Sometimes, the cause is the preferences of other physicians in the system. Having the burdens of practice and care already on them, attending physicians would prefer to have all necessary diagnostics available prior to taking the patient and making their official "admit" decision. Thus they demand multiple sets of diagnostics until a precise treatment plan can be developed prior to making even a preliminary admit decision.

Furthermore, the final admission decision is often left to hospitalists or specialists who must "lay hands" before they will allow an admission. If these resources are not local and do not have good, mutually trusting relationships with the ED physicians, as a group or individually, there is often a requirement that a full workup be completed before a disposition decision is rendered. This may also require numerous, often relatively needless communications between ED and external physicians, and/or a wait for that physician to arrive and see the patient. All too often, this results in still more tests and longer delays. To be fair, these specialists may want all necessary information available to them prior to their arrival on the scene, such that their workload and time requirements are reduced, and they can speed through their own processes. However, such lack of cooperation and trust means an inherently and unnecessarily extended length of stay for precisely those patients whose stay needs to be the shortest.

Hospitalists are notorious for both cooperation and lack thereof. Some groups cooperate fully with the ED physician teams, especially when both groups are deployed by the same contract employer. Here, physicians are often instructed on the necessities of cooperation, communication streams, and mutual trust.

Alternatively, when ED physicians and hospitalists are not of the same mind, and mistrust exists on either or both sides of the ED walls, the bottlenecks can be long and tedious. Lack of trust drives more and sometimes unnecessary tests, delays in patient movement, and bickering over who could and should initiate the admission decision.

Where they exist, some of these conflicts are due to historical frustration with inappropriate admissions or refusal to admit. True, there will always be those patients for whom the initial disposition was incorrect and who were inappropriately admitted. But statistically, this is a very small percentage. Our natural tendency to recall the hassles and frustrations of those errors yields an unwillingness to allow for these mistakes by denying ED physicians decision control or claiming intransigence on the part of the hospitalists.

In a recent project, neither ED physicians nor the hospitalists trusted the other. We arranged for a monthly "Blue Angels" review of all admissions and denials that were considered by either side to be inappropriate or clinically flawed, led by the hospital CEO and CNO. This format, made famous by the Blue Angels fighter jet squadrons of air show fame, allows for open, frank, and intelligent discussions about the issues pertaining to various decisions. Through this, both sides could present clinical opinion and evidence, describe the situations they faced, and learn from one another. This helped heal some very old wounds and develop a more symbiotic relationship between the parties.

Lastly, there may be some debate as to where the patient will ultimately reside. It is not uncommon for a "belly pain" or "lower back pain" patient to have several potential destination units upon admission from the ED, depending on the diagnostics and segmentation of units. While absolutely true in many instances, this need for precision becomes its own bottleneck in the "Eyeball Disposition" processing of patients. Even if the final workup is complete and the patient is ready to be admitted, there can still be debate as to where a patient can go. But this debate slows the process, as the discussion doesn't really start until hours after the patient's arrival and expression of a chief complaint. Thus, if several units need to be notified of a potential admission, so be it. The key is for the communication stream to be maintained after the eyeball disposition is put forth, such that units can keep up with which patient will be going where.

Indeed, communication is a key element of this process. Sadly, our new IT systems are sometimes so inflexible that new processes like this cannot be melded into the IT workflow and made to support better patient care. I recently worked in a hospital wherein their "brand-name," "top of the line" EMR caused them to delay implementing this change because of the way the EMR registered the ED physicians' preliminary decision to admit. At this facility, if the physicians were to use the EMR at all, even their preliminary decision had to be logged in the system. However, in the EMR's "mind," this cut short the work-up time and greatly lengthened the time required to move a patient out of the ED. For instance, an admitted patient might be seen as having been quickly dispositioned but then languishing for hours before moving to an inpatient bed. The system simply had no way to record a disposition decision as anything other than final, and the IT staff had to develop a work-around to prevent the reportable numbers from looking bad. Thus you should beware that this and all your efforts to improve processes must be supported by your IT systems.

Eyeball disposition is so important because of what it can do to expedite the flow of patients out of the ED to inpatient units. It is critical if you are going to impact the capacity of both your ED and the inpatient units, and the ability of the latter to support the former will smoothen the flow.

PROACTIVE MANAGEMENT OF "FREQUENT FLIERS"

Frequent users of your ED often stand out in your data. These are patients who come to your ED dozens of times each year, often seeking the same care each time. Indeed, you likely already know the top 10 or 20 visiting patients in your population. But though commonly low in number, these patients can require large amounts of work, resources, and expenditures. If you are not properly addressing this small but impactful population, you may be missing opportunities to both provide better care for these patients and reduce the stresses of high-cost repeat visits.

To better address this population, first identify these patients in your ED population. Make a list of your top visiting patients, along with a detailed clinical history. Study their arrival patterns, chief complaints, clinical needs, and social and familial contexts. Examine how much capacity each uses, and the implications and risks associated with continued ED visitation.

Then, consider how their needs might be better met through external resources, including community health organizations, churches, extended family, or mental health professionals. Examine their respective social contexts and any gaps that may be leading to the need for ED visits. You may find that there are organizations within your community that are willing and able to help you address the needs of this small, outlier population and thus provide better care at a much lower cost.

Our clients around the country are routinely finding that these few patients can find better care externally if it is properly coordinated and proactively managed, yielding reductions in ED visits and unnecessary costs. As an example, one patient was clinically depressed, diabetic, and had very poor eyesight. Though she was largely mentally capable of managing her diabetes herself, she has not been to an eye doctor in years due to cost and a lack of insurance. Thus her lens prescriptions were incorrect, leading to an inability to see well enough to use glucose monitors and manage her health. This exacerbated her feelings of depression, which led to repeated health and wellness issues and subsequent visits to the ED. By coordinating the care among local volunteers and physicians, she was able to get new eyeglasses, training on managing her health and diet, and proper medications for her depression, which dramatically reduced her visits to the ED. Simply delving deeply into this patient's overall wellness needs, rather than just managing the immediate health situation, helped to improve this patient's life and health.

This approach will require some work and time on the ED and hospital side. Yet depending on their impact on ED performance and workload, better managing this small population may pay off in efficiencies, staff satisfaction, and patient wellness.

RESULTS WAITING AREA

Patients awaiting lab results and radiology reads can take up critical clinical space, especially during busy times. Routinely, relatively low acuity patients can be seen lying in beds awaiting urine tests, x-rays for sprained ankles, and other testing. Some of these patients are not sick enough to warrant an ED bed, and could wait for their results elsewhere. To avoid this ineffective use of clinical space, a "Results Waiting Area (RWA)" or "vertical area" is recommended as a means to free up capacity for more patients. These are simple areas or rooms where patients who are only waiting on results, or consults and prescriptions, can wait before being discharged.

Depending on the patient population, the available space, and your current layout, these spaces may be closed or open, with comfortable chairs or even stretchers, depending on the patient need. These spaces are commonly built nearby to clinical resources, such that visual monitoring can be maintained, and quick and ready access to patients can be had. Of course, this area needs to come with a private consult space such that physicians can share information with patients while avoiding HIPAA violations and maintaining general privacy. Registration might even have a role to play here, as the waiting period is an excellent time to complete the full registration process.

Hospitals commonly make these areas curtained rather than walled, and most don't seem to mind relatively tight configurations, with as many as 10 places in what was a normal ED room. Some don't seem to mind the idea of standard waiting room chairs, without televisions or other "creature comforts." That, of course, is up to each facility. Certainly, one must consider sterility and cleanliness, as well as comfort, noise management, and of course, privacy.

As patients' results come back, they are escorted to a consult area, after which they are escorted to their next destination.

Thus, rather than waiting in an ED bed, patients who might need a "yes" or "no," or who are waiting for clearance from allergic reactions, etc., can wait in a comfortable, "non-clinical" space, yet still be within the confines of the ED.

Used effectively, the RWA allows for quicker bed turns, higher volumes in the same time, and reduced total LOS. Even minor time savings (i.e., 10–15 minutes) add up over the course of a busy day. This can be especially important during busy times when clinical space is at a premium. This space might also be important for high-volume, low-acuity patient populations who need labs and testing for diagnostics, but who don't necessarily need a private ED bed at all.

INTEGRATING CASE MANAGEMENT IN ED ADMISSION DECISIONS

Case managers (CMs) have more recently been used in the ED to perform a variety of duties, from assessing the legitimacy of admissions to planning for the discharge of patients back into the community. In this day and age of growing scrutiny of admissions, the growth of the use of observation as a means to reduce the cost of unnecessary admissions, and the use of financial incentives to improve the throughput of contracted ED physicians, CMs could and should be taking a larger role in the decisions to admit.

If nothing else, a good CM can use InterQual or other tested criteria to assess the appropriateness of an admission, which in turn might increase the likelihood of reimbursement for the inpatient care. Unfortunately, many ED physicians view this as a direct intrusion of their clinical decision-making "turf" by nurses with thick books and regimented formulae.

Yet, CMs and physicians needn't clash. Indeed, as we move slowly away from fee-for-service payment models and more toward what might be a Canadian- or managed population reimbursement model, limiting admissions to those patients who truly have need will become more and more important. Physicians should actually support the input from the CM partners, accepting the "realties" of standards as part of their overall decision criteria. Yes, there will be those instances when the InterQual criteria doesn't match well with the decisions of the ED physician and his admitting physician counterpart. But there will be many instances in which the aid of a CM can help direct the testing and diagnostics so as to aid rather than hamper physician dispositions.

Thus for clinical, financial, and patient care reasons, CMs should be integrated into the overall flow of ED admissions. The best way to do this is to use eyeball disposition, so as to integrate the CMs with the patient's diagnostic workup as early as possible, giving her the best chance to offer assistance, advice, and input.

Unfortunately, the CMs are only brought into the decision-making process after the physicians admission disposition has been made, and thus at a time when a battle must ensue, complete with egos and public proclamations of errors, in order for the decision to be reversed. This leaves both the ED and the CM in the awkward position of working against one another rather than together. Better to have the CMs directly engaged with the physicians and ED staff early on in the potential admitted patient's visit, to prevent unnecessary admissions and make use of appropriate and cost-effective treatment options.

Predicting and "Managing To" Demand: Using Front-End Processes to Manage Back-End Delays

Now that you have studied your arrival patterns thoroughly, and know how to use data and concepts such as eyeball disposition to predict admissions with a high degree of accuracy, you can go to the next step of ED capacity management and begin strategic communications with downstream (a.k.a. inpatient) providers.

Of course, you needed a solid understanding of the arrival patterns *into* the ED so as to understand the admission patterns generated *by* the ED. The former obviously impacts the latter. As we analyze the arrival patterns and break them down into the aforementioned categories, we can begin to see the correlation between arrivals and inpatient demand generation. This correlation should help you to discern the inpatient demand patterns the ED is generating. And as we discover these downstream demand patterns, we should analyze *how those patterns might be influenced or managed*.

For instance, take the demand pattern from the ED to a given inpatient unit shown in Figure 9.2.

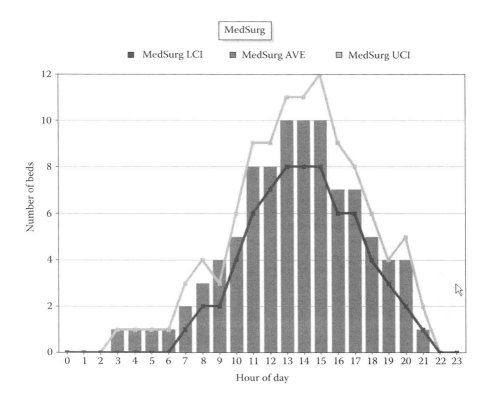

FIGURE 9.2   Patterns of the average number of admissions from the ED to an inpatient unit, by HOD.

Figure 9.2 shows the pattern of admissions averages from many weeks of data. These patterns should always be broken down by DOW, inpatient units, and patient and bed types to offer the kind of granularity necessary for full capacity analytics.

The graph shows the average number of beds required on this sample inpatient unit by HOD (the bars in the graph), as well as typical range of demand around the average, shown as the two lines, one above and one below the average. The upper line is referred to as the UCI, or upper control interval, and the lower line is referred to as the LCI, or lower control interval. These represent, in this case, the ninetieth and twentieth percentiles of volume, respectively, in the data set. So, as per the example (Figure 9.2), the ninetieth percentile of volume at 1400 is 11 patients. Likewise, the LCI at 1400 is roughly eight patients. This offers us the range of demand for a given hour over a period of time, and allows us to better understand the actual variability within a given time period during the day. As you can see, we can better understand the patterns of demand by using percentiles of higher and lower volumes and thereby gauge the range of demand to a given unit over time. This is far more meaningful than the average alone, as you now know. One can also use a maximum and minimum volume over time to show the extremes in the demand range and compare that to the selected percentiles to discern the total range of variability over time.

Each of the patients in this particular inpatient demand pattern came to the ED within some arrival pattern. Correlating the initial ED demand, in the form of arrival patterns, with the inpatient demand will reveal a great deal about the function of the ED, the consistency of the disposition time, and any significant variations with which we might need to deal. We can use this information later as a means to manage both ED capacity and inpatient demand.

To explore these relationships between ED arrivals and downstream demand for inpatient beds, first we want to get an accurate measure of the actual inpatient demand time. Of course, we already know when our ED patients arrived. However, most electronic health records (EHRs) only tell you when the patient actually left the ED, not when the disposition decision was actually made. This is important because, in an ideal world, the patient would leave immediately or very soon after their "official and final" disposition was made, not once all the admission I's were dotted and T's were crossed and someone got around to transporting the patient upstairs. Thus we want a measure of the time at which the disposition decision was actually made. If you are like most and don't have this timestamp, there are a number of proxies available, though I won't list those all here.

First, of course, we want to break out DOW and seasonality (if applicable). We've already seen how the patterns of demand can vary by DOW and HOD, so we want to continue with that differentiation here.

Next, we want to compare the arrival and admit times and look for lengths of time that can give us clues about not only our ED processes but the general time required to work up a given patient. This will help us assess and predict the time at which a given to-be-admitted patient will be ready for his inpatient bed. To do this, we need some additional granularity. We'll need to break out the analysis into patient types, preferably corresponding to the inpatient unit patient differentiation. So, if I have cardiac, ortho, and GI units in my hospital to which the ED admits, I want to segment patients going to those units into groups so as to better predict admission patterns by unit.

For instance, we may have a situation in which cardiac patients take an unusually long time to be worked up and seen by our attending/hospitalist/specialist. This might lead to some intra-ED process change, regimentation, and waste reduction efforts for specific patient groupings/types. Or, if the constraints are on the inpatient side, you will want to home in on the specific areas of the hospital that generate the most constraints to flow.

You may also want to break this analysis down by shift so as to determine practice patterns of various combinations of staff and a variety of physicians. Certain ED physicians and teams may simply be causing more constraints and delays than others. Some ED physicians just take longer to disposition patients, feeling that they need to be very sure about their decision to admit.

Alternatively, you will want to examine your hospitalists and attending physicians individually, as some hospitalists and specialists may require undue amounts of testing and documentation before they will admit a patient. We have seen glaring differences in the number of consults required and the number of tests ordered, all centered on a very few hospitalists.

From this analysis will come an understanding of the demand patterns your ED generates. The next step is to make use of this information in promoting the balance of the demand–capacity continuum. This can be done through setting up process steps, communication streams, visual cues, and other tools to aid in moving patients. We won't go into the details of all these herein, but the following are the basics:

- As a potential admission is "Eyeballed" appropriately, immediately notify the inpatient unit(s) of the expected time of admission, the patient's chief complaint, and the ED physician.
- Immediately involve case management in the decision to admit.
- Notify the patient's PCP and hospitalist of the potential admission, and communicate a diagnostic plan so as to preempt future requests for clinical data.
- Notify other involved parties, such as transportation as needed (if they are known to be bottlenecks in the admission process).
- Continue communications between the ED and the inpatient units throughout the work-up period, particularly if the admission decision changes, or the patient's destination unit changes. This is critical to ensuring that the units are not holding beds or even anticipating arrivals of patients who will never turn up.

Scheduling Admissions

Taking this concept one step further, it is quite possible to actually schedule admission before patients ever arrive! If volumes are high enough and your demand patterns consistent enough, we may find that it makes sense to actually *schedule* some of the admissions to specific units based on the historical patterns of demand, still recognizing that variability will have its usual impact.

This is best achieved by examining the arrival patterns, LOS, and downstream demand in a simulation model. The simulation can better predict the outcomes of various changes you might make in the processing of to-be-admitted patients, and quantitatively demonstrate the results of these changes. From this, we can determine if there are opportunities to schedule admissions. Let's look at the outputs of one of these models in Figure 9.3.

This graph requires some explanation. The simulation model calculated the admission times for all admitted patients to a sample inpatient unit over the course of a given period, *prior to process changes being recommended*. Thus this graph represents the then-current state of the demand patterns for beds on this unit.

The darker bars represent the likelihood of an admission during a given hour (with the vertical axis representing probability percentages). So, in the 1600 hours, there is roughly a 48% chance on an admission.

The lighter bars represent the likelihood of an admission during a 2-hour period. So, the 1700 bar represents the probability of an admission during either the 1600 hours or the 1700 hours, which is roughly 91%.

If we use a cutoff point of 70% probability of an admission to this unit, we can see that there are five 2-hour periods during which an admission is highly likely ... those lighter bars whose probabilities are above 70%.

This important data can show us several things. First, there are opportunities for scheduling admissions based on the arrival patterns of patients. For this project, we traced the arrivals of admitted patients back and found when the high-probability hour admissions arrived. Thus, we could determine roughly how long they were in the ED before they were admitted. Next, we changed processes in the ED to reflect more of a "predictive" rather than a "reactive" environment, so as to take advantage of the eyeball disposition information. Finally, we took the arrival patterns, added an appropriate ED LOS for workup, added an appropriate amount of time for the admission process itself, and created a pattern of expected scheduled admissions for this unit. The final product was a schedule of three to four admissions (depending on the DOW, excluding weekends) which could be relied upon by both the ED and inpatient unit.

This was helpful for several reasons. One, it obviously greatly opened up communications between the ED and the inpatient units, particularly those whose admission patterns created bottlenecks for the ED. Second, it gave some semblance of regularity to the stream of patients coming to the unit. No longer did the unit manager have to guess about at least some of the admissions (this particular unit received as many as 10 admits from the ED on an outlier day). She could plan staffing and workload for at least a few of the daily patients, and thereby space out the work of admissions coming from the ED and other clinical sources such as surgery.

For the ED, it allowed for an expected admission during certain hours of the day, regardless of how busy things might be. Thus it allowed for an expected decompression during busy times, while generally putting guardrails and goals on work-up LOS and helped maintain workflow. It also helped offer guidance on all other workups such that LOS was managed by the expectations of admission rather than a "whenever" mentality that had pervaded before.

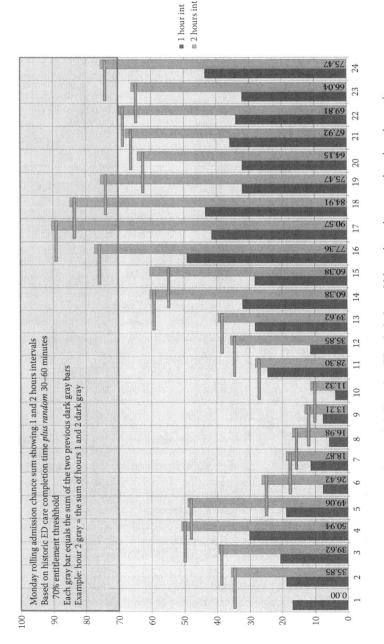

FIGURE 9.3   Graphical representation of the probability of an ED admission within a given time to a given inpatient unit.

That said, I am not so unrealistic and fanciful as to assume that scheduling of all admissions from the ED will work in every situation, or even in more than a few. However, it is the *concept* of the demand–capacity continuum that is critical for both ends of the ED's demand pattern to understand. *There are arrival patterns, and therefore there are admission patterns.* These latter are, surprisingly, largely under your control if you choose to take control. Identifying and, to the extent possible, *managing to* the arrival patterns is the key to getting a much better grasp on the demand–capacity continuum, such that both ends of the admission process can see how they can impact the system's workload and workflow. This concept of predictability of arrival patterns and the subsequent predictability and manageability of the downstream demand is critical to the successful management of our systems. To the extent this can be achieved, both ends of the continuum will recognize benefits in anticipating and better managing workload, resource and task allocations, and workflow. Importantly, to the extent that either end of the continuum recognizes and controls any discernable patterns, the system's optimization will be enhanced.

OTHER ED PERFORMANCE IMPROVEMENT CONCEPTS

Because of my focus herein on system-wide capacity, there isn't space or time to cover all the good ideas for improving ED performance. We can only detail a few of those that are directly and consequentially related to the "rest of the house." So, I'll simply list a few of the more popular ideas and allow you to delve deeper as you see fit. Of course, this is not an exhaustive list, so you may have implemented ideas that are better than the ones below. If so, please share with the rest of the world ... we all need new ideas! There is a group on LinkedIn specifically dedicated to dynamic capacity management. If you would like to add your thoughts, please join us!

Split Flow

Split flow is called by many names, but generally refers to the concept of creating different process flows for different kinds of patients. Low-acuity patients have one flow that encompasses rapid processing, the use of physician extenders (NPs, PAs) and nurses who "treat and street" patients quickly in areas designed to maximize throughput and productivity. For higher-acuity patients, a different flow sends them directly to physician interventions where special equipment and processes await. Some even use a third and fourth flow for trauma, mid-acuity, and/or observation patients.

With the correct staffing model, processes, and administrative support functions, these split flow systems can be quite effective in maximizing resource and space utilization as well as throughput.

Physicians in Triage

This is normally reserved for the busiest of EDs, but placing a physician in triage can expedite not only immediate physician contact for those patients needing it, but also allows physicians to better direct the flow of patients into Split Flow systems.

ED flow is obviously heavily influenced by the "up-front" or "front end" processes. Failure to cycle patients efficiently through the triage, registration, and initial assessment phases of their visit can significantly delay the overall LOS. Furthermore, many patients need only minor care and treatment, and need only to see a physician for "sign-off," if that. Thus the idea is to have a physician resource as far out into the initial patient interaction as possible. Dubbed "Super-Fast Track," or "Ultra-Fast Track," or simply "Physician Triage," these flow concepts all involve the use of physician expertise to perform "eyeball" triage and immediately treat low-acuity patients and manage the routing of all others. Patients are discharged from the front-end treatment areas without ever seeing the "main" ED or crossing over into "the back." These expanded front-end systems help to reduce the number of process steps and staff with which the patient must interact, making the ED's front-end parts much like the "Doc in a Box" clinics popping up around the country.

There are significant process constraints to overcome here, however. These normally require special staffing patterns and process flows. Some users of this method heavily staff these front-end systems with, for example, a physician, two nurses, and a tech. Volumes must therefore be very high in order to justify the higher staffing expense. Thus, careful consideration must be paid to the community demand patterns to avoid overstaffing and unnecessary excessive costs.

Furthermore, process issues can arise as the speed of the treatment process overwhelms the parallel and downstream processes, particularly the registration process. It is not uncommon for a patient in one of these split flow and/or physician-in-triage systems to be treated and ready to leave before registration can complete its tasks. Likewise, labs and ancillary support services must be made to keep pace with the improved throughput, else the bottleneck simply moves around within the system, yielding little impact.

Ironically, the use of physicians in the process can actually slow the process down. One hospital instituted a physician at triage at the suggestion of an external Lean consultant. The physician was placed in a four-room triage area along with a triage nurse, registrar, and PA. However, the physician functioned at the tail end of a serial process flow behind the three other major triage and registration process steps, which themselves were very regimented and inefficient. By adding a new physician interaction at the end of these other serial processes, this new system actually added to the overall LOS as the diagnostic process was lengthened serially rather than shortened. Thus, because the physician was added to a broken process, she served to further slow the process rather than increase throughput and reduce LOS.

The Holy Grail is Here: A 60-Minute LOS ED

As I mentioned very early in this chapter, even the most famous Lean hospitals show ED performance metrics that are no better than the average U.S. hospital. In this chapter, I have offered you just some of the means by which to make leaps in performance by taking on the largest constraints to ED flow. You can expect much better performance, quickly, by implementing just one or a few of these new operational models. But can you get even more? Can you make truly game-changing leaps in performance and create competition-crushing metrics and service levels?

Our latest work indicates that indeed you can! If you simultaneously attack the key constraints throughout your ED and hospital, make these and a few other key changes to your processes, and really go after these new operational models you can achieve a 60-Minute LOS for nearly all your patients. That's right ... depending on your physical plant, inpatient capacity constraints (with optimized performance) and staffing models, you can get most or even all of your patients in and out of your ED within an average of 60 minutes!

Be warned, however! This seemingly bold goal (which isn't really all that bold!) requires that you completely blow up your current operational models and change much of what you do in the ED. It requires that you institute a new way of thinking about your ED and your hospital, and how patients move within and through it. And it requires full senior management engagement, collaboration and support. But make no mistake about it ... it IS possible!!

SUMMARY

The ED has been called the "front door" of the hospital, and its ability to see and process the community's care needs is critical to the service commitment hospitals make to the communities they serve. Without proper interaction and engagement with other "downstream" departments and staff, the ED can easily become isolated within its own operational silo, making the ability to efficiently and effectively triage (by its broader definition) patients to the proper clinical areas more difficult, slower, and much more costly.

Alternatively, looking at the system as a system and working to understand and "manage to" the inherent variability in demand and capacity patterns will help us to fully integrate the ED and other source areas into the system-wide operational model. This will help you to develop strategies that will improve your "capacity to care," and ready you for the future world of payment reform, whatever form that takes.

10 Blocking and Tackling of Capacity Management in Surgical Services

Note: Although throughout this chapter I use hospital surgical services as the basis of the discussion, these recommendations, tools, and blocking and tackling steps can and should apply well to outpatient surgery centers. Just change the location of the analytical work and everything in this chapter will apply relatively smoothly. Note also that I will commonly make reference to the current FFS reimbursement model, and do not regularly reference the use of surgical services in a reformed payment scenario. Nonetheless, these concepts can and should apply to the future world of reimbursement in whatever form that takes. Having worked in the world of bundled payments, I know well how changes to reimbursement models will alter the healthcare landscape and force collaboration where it does not currently exist. Thus, any model you adopt should be readily adaptable to the new worlds of population health reimbursements.

The optimization of surgical capacity is one of the few topics that will always light up the eyes of the C-Suite executives. Surgeries are, after all, currently the lifeblood of the financial viability of the hospital and essential to the hospital's relationship with, and breadth of scope of service to, the local community. Thus surgical services generate tremendous competition between hospitals fighting for the loyalty of surgeons and their patients, and is very often a significant source of contention and controversy. Furthermore, of all the areas of the hospital, surgical services is one wherein optimal performance is required such that the entire system, from pre-op through discharge, runs like a well-oiled machine. This will, in turn, enable the full potential for revenues, market position, and community service. Thus hospital leadership must ensure that throughput, turnover times, and utilization of space and time are optimized in order to gain the most opportunity from the available capacity. Failure to run a well-managed department leads to, among other issues, surgeon disloyalty, frustration, and loss of current and future growth opportunities.

Furthermore, so as to keep well-paying patients coming to their doors, hospitals want to be known for their surgical capabilities and quality relative to local competitors. Thus they strive for various certifications and awards that speak to their skills and ability in key, highly profitable service lines such as cardiovascular and orthopedics. This extends to the use of highly specialized equipment, like surgical robotics, which can draw attention to clinical differentiation or a "high-tech" approach. (More on the use and misuse of robots later.) Indeed, the highways of many cities are littered with hospitals advertising their accreditation as an

"XYZ Center of Excellence" or an "ABC Top 100" surgery program. These are typically high-revenue service lines such as cardiac, open heart, orthopedics, or robotics, to name a few.

In order to boast of surgical capabilities and thus drive patients (and their families, money, and loyalty), hospitals need qualified and competent surgeons to meet the demand from the community that their reputations are supposed to generate. As in many cities across the United States there is a dearth of certain specialists and/or the competition for available specialists is so fierce, surgeons can often ask for and receive specific favors and preferences from hospital administrators. This can be especially true if surgeons are willing to move their business from one facility to another, in whole or in part. Thus, in many cases, surgeons can negotiate and get whatever they want. This issue is particularly important given the current market consolidation trends and physician-centric business models that are a by-product forced by the PPACA (a.k.a Obamacare), which are driving even more strategic alignments and increased concentration into healthcare markets.

Therefore, surgeon preferences in the OR are commonly respected (some even more than others) even if these preferences mean some detrimental impact on efficiency, cost of operations and supplies, staff, or even other less-profitable surgeons. These can include preferred choices of relatively costly orthopedic implants, the provision of surgical assistants and extra staff, preferred surgery and block times, preferred equipment and/or the purchase of the newest equipment, the provision of robots, etc. These preferences can serve to attract surgeon loyalty or, in cases in which the preferences go to "the other" surgeons, drive it away.

Typically a hospital will want to keep a wide range of services available to the community to ensure that highly profitable cases come along with the less-profitable volumes. This also helps prevent encroachment of competitive facilities and promotes a broad loyalty among surgeons and other specialists. A broad and deep "footprint" in the community can help providers who are within that footprint, whether via pricing power, spreading "on-call" requirements, concentrating spending and capital improvements, and creating efficiencies of service provision.

However, physician preferences have led to an overall degradation of performance in some facilities. Physicians are the number one obstacle to performance improvement in most hospitals. And nowhere is bad behavior, intransigence, and obstruction more evident, relevant, and impactful than in the OR.

Late starts, longer-than-normal cases, costly supplies, expensive equipment, bad attitudes, and even staff and patient abuse (verbal and otherwise) are sometimes tolerated (and thus rewarded) to keep surgeons bringing high volume and profitable cases to some facilities. This has all led to the abuse of the potential of the facility to serve the community and its surgery patients and a selfish and uncooperative manipulation of the available community's "capacity to care."

Of course, I am not suggesting that all surgeons are "bad apples." Indeed, most surgeons are cooperative, congenial, and willing to accept changes that are suggested to them or being forced upon them. Most surgeons still put patients, quality, and outcomes first, and try to keep a congenial relationship with the hospitals in which they work. Keep in mind, too, that hospitals may have fostered these bad behaviors over the years through antagonistic relationships with physicians that have resulted in an "us vs. them" mentality on both sides. Nonetheless, without a positive and cooperative culture, strong physician leadership, and collaborative relationships with physicians, life can quickly become difficult for the OR and its operations.

Furthermore, it should be noted here that as the U.S. healthcare system evolves toward a capitated, population health-based model, the opportunities for such abuse must necessarily be reduced. In the (perhaps distant) future, arguments will be less about who is bringing in the most revenue and more about efficiencies, capacity optimization, and community service via surgical services. Cases will be scheduled based even more on patient need and even less on surgeon greed and hospital revenues. Capacity will be better managed and the location and type of a given case will be determined by the appropriate environment and best patient outcomes and less on cost, revenues, and income. Similarly, those who utilize the hospital's capacity will have an inherent synergy with the facilities they use, and see them less as unpleasant obstacles and more as partners in patient health. In the meantime, of course, we must deal with the realities of our often bizarre reimbursement and "costing" mechanisms that drive so much of the inefficiencies and seemingly crazy motivations within the system.

Yet, while all these and other issues, from turnaround times (TATs) to implant costs to the late starts, are all important to the strategic planning of a given facility and its financial resources and infrastructure investments, herein we will focus on only a few. Specifically, we will focus on the use of OR time and a few key expenses in the context of the basic blocking and tackling of surgical services capacity management. Thus, I will leave supply chain management, OR TATs, staffing optimization, and several other operational issues to other authors more focused on these topics.

BLOCK-SCHEDULING OVERVIEW

Many years ago, as a convenience to surgeons, hospitals, and schedulers on both ends of the phone, "blocks" of time on the surgical schedule were developed and given to surgeons. Block schedules have become very common as a means to help surgeons avoid the chaos of scheduling cases each week, lend regularity and consistency in the days and hours of work at a given facility (ironically allowing them to work with competitors more readily), and to keep the hospital as a preferred source of OR time. Blocks are given to both individual physicians and/or physician groups, and can last from an hour to an entire 10-hour shift. Blocks can be given to surgeons irrespective of specific rooms, such that a surgeon only knows the specific time slot(s) he has during the day or week but not the room in which surgeries will be performed. Alternatively, blocks can be associated with specific rooms or equipment, such that both a time and specific OR are allotted in a given block.

Blocks can occur daily, each week, biweekly, or on some other pattern, as needed. On certain days of the week, blocks are often preferred by certain surgical specialties. For instance, many orthopedists prefer to perform their total joint cases earlier in the week, as inpatient recovery time may require an LOS that might extend into the weekend, thereby requiring weekend physician rounding were surgeries performed on, say, Thursday. Because many physicians prefer to avoid working on weekends, they prefer to have their patients discharged rather than admitted on Thursday or Friday.

Even more importantly, clinical outcomes suggest that group rehabilitation for lower extremity joint replacement is beneficial to patients, thus promoting a "joint day" early in the week. As the theory goes, "communal" rehabilitation promotes positive reinforcement of good habits, encourages competition and group support, and generally promotes faster and more effective rehabilitation and shorter LOS. While perhaps clinically effective, this requires some unique scheduling practices and policies, which can be a nightmare for both orthopedists as well as other surgeons who want Monday block time.[*]

Occasionally, surgical blocks are simply "broken." For instance, blocks are based less on a physician's historical use of OR time than their ability to coerce hospital and department managers for as much OR time as they can get. These blocks are based more on politics than utilization or other more standard metrics. This naturally leads to an inefficiency in scheduling and reduced OR utilization. Perhaps even more commonly, blocks are established and then only occasionally revisited and revised, despite changes in surgeon practice patterns, utilization rates, and volumes. These are the block schedules that cause the most inefficiency and constraints to the system, as they can prevent new surgeons from getting preferred OR time or any time other than the leftover "add on" time (usually at the end of the day). And this obviously limits growth and opportunities to serve new surgeons and their patients.

In still other cases, blocks are assumed to exist even when they do not. That is, a surgeon might receive a given slot of time every week even though no block has been officially established and codified. Alternatively, a surgeon's time is officially listed on the schedule for, say, Thursday mornings, but the OR scheduler knows that he/she actually tends to operate every Tuesday, and thus a slot is largely kept open and available on Tuesdays rather than Thursdays.

Or, a busy surgeon may prefer to avoid having block time so as to keep flexibility in his/her schedule and make movement from hospital to competitive hospital easier and less constraining. This is not common but it is a tactic of high-volume surgeons who know that their volume of surgical business means they will get whatever they ask for.[†] Thus, these surgeons will push the limits of local hospitals, take whatever leeway they can obtain, and use it for their advantage.

Generally speaking, as block time is considered a valuable commodity, it is jealously guarded by surgeons. Nothing will initiate a threat of "taking my business elsewhere" like a discussion of the removal, reduction, or alteration of block time. Yet block time is equally valuable to the hospital (its *real* owner!) as it, in part, determines much of the OR and thus how much surgical revenue the hospital can

---

[*] Our firm has done a great deal of work in these environments in an effort to create realistic and usable surgical schedules within the context of "joint program" parameters. While difficult, it is possible if proper data analysis and schedule simulation is completed.

[†] I recently worked in a facility in which the highest volume physician wanted NO block time, but routinely scheduled cases for late in the day, then showed up late after he finished work at another facility. This lead to the tacit creation of a 1900–2400 shift achieved through the use of overtime and call-in staff. This was perhaps one of the most egregious abuses of OR scheduling I've witnessed.

generate. Therefore, block time must be effectively and collaboratively managed in order to ensure its optimal contribution to both surgeons and the facility.

Alternatively, there are still facilities around the country wherein there are no official blocks. Indeed, in some facilities, the word "block" is a taboo and should not be mentioned within the four walls of the OR. This attitude is sometimes driven by surgeons who have been "burned" by poorly managed blocks in the past, or who prefer the freedom their high volumes and preferred status allow them. Yet, even though there is no official blocking of time, there may be "de facto" blocks ... those allocations of OR time based solely on the physicians' historical preferences. In these cases, physician longevity, political weight, and importance to the facility's revenue often drives who gets what at 0730 start on a given day of the week, who gets which OR, and who gets to use "flip" rooms. But whether official or not, there must still be a scientific approach to the analysis of "blocked" (allocated) OR time to ensure that capacity is being optimally used and the community is best served.

Herein, we will deal with the more "official" block allocations. Yet, if your facility does not use blocks, you can still benefit from the analytics described in this chapter.

BLOCK ABUSE

Blocks can be and are abused. That is, a surgeon may have hours of blocked time each week in the OR, but does not consistently use it. This is common where surgeons have, over time, shifted case volumes and allegiances to other hospitals or outpatient "surgicenters" wherein they have a vested financial interest or where they find it more convenient and more profitable to work.[*] This is also common when a competitive hospital has wooed a surgeon's business away from another hospital, perhaps offering newer equipment, even better OR time, better or more skilled staff, or other perks. Or, a surgeon's volume might slip as he/she nears retirement and winds down the practice. Or, in some cases, new surgeons have taken volume away from the more established physicians. Practice patterns may have changed, partners may have been added or moved on, and/or old schedules have failed to keep up with new practice patterns.

Regardless of the reason, the underutilization of block time leads to significant losses of opportunities for growth, revenue, expansion of the surgeon base, and competitive advantages. Yet, despite the high cost of these constraints, many hospitals fail to reexamine their block schedules on a regular basis. I have seen blocks that are literally 7–9 years old still in place, largely as they were when they were created. This is an egregious failure of community service, not to mention hospital operating revenue and cost.

Fortunately, there are ways to use the block schedule to both motivate and manage surgeon behavior for the betterment of the utilization of the ORs and the capacity of the entire department to serve the community demand for surgery.

---

[*] As the U.S. healthcare landscape continues to form, the use of various facilities within the community will evolve. Many surgeries have already moved from the higher-cost hospital environment to a lower-cost outpatient surgical center. Still more changes are likely, as these latter facilities morph into "shopping malls for healthcare," and hospitals create specialized surgery facilities and units within or close by so as to better compete in the market for profitable patients.

BLOCKING MANAGEMENT PRACTICES

There are a number of blocking practices within hospitals across the country that influence how well block time is utilized. Smart, effective OR managers, along with the elected or assigned members of the physician oversight and executive committees, will set up parameters for block utilization requirements and regularly monitor the use of block time among the blocked surgeons (monthly, at least). Eighty percent or greater is preferred, and 90% or greater is not uncommon. When block time slips below a certain threshold (say, 50%) for more than one or two predetermined periods, block time will be reassessed and, if necessary, removed and reassigned.

Block "release time" is also used to manage block utilization. If a surgeon has not scheduled a full block by, say, 72 hours before the day of surgery, the OR scheduler will release all or a portion of his block allocation and open it to other surgeons for scheduling cases. This release time varies between facilities, and can vary between specialties, as certain specialties have unique patterns of scheduling cases.

Some hospitals will only block in 4- or 8-hour increments. Surgeons who need less than 4 hours of time are asked to schedule into commonly available "add on" or "open" time on the schedule, even if it falls late in the day. While this saves hassles for the schedulers, it often leads to low block utilization, especially for the longer 8-hour blocks, and can lead to physician frustration due to the lack of consistent availability of OR time.

Of course, these and other OR management structures require ongoing management and maintenance by competent OR managers, backed by surgeon and hospital leadership.

Other block approaches exist, and some work better than others. Dexter et al.[*] and this author have used mathematical models to analyze scheduling practices for over a decade, and this author has used simulation and other analytical tools for a similar period. Many variations on these exist, but all point to the need to actively and deeply analyze the schedule, manage it closely, and change it regularly. There comes a time in which the schedule must be changed to allow for the kind of efficiencies and revenues of which the facility is capable of generating.

WHEN THE BLOCK SCHEDULE NEEDS CHANGING

When hospitals do decide to examine their schedules, it can be a painful process, especially if the schedule has not been regularly monitored for lags in utilization performance and surgeon behavior has not been properly governed. Part of the reason that a wholesale evaluation of the surgical schedule is avoided is the controversy it can stir up. And the more dramatic the change, the more controversial the changes. Remember, there may be decades of physician preferential treatment serving as a backdrop to the serious evaluation and dramatic improvement of the surgical schedule. Thus, schedulers replace difficult block decisions with their knowledge of the physicians, scheduling habits, and surgery volume trends to create

---

[*] Dexter, F., Macario, A., and O'Neill, L. 2000. Scheduling surgical cases into overflow block time—Computer simulation of the effects of scheduling strategies on operating room labor costs. *Anesthetics Analgesia.* 90(4):980–8.

their own pseudo new block schedule in practice even though the current block schedule might remain in place on paper. The dangers here are numerous, not the least of which is the loss of the knowledge ingrained in the scheduler's head. Many ORs are one career change or car wreck away from a scheduling and operational disaster lasting for weeks or even months. More importantly, without an "official" block schedule, management, oversight, and governance are more difficult, leading to the aforementioned block abuse.

Yet, there is often very little to fear from a remake of the schedule. Physicians are, if nothing else, realists who commonly respect data. They know their practices, or can be made to know them based on some good data analytics around utilization. This can lead to healthy discussions of revisions necessary to bring the OR to a more optimal performance, better serving the community and all surgeons who work there. If they respect nothing else, physicians tend to respect good, defensible data analytics.

Thus if you choose to "go there," a critical component of block analysis and redesign is deep and dynamic data analysis. It is not enough to take a few metrics, such as surgeon start times, OR utilization (which is often grossly miscalculated or inaccurately averaged), and volume and make critical decisions. Such "data-lite" decision-making will inevitably lead to revolts among the surgical staff and yield damaging disruptions in physician culture and attitude and even in the department's performance. In the sections below, I will describe some of the data and analytics we commonly use for our capacity optimization efforts. Keep in mind that much of this data is not easily obtainable unless you know how to properly construct it, and/or unless you have the right OR management systems in place. Ironically, we have found that the newer EHRs that tout themselves as "one stop shops" for data are in fact the worst at the production and availability of the kind of raw data this analysis requires. So many of the facilities in which we work are wholly unable to extract data from their electronic medical records (EMRs) and thus unable to do anything but rely on the canned reports these systems generate, which are routinely inadequate. Thus, as you seek the data I suggest herein, understand that some or much of it must be "constructed" from single or multiple data sources, and/or by using highly advanced data manipulation techniques and tools that provide the level of granularity required.

OR DATA ANALYTICS FOR OPTIMIZATION

Let's look at three essentials of analytics for the basic blocking and tackling of surgical services.

BLOCK UTILIZATION

As mentioned, the block schedule is a key component of performance optimization, and a critical piece of physician relations, volume and revenue growth, future expansion opportunities, and longevity in the future of capitated reimbursement models. The utilization of surgeon blocks is therefore a critical element in the overall ability of the facility to optimize its capacity to serve the community's surgical needs, especially in the coming world of capitation and limited per-patient revenues. Keep in mind … block utilization is not just about OR time. To truly measure block utilization, we need to look deeper at the activities, cases, case types, revenue potential and payor mix, etc., to gauge how we want to fill our surgical schedules.

Block utilization can be calculated a number of ways, depending on the goals of the analysis and the objectives of the OR manager. Commonly, and using most OR IT systems, one simply takes the average weekly (or daily) case time of a particular surgeon or group, and divides by the total daily or weekly block allocation. This simple approach typically uses an average to represent the OR time used per week or month, and captures a single metric by which relative surgeon activity is judged. Thus, if Dr. Abraham has 1100 minutes of allocated block time per week, and uses an average of 840 minutes per week, the block utilization percentage is 76% (which might be considered relatively high in many facilities, depending on the specialty). However, it often makes sense to go one or more steps further in order to better ascertain the changes required to promote more optimal utilization. Let's look at some ways in which you should be analyzing your block utilization.

Of course, you start with the individual physician blocks. If your blocks are given to groups, first break those groups apart into the individual physicians and study their utilization. You may find nuances in these analytics that lead you to adjust blocks for the group or individuals or both. For instance, in a recent project, we found that the dynamics of a large orthopedic group were changing. Overall, their utilization was down significantly, and other surgeons competing for time were pushing the hospital to shrink their block allocation. Of course, the orthopedists were telling their peers that there were legitimate, short-term reasons for the decreased utilization, but they had no data to back up their claims and dispel the notions that had arisen. Both sides were partially correct.

By delving deeper and analyzing the practice patterns over time, we found that some of the "more experienced" physicians were slowing down and heading toward retirement while new, younger group members were building their practices, and still others were taking their business elsewhere. We negotiated on behalf of the hospital to change the group block to several individual blocks, freeing up critically needed OR time while maintaining relationships with the older orthopedists and making the newer physicians feel welcomed and important. Without deep data analysis, this situation would have likely devolved into a battle of wills, politics, and back-biting sessions between this orthopedics group, other physicians, and the hospital and OR managers.

Once you have all your individual surgeons separated, the next step is to list out each block for each physician for each DOW. Look historically at the utilization of that block over time (which can be as simple as subtraction!). Analysis done by DOW should be used if there are one or more blocks per week, so as to ascertain if a surgeon is using a particular day more heavily than others. Many busy surgeons have several blocks throughout the week, but prefer to fill some over others, leaving some blocks less heavily utilized than others. If we were to only look at average utilization over time, we would miss the trends that show the reduction in utilization on specific days, and might misallocate time across the week. Alternatively, a reduction in percentage of cases by DOW might indicate changes in practice patterns or the movement of some cases to other competing locations. Thus, this may also show you changes to the practice focus, patterns of behavior, or changes to loyalties and surgery location preferences.

Next, you should examine the volumes of cases per day relative to the blocks over time.

Figure 10.1 shows one of several trending analytics we run for our clients. Here, we study the number of cases surgeons are bringing during each of the blocked periods to help ascertain trends and case type change.

This metric lets you see the variation in volumes per day over time so as to look for signs of deterioration in loyalty, expansion or contraction of practices, and potential for changes to the block allocation. This also allows you to see which surgeons are more consistent in their business and which are more sporadic, which can in turn lead to decisions about block allocation rankings based on utilization consistency. Additionally, this analysis will help you justify block allocations which, on the surface, might appear to be too high or too low. We commonly find trends in the activity of specific surgeons and even certain case types over time, which will help us to ascertain solutions that help drive up utilization and reduce abuse.

Lastly, as we'll see later, you can also examine your payor mix within blocks to help determine how relatively profitable your utilization might be. As you examine this data, you can do so within the context of the block schedule and the surgeons themselves. What percentage of the block schedule is filled with what payor mix? Do some surgeons bring higher or lower percentages of high-paying cases to their block time? Are some trending toward predominantly government-funded or low-reimbursement patients or well-paying privately insured patients? You'll want to examine what percentage is coming to *your facility*, as it is not uncommon for some physicians to take their better-paying patients into their self-owned surgery centers or preferred hospitals, leaving less-profitable patients for your facility to handle.

TRENDING AND PREDICTING FUTURE DEMAND

Much of this can be trended using forecasting and predictive analytics. As you look at historical data and try to envision your future, you can begin to ascertain which practices are likely to see growth or decline, and which ones will need more or less OR time in the future. This is especially important as facilities expand or build new physical plants. It's not just a matter of how many surgeries you currently do, or even the expected volumes of the future. You should also consider the types and mix of cases, the payor mix, and the needs of surgeons in order to effectively design new space.

It is worth noting that there are a number of firms who specialize in the analysis of demographic trends and patterns which can offer you further insights into your future need for surgical capacity. Some will offer you a deep analysis your market and the expectations of growth of certain morbidities such as cardiac and orthopedics. Others are better at the analysis of current and expected market conditions, and may point you towards the emphasis on untapped potential or "leakage" to other hospitals.

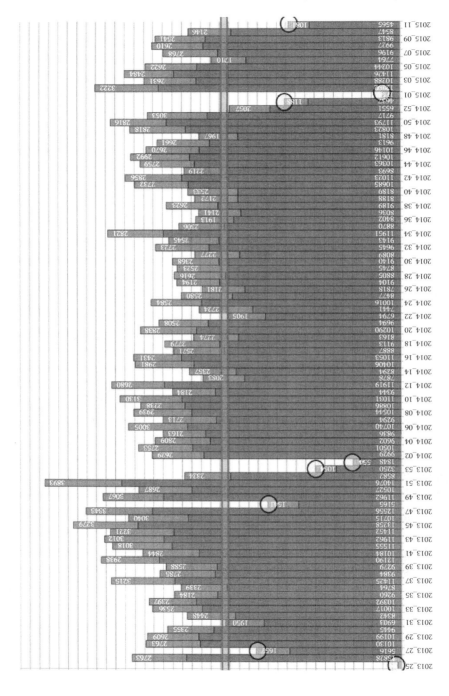

FIGURE 10.1   Weekly surgeon volume trends.

SURGEON UTILIZATION

This might seem odd data to analyze, as the utilization of a surgeon is relatively similar to block utilization analysis and may not be at the top of mind for hospital executives. However, let's pretend that you are creating a new block schedule without any references to previous blocks, as if it had never been done before at your facility. Where would you start? Wouldn't you want to consider how the surgeons used their time throughout the week? Wouldn't you want to know on what days a given surgeon practiced, and how much variation there is in the amount of time he/she uses throughout the week? You might also want to know how regular their utilization patterns might be, and how regularly they darken your OR doors versus those of your competitors. What are their start times (often an indicator of the location of choice), and how often do they show up and start on time as scheduled? Are they seeking additional time or are their volumes, OR time, and percentage of weeks practiced waning?

In our dozen-plus years of this work, we have rarely found facilities in which there is consistent and accurate matching of block times with actual surgeon/practice need. Most commonly, we find surgeons are under- or overblocked, meaning they have either not enough or too much block time for their typical case load requirements. When this is bad enough, the difference can be thousands of minutes per week of mismatched OR time. Of course, a nurse manager and scheduler will scramble to fill holes and shift case load around between used and unused ORs, but this is neither efficient nor particularly satisfying for schedulers, staff, or surgeons. Rather, this can lead to staff burnout, poor staff attitudes (from working overtime or call off's), and surgeon frustration.

Surgeon utilization analysis obviously overlaps to a certain degree with the aforementioned block utilization analytics, except that the reference point is no longer the block ... it is now the surgeon himself.

So let's start with a very clean slate, as if we've never built an OR schedule before. For our work, we normally break every case down into micro-subcomponents of time, such that we can discern at a highly granular level the activities of each surgeon on each day she operates over time. (While this requires some complex analytics and simulation tools, the effort yields an enormous data set, rich in information and ready to create solid recommendations!)

Typically we start at a high level, and drill down to varying levels of detail in order to best give the client the information they seek. First we look generally at overall activity, and would commonly begin with the time the surgeon uses for cases each day of the week, throughout a given period. For this sample surgeon in Figure 10.2, we can see that his weekly minutes varies over the 2 years of data. The spread is very near a traditional, normal "bell curve" indicating that he has short case days and very long case days, and a great deal of his activity occurs within a given range.

Surgeons routinely practice on several week days, and their volume of cases and OR time varies between days. Different days can see different case times and case types. Furthermore, their volumes can wax and wane each week, depending on the consistency of their own case load. One week is high, another low. Thus, we need to analyze the volume and case times, as well the variances in both, across some span of time. This will help us determine the regularity of volumes and the consistency of

Dr. Busyness, weekly total case time over 2 years of volume

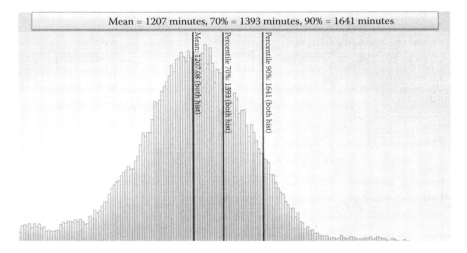

FIGURE 10.2 Sample weekly case minutes histogram.

case time and help us to ascertain the relative need for the allocation of block time on a given day of the week.

Note that the mean (a.k.a. the average), the leftmost line in Figure 10.2, is the smallest of the three numbers depicted. This is to be expected, as it is the middle point on the curve. The average on a bell curve like this one depicts the value above and below in which roughly 50% of the values of the data set lie. That is, 50% of the values lie under 1207 minutes, and 50% is higher than 1207 minutes.

Sadly, many managers use the average to offer block time. However, if we only give Dr. Busyness a total of 1207 minutes (or something rounded close thereto) he would go over that 50% of the time, causing delays in to-follow case starts, overtime pay, and extended hours of operation. Or, he would have to cut the number of cases he did during his block time (else routinely go above it), ask for more time, shift to a new block, or scramble to find add-on time, or perhaps take his business elsewhere! We routinely see the busiest surgeons with insufficient blocks times, and the least busy surgeons with latent capacity.

Note then the percentiles that have been added into the analysis. These indicate the amount of the curve that is captured to the left of the given line. That is, they tell us how much of the potential variation in total weekly case time is captured within the given percentile. So, for instance, we see that Dr. Busyness would use 1393 minutes *or less* 70% of the time. If we gave this physician a block time of roughly 1400 minutes, he would only go over that 30% of the time.

However, some surgeons aren't so easy. Dr. Busyness had a nice, smooth case time histogram. You will find that this is relatively uncommon, and that many surgeons have odd case time patterns. For instance, see the example in Figure 10.3.

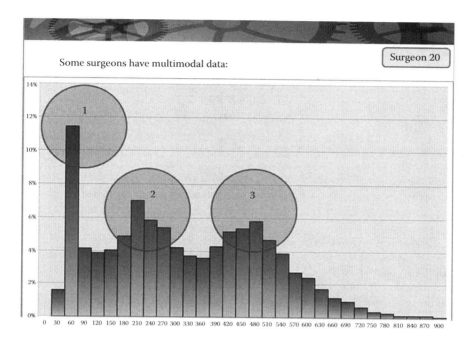

FIGURE 10.3 Multimodal distribution of case time.

The graph (Figure 10.3) represents the distribution of case length for a single surgeon over a 1-year period. You can quickly see that there are three distinct "humps" in the distribution, meaning that there are three peaks in frequency of case length across the entire data set. This would likely mean that this physician does at least three different case type groupings which yield three distinct and similar case length patterns. In such a scenario, we would use the data to identify the patterns of each of the three different case length groupings so as to enable a more informed decision as to the "when" and "which" of this surgeon's utilization. Thus, each of these three groupings would become its own data set and analysis, which would in turn allow for better decision-making on when, where, and how long this surgeon's block or blocks would be. In this case and most others, before we go about estimating block time for each surgeon, we would want some additional information. We would want to go back to the aforementioned block analysis and look at the cases each surgeon performed. In the case of the multimodal case length analysis, we want to allocate block time to a surgeon's case types rather than to all cases. Are some of your orthopedists using more or less block time due to the types of cases they perform? Some high-volume surgeons perform less complicated cases yet need the same amount of OR time as those who perform long, complex cases … yet the former often makes more money.

Case-type analysis leads to case time analysis. So, a little deeper dive into the actual case types over time will help offer insights. Again, this requires a greater granularity of data than is normally pulled for typical reporting, thus it may be difficult to obtain and analyze without the right resources. In this analysis, for example, you may find that an orthopedic group is increasing or reducing their volume of total joints versus shorter, more numerous cases. This trend should be examined within the context of the size of the allocated blocks and the potential financial impacts to the hospital. Easier, high-profit cases could be moving to local surgicenters, leaving only larger, more difficult cases for your hospital (which is fine if you happen to own or co-own that surgicenter, but concerning if you don't).

Thus we commonly add a deep dive on case types, which leads to an understanding of subtle changes to practice patterns that need to be understood for the sake of future strategic and capacity planning. For instance, some General Surgeons will use several room types on a given day, e.g., a "normal" OR, an Endo suite/OR, and a robot. Thus a schedule would need to reflect the utilization pattern of each physician relative to the utilization of a particular room type, especially if "flipping" occurs. This will require additional analysis to determine the precise utilization patterns of surgeons *and* room types in order to establish proper block allocation parameters.

Even if you know that surgeons are "leaving the building," you may not know the extent or impact of the changes, or specifically how much capacity you now have to fill. Deep data analytics can reveal changes to case types or lengths of surgeries that may constitute more or less OR time; the slow migration of certain case volumes elsewhere; or the increases of certain profitable case types of younger, growing practices. Of course, the evolution of case types within a practice is to be expected. However, trends towards more profitable surgeries or generally higher volumes should be rewarded. Those who selectively bring your facility cases can be encouraged or pressured to bring more through the use of data and the rewards available in the schedule.

Also, here you'll want to pull industry data so as to gauge how well your surgeons are utilizing your highly valuable OR time. Due to the number of facilities we've worked in, we have our own surgery databases that include case types and time for each specialty. There are also commercially available databases for purchase should you need that data. Are your physicians slow or on par or even faster than their peers? Does it simply take one of your heavily blocked surgeons more time to do a given case? As you examine surgeon utilization and the resulting block allocations, you should never reward bad behavior! Though not common, this can happen if an unusually slow surgeon is given more block time than his peers simply because he is slower than they are. While most OR managers know better than to reward the slow with more time, this habit can creep in over time. A surgeon who consistently practices outside her block due to relative slowness rather than expanding volume is too often accommodated rather than offered alternatives, such as breaking up a long block into several short blocks, or leaving longer, more complex cases to slower OR days. Regardless, such a scenario can lead to significant conflict without the backing of solid data analytics, and an objective and engaged OR steering committee made up of physician peers.

Next, as mentioned above, we'd want to break down time into days of week and case types. Is a surgeon relatively busier on Mondays or Wednesdays? Does he practice elsewhere, perhaps at a local surgicenter or another hospital, during certain days of week, after which he comes to your facility? From the second example in Figure 10.3, "Dr. Threehumps" may be an orthopedist whose case times are distinguished by totals, revisions, and scopes. He might do all his totals on Mondays and other cases throughout the week. Therefore, we would want to track his activities *and* case types throughout each week in order to fully assess his block requirement.

Figure 10.4 depicts the number of cases starts for a surgeon by HOD and DOW, with each line representing a particular case type. The surgeon in this chart shows heavy activity on Thursday mornings for a given case type/grouping. This can become vital information for laying out a block schedule.

We find that this degree of detail is commonly left incomplete, perhaps due to the complexity of the analysis, the politics of changing block allocations, and/or weakness in the C-Suite. Yet, if your surgical schedule is to go from a "rough estimate" to a precise, capacity optimizing program, this degree of attention to detail will be required.

Finally, we would typically group active OR time into time segments for more meaningful analytics. Depending on the client's needs, volumes, and activity levels at various points in the day, we might group activity into "Core" and "Non-Core" time, or other segments that allow the OR to better allocate block time. Proper staffing alignment would require an examination of the non-core hour and weekend volumes to prevent underutilized staff and balance the use of overtime.

CONTROLLING (FIRST) CASE START TIMES

Here it may be worth mentioning that start times matter. When a physician starts her surgical day is as important as how long her day lasts. We all know the vagaries of late starts, but it is still worthwhile to say that consistently late starts should not be tolerated under any circumstances. Most OR managers track first-case starts, yet it is the late-morning and afternoon starts that can throw off the end of the day and cause unnecessary overtime pay. Physicians who practice at other facilities and come to your OR in the late morning or afternoon should be held as accountable as those who start at 0700. It is unacceptable to allow a surgeon working at another facility to routinely arrive late, start late, and end during nurse overtime hours.

In Figure 10.5, we show the severity of the late-start issue. In this rather chaotic and poorly managed OR, late cases dominate the schedule, with the most common relative start time being 20 minutes late as shown by the line with a steep peak, which represents about 10% of the total volume.

Of course, there are many causes of case start delays, only one of which is the surgeon. Your staff, poor pre-case prep, delays in pre-op, anesthesiology, and holding can all lead to first-case start delays. This can become a downward behavioral spiral, as surgeons frustrated with other root causes quit showing up on time, leading to additional delays when the other causes are fixed or mitigated.

Thus, you need to track the issues that plague the system and avoid using a single cause, as there may be many. Though most EMRs rarely track more than one cause, you should keep an ongoing log of ALL the reasons for delays in start times.

Finally, remember that your start times need to be well-defined and understood by the staff and all surgeons. In too many facilities, start times are assumed to mean different timestamps by various players. Whatever you decide to make start time, whether wheels in, cut time, etc., make sure that it is well known and understood by all so that tracking can be consistent and manageable.

FIGURE 10.4 Number of case starts by surgeon by DOW, HOD, and case type.

C1	C2	C3	C4	C5	C6	C7	C8	C9	HOD	DOW
9	5	85	5	42	4	1	25	4	07	Mon
7	1	35	1	83	1	1	143	5	08	Mon
2	1	17		72			42	5	09	Mon
2		22	6	66	1		70	8	10	Mon
13		46	5	69	1		62	9	11	Mon
28	1	30	17	50			54	9	12	Mon
16	1	27	7	55		2	47	9	13	Mon
7	3	26	2	39	1	1	59	7	14	Mon
3	1	15	1	20	1		42	1	15	Mon
2	3	14	2	17	2	1	45	4	16	Mon
	1	5	2	6		6	28		17	Mon
		6	5	5	1	1	17		18	Mon
		4	1	1	4		17	1	19	Mon
6	37	1	108	2	117	49		12	07	Tue
3	90		74	1	14	108	1	49	08	Tue
1	27		80		20	136	1	29	09	Tue
2	35		95		40	106		51	10	Tue
17	48		53	1	34	80		43	11	Tue
29	35	1	84	18	23	66		38	12	Tue
14	32		77	6	32	61		51	13	Tue
6	30	4	65	2	24	45	2	37	14	Tue
1	14	1	32	1	15	28	2	25	15	Tue
	14	3	17	5	5	14	3	13	16	Tue
	8	2	15	4	5	5	1	12	17	Tue
1	1	1	6	3	3	2		10	18	Tue
2	2	2	2	2		1	3	6	19	Tue
8	1	41	8	10	16	4	2	21	07	Wed
8		25	2	20	11		8	95	08	Wed
6	1	23	1	15	17	1	1	40	09	Wed
23	1	20	2	22	23		1	43	10	Wed
12		34	5	20	5			43	11	Wed
8		30	13	14	18	1		43	12	Wed
2	3	26	6	3	21	2		31	13	Wed
	2	17	2	4	10		2	20	14	Wed
	2	15	5	1	8		5	10	15	Wed
	1	14	9	1	5		5	15	16	Wed
	3	7	11		2	5	1	9	17	Wed
	3	8	5		1	3	6	2	18	Wed
	2	1	9		1	2	1	5	19	Wed
71	47	5	14	4	1	50		1	07	Thu
175	61	1	8	1		131		2	08	Thu
159	34		11	1		128		5	09	Thu
155	39		5	1		120		1	10	Thu
127	37		7	2	1	104		3	11	Thu
105	29		4	12	1	65		17	12	Thu
70	28	3	5	3		56	4	16	13	Thu
28	32	5		1	4	38	41	8	14	Thu
9	21	1		1	2	19	21	6	15	Thu
7	13			7	3	10	15	6	16	Thu
	7	6		5	1	3	6	5	17	Thu
2	5	2		3	2	4	4	1	18	Thu
	1	1		1	3	2			19	Thu
19	2	9	13	12	64	93			07	Fri
38		5	1	21	4	148	4	1	08	Fri
35		6	1	24	18	151	3	1	09	Fri
39		3	1	37	31	118	2	1	10	Fri
28	1	6	5	23	18	85	1	7	11	Fri
17		4	9	22	11	46	5	12	12	Fri
9	1	6	11	11	16	32	6	6	13	Fri
7	7	7	6	2	9	17	7	2	14	Fri
6	4	4	13	9	7	10	7	14	15	Fri
1	8	2	7	3	2	5	3	6	16	Fri
4	3	6	6	4	2	2	7	6	17	Fri
1	4	6	2	3	1		7	3	18	Fri
	3	1	1	1	1	1	2	2	19	Fri

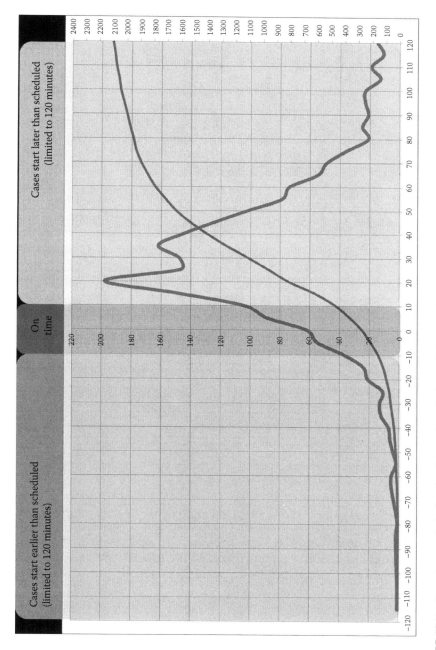

FIGURE 10.5   Start-time analysis showing the number of minutes before or after the assigned start time, which is shown as "0" on the x-axis.

Non-Blocked Surgeons

Remember that there are other surgeons in your community who use your facility but who might not have block times. These surgeons might like to have block time if some were available. But commonly they will use "open time" or "add-on" time to get onto the schedule. It is quite important to allow for open time within the block schedule in order to accommodate new surgeons, smaller but important practices, and blocked surgeons with inordinately busy weeks.

Importantly, there may be surgeons who currently have but do not deserve block time on the schedule. Their volumes may have dropped or their business might have moved elsewhere and thus they need less than your standard block would allow. Alternatively, your hospital may have made the decision to move away from a particular low-revenue service line, thus creating the need to remove block allocations and let those surgeons use open time. Regardless, these physicians may still be accommodated via the block schedule if an adequate amount of open time is not allocated.

In supporting the decisions around the need for open time, we commonly study the percentage of add-on cases that will fit into a specific time period. This analysis will provide information as to how long your open time slots should be, and what percentage of cases would fit into that amount of time. Then, we examine the historical patterns of utilization of non-blocked surgeons to gauge the DOW allocation requirements of the non-blocked group. We will then examine the types of cases being added on to gauge their emergent status and whether or not add-on cases might be better scheduled into an existing block or open time or if they are truly emergent. Commonly, we see non-emergent cases added onto the schedule as emergent by blocked surgeons, which takes the open time away from the non-blocked surgeons for whom that time is intended. This, of course, can be managed with proper governance and scheduling policies. Lastly, using simulation analysis tools, we "assign" non-blocked surgeons their preferred day to see if each non-blocked surgeon can be accommodated on their preferred day. This helps the client to gauge how many non-blocked surgeons will still vie for time on the schedule.

The extent of your open time, and its availability during the day, will depend on the need and number of surgeons in your community, whether you are actively recruiting new surgeons, and the rigidity of your block allocation policies.

Depending on the scenario, we will recommend scheduling allocations of open time during core hours, 0700–1500, so as to prevent overtime caused by end-of-day starts, allow for predictable access, and promote efficient staffing. Providing regularly staffed open time allows consistency in availability for non-blocked surgeons while permitting your blocked physicians the time they need. This also relieves the pressure to add blocks onto the schedule for those surgeons whose usage patterns do not warrant a regular block.

OTHER ANALYTICS

Though several years ago it was considered a taboo, many of our clients want us to evaluate the payor mix of the surgeons using block time. This is particularly important when competing groups are in different insurance plans or company coverage, or in areas with large concentrations of employees of a single employer. Let's face it ... some pay better than others. Should some get preferential block or OR time based on the revenues they bring? That, of course, is up to the facility and its management team. But the analysis is worthwhile in areas where the lineup of payors tends to send volumes to one surgical group or practice over others.

Additional analytics that you can include in your assessment of physician utilization are similar to those mentioned previously in this chapter. Recall that we used analysis of case type, case length, end-of-day time, relative cost to the hospital (particularly and especially implant costs), inclusion with key payor(s), volume and case trending, and profitability of current and future cases. These can obviously be completed, by physician and time period, to assess the relative utilization, value, and growth potential of each surgeon.

OR UTILIZATION

The analysis of OR utilization is an entirely different matter. For these analyses, we forget who is using the space and only focus on how much the space is being used. Here again, we will want to break down the analysis into smaller pieces so as to ascertain how we might expand the use of OR capacity.

OR utilization can be a deceptive analysis, as most hospitals use a single average number to represent the system. However, utilization can go up or down dramatically if we consider the variables that can play into this number. For instance, the average utilization can vary widely if we look at different days of the week. This is pretty obvious in many facilities, yet the common practice is to report an average across the entire week. DOW may also drive the number of ORs that are in use. So, Mondays and Tuesdays may require more space and resources than Friday.

Similarly, HOD can matter as well. It is not uncommon for activity to drop significantly after midday in many ORs. This is relevant as you examine how many ORs you keep open and during which hours. Unfortunately, hours of operation are sometimes driven more by nurse shifts than the actual surgical case time requirements, and thus ORs are kept open but remain largely underutilized. It is rather important, then, to examine both HOD and DOW as you look at your utilization.

Of course, you'll want to look at the utilization of each room as well. In many facilities, there is plenty of unused space. Sometimes, ORs are aged to the point that significant financial investments would be required for their ongoing use. Or, volumes might have slowed to the point that there is excess and latent physical capacity ... space that simply isn't being used. I have worked in facilities in which accounting for the low utilization of some space makes a tremendous difference in their average overall utilization, often doubling the larger, gross average. Older ORs, used only for certain cases by certain physicians, decreased the overall utilization and the utilization of newer, more modern space, thus creating a misunderstanding of the actual chaos of the busiest areas and the relative inefficiency of the older areas. This was magnified in one client's OR when, per one of our recommendations, older ORs were shuttered through the creation of capacity in the "newer" ORs via schedule redesign.

Alternatively, some ORs are busy all day, every day, including weekends. In these facilities, space and time is precious, and therefore the management of OR time in these constrained capacity scenarios is crucial for financial survival and the maintenance of physician relationships. Indeed, in some of these facilities staffing is the biggest constraint to growth and volume maintenance. Yet, surprisingly, even some of the busiest departments fail to properly and regularly monitor their performance and utilization metrics in something more than a standard IT output report.

Thus the tendency to use averages should be avoided *unless* you are looking at a highly granular level, such as HOD. Average daily OR utilization is *highly deceptive* as it masks those ORs that are not preferred due to their spatial constraints, equipment restrictions, or access to the rest of the OR. Instead, an appropriate level of detail should be attained such that variation in operational patterns and trends can be readily discerned and made actionable.

To do this, we start with the variance in utilization by DOW and room. We want to examine how often a given OR is utilized, and during what hours of the day. See Figure 10.6.

The chart in Figure 10.6 represents two ORs and their utilization by DOW during core and non-core hours. The spread of utilization is obvious and should offer clues as to opportunities for capacity expansion. We see that Mondays, Wednesdays, and Fridays are relatively poorly utilized, except for OR4 which is relatively busy on Friday. Likely, one surgeon has a busy Friday schedule here and likes OR4. Tuesday is the busiest day and the day most likely to see activity into the evening hours (and, in this client's case, the day that surgeons complain the most about available capacity, delays in case starts, and general lack of optimal flows).

Concurrent utilization can be an important metric when examining the OR and its schedule. Concurrent utilization simply refers to the number of ORs being used during a given period of time (e.g., one 30-minute period), and helps point to staffing inefficiencies, the use of "flip rooms," and the overall "busyness" of the OR. Commonly, there are "down" ORs throughout the day as surgeons finish their block times early, cases cancel, physicians run late, and staff is unavailable to turn over or even staff rooms. Concurrent utilization can be represented in a number of ways, one of which is shown in Figure 10.7, which shows the concurrent utilization of an orthopedic group with multiple physicians practicing on the same day.

A WORD ON SURGICAL ROBOTS AND UTILIZATION

As robotic surgery takes on a larger role in our hospitals, the utilization of these very expensive machines can be critical to their value and revenue generation. If not well utilized, this equipment can quickly lose its marketing and clinical advantages. The equipment is expensive to purchase, expensive to maintain, and expensive to use, depending, of course, on your definition of "expensive." In many cases, the extra cost is justified by clinical outcomes when patients see better long-term results and quicker recoveries. Furthermore, robots make for good marketing, so the potential benefits of consumer choice may well play into purchase decisions. However, payors typically do not offer any more for a robotic surgery than a non-robotic surgery. Thus one must examine the entire cost–benefit equation, including start-up costs, turnover times, case lengths, upkeep/maintenance costs, marketing benefits, competitive landscape, and surgeon attraction/retention relative to non-robotic surgeries.

Room by day	Room	Core AM	Core PM	Extended 5P	Extended 7P	Evening	On call
OR 03_01_Mon	OR 03	41.92	34.76	17.99	15.24	3.58	2.10
OR 03_02_Tue	OR 03	63.72	50.30	24.39	14.33	6.17	0.95
OR 03_03_Wed	OR 03	42.15	37.73	21.34	11.59	8.16	1.11
OR 03_04_Thu	OR 03	60.29	41.23	14.79	15.40	6.48	0.72
OR 03_05_Fri	OR 03	42.07	32.16	23.63	14.02	2.44	3.01
OR 03_06_Sat	OR 03	15.17	9.83	12.80	4.12	2.13	1.91
OR 03_07_Sun	OR 03	10.52	8.77	6.40	3.81	3.13	1.91
OR 04_01_Mon	OR 04	37.88	34.68	18.75	10.52	3.96	1.91
OR 04_02_Tue	OR 04	60.21	50.00	22.56	10.67	6.63	2.13
OR 04_03_Wed	OR 04	44.97	42.15	18.60	10.82	4.04	1.07
OR 04_04_Thu	OR 04	59.76	38.49	11.43	11.43	6.33	1.33
OR 04_05_Fri	OR 04	61.66	36.89	16.01	11.28	4.57	0.88
OR 04_06_Sat	OR 04	3.20	4.50	5.18	4.73	3.43	0.34
OR 04_07_Sun	OR 04	7.24	5.87	3.05	4.27	2.06	0.84

FIGURE 10.6   OR utilization by DOW and core/non-core hours.

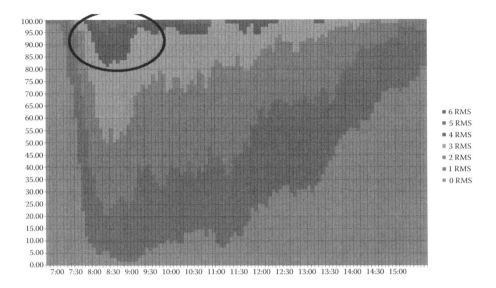

FIGURE 10.7   Concurrent utilization by HOD shows the percentage of historical concurrent utilization of a given number of rooms.

Of course, robots should be used for the right surgeries. Surgical robots were originally developed to perform prostatectomies, specifically radical prostatectomies, such that a man needing surgery to remove prostate cancer might still have hope of normal urinary and sexual function. Utilization spread as the U.S. Food and Drug Administration (FDA) approved other uses such as Ob-Gyn procedures.

With these markets quickly peaking for robot manufacturers, there is a push to advance into other surgical specialties. For example, there was and is a push to get into cardiology. Unfortunately for those manufacturers and their shareholders, cardiology has, in most areas, largely rejected robotic surgery. Yet the search for new markets continues on, including general surgery. Thus we are continuing to see experimentation in robotic surgeries for procedures that are not often associated with the need for the precision and technical expertise of robotics. A close examination of the use of a robot in one hospital reveals that general surgery is the dominant user, with few, if any, prostatectomies being performed.

Figure 10.8 shows the relative number of surgical minutes used by each of the three specialties (general surgery, Ob-Gyn, and urology) for each week of the data period (mid 2013 to late 2014). The data show a limited but relatively steady use of the robot within Ob-Gyn, and sporadic and low utilization by urology. The interesting data element is the rapid and pronounced increase in robot utilization by general surgery.

This begs for further examination within the data set. There may be great growth opportunities in "traditional" robotics markets if new urologists and Ob-Gyn's can be enlisted. Or, there may be a general surgeon who is doing research into the potential uses for robots in general surgery. Either way, at least on the surface, the hospital was not making what it should on the equipment it purchased, given that the average cost per surgery was known to be between $1500 and $2500 per case, and the most

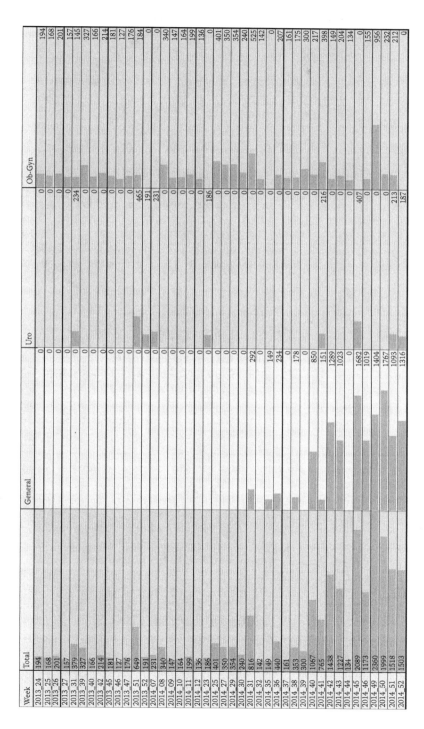

FIGURE 10.8 Weekly utilization of robots in three specialties over time, in minutes.

common robotic case type was not a high-revenue case type. Furthermore, these robotic cases and their turnover times were routinely longer at this facility than non-robotic cases of the same type, regardless of the specialty or procedure.

Therefore in analyzing this situation for cost–benefit or capacity management, we would typically examine the revenues per case (to date, few insurers are paying for robot assistance upcharges); cost per procedure with a separate line item for robot costs inclusive of annual maintenance costs, per procedure supply costs, and ongoing regular maintenance costs; patient satisfaction scores; OR and robot turnover time by case type (compared to non-robotic cases); procedure length by procedure type (compared to non-robotic cases); post-procedure LOS; inpatient LOS, if any; and other post-op metrics that might lead to an understanding of relative value. Such an analysis may reveal some surgeries for which robotic assistance is highly valued, and others for which there is little or no additional value to justify the increased expense.

Great planning must go into the use of this kind of equipment, such that those patients who could benefit most from the advantages of robotic surgeries are allowed as much access as possible. Care must be given to ensure that prioritization is given to those surgeons and their patients for whom the value of the robot's additional cost can be best and most readily justified.

ADDITIONAL ANALYTICS AND TIPS

Feeling overwhelmed with data yet? Don't! This is not that complex, really. But it is a requirement if you are going to go to any of your surgeons and have a legitimate discussion about your surgical schedule, block allocations, and their place in the hospital. Let's face it. The schedule is the heartbeat of the OR.

But our analysis is still not yet complete … there is more to be done for many of our clients.

"FLIPPING"

In many facilities, "flip rooms" (a.k.a. "dual rooms") are used by surgeons to increase their productivity. This is rather common with orthopedists and ENTs, who move from case to case without the need to wait for what can be a lengthy room TAT. Other short-case specialties can benefit from the ability to move quickly between cases, as their cases are shorter than the room TAT. Extreme examples of this can see one "main" orthopedist performing joint replacement surgeries moving methodically between four to five ORs, allowing the opening and closing of each case to be done by his first assistants and/or other surgeons. The "main" surgeon comes into each room only long enough to place the implant, then leaves to move to the next case while others close the case and complete the post-implantation surgical processes. In extreme cases, one physician can perform dozens of joint replacements in a given day within a well-regulated, precisely planned, and executed "surgical factory."

Of course, most hospitals don't see this kind of volume (but would love to have it!) Nonetheless, the push for flip rooms is strong. If they actually use the system as designed, surgeons can often benefit from reduced time in the OR and even a greater number of cases each surgical day. The hospital's benefits are lesser, given the cost of keeping two ORs running for one surgeon. Flip rooms can lead to notorious reductions in OR and staff utilization, especially when a surgeon's volumes are inconsistent from week to week, which in turn leads to staff call off's, overtime, and loss of potential revenue. Furthermore, flip rooms take valuable real estate and staff that could be used for other surgeries. Only when a physician has consistently high volumes (and thus can generate more cases per day using flip rooms) is such an arrangement even appropriate to consider.

Commonly, hospitals use flip rooms informally, making them available when staff and available rooms allow. This keeps the surgeons guessing about whether or not they will be able to keep moving quickly or will be delayed as a room is turned over, and keeps staff guessing about the next case. At one client, an orthopedist would routinely announce his arrival by shouting "Do I get to flip today?" as he approached the OR nurse station. Such environments tend to be more chaotic and less satisfying to both surgeons and staff.

Furthermore, due to the cost of running two rooms per surgeon and the high cost of space and resources, flip rooms cannot typically be used extensively in space constrained environments wherein costs and space need to be highly controlled. In these situations, there simply aren't enough ORs and staff available to allow for all physicians to operate in the purely flip room environment.

Alternatively, good OR managers and Board Runners will "squeeze" additional cases between, for example, orthopedics cases. So, while Dr. Bones is working on a hip replacement, a scope case can go into her second flip room without the risk of creating a conflict for her when she is ready to flip to that second room. This allows the benefit of flip rooms for Dr. Bones while allowing greater volumes and productivity for the OR.

However, these are rarely formalized and set forth in the surgical schedule. OR managers fear the inevitable scenario in which Dr. Bones exits her first case to find Dr. Scopes still operating in Dr. Bone's second OR, delaying her next start. Thus creating a situation in which two surgeons consistently and regularly share a third "flip" room is difficult if not impossible without some advanced analytics, even though it may make intuitive sense. The inevitable fireworks and the unknowns of officially pairing physicians into a "Shared Flip Room™" (SFR) makes it risky if not impossible to implement unless you first ensure that the concept works with *your surgeons* and *their specific historical volumes, utilizations, and practice patterns.*

We have discovered over many years of work and research that such formalized implementations are quite possible. While it doesn't work with every physician pairing, we have proven that certain physicians will pair well together if they share a third "dual" room. Essentially, the theory goes as follows: Two physicians begin working at approximately the same time in two ORs. The first to finish goes to the third "shared" OR, and her first OR is cleaned. The second of the two surgeons to finish then goes into the now cleaned first room. That surgeon's OR is cleaned and made ready for the next surgeon to finish. And so the "ballet" continues, with physicians flipping to the next clean and available room throughout the day. With effective board runners and proactive management of next case starts and room turnovers, certain pairings of physicians can work very well.

To prove whether or not a pairing will work, we use sophisticated and elaborate simulation models that allow us to accurately predict the outcomes of two physicians paired in an SFR scenario over the course of long periods of OR time. As you might expect, the use of estimates, averages, and other generalized data will NOT suffice in proving the efficacy of a pairing, nor will it convince any knowledgeable physician to try it. In our models, we will use each physicians' practice patterns, volumes, and case times (as derived from a second analytical simulation model), OR constraints and limitations, staff and equipment requirements and limitations, etc., to accurately predict the long-term impact of various physicians pairings. Some, of course, work out better than others. Some are just not meant to be paired together at all. Yet, when appropriate and thoroughly vetted, we have found that implementing this concept allows for much greater capacity, much higher utilization, and nearly all the benefits of a "true" dual rooms scenario without the added costs and reduced capacity of the traditional model.

Indeed, our work indicates that, under the best pairings, there is virtually no difference in total OR time for a surgeon in an SFR versus a true dual-room scenario. More commonly, the difference in total OR time is quantifiable but negligible, making the traditional model very difficult to justify to a CEO trying to control OR staff cost and utilization. Of course, as the simulation models accurately predict, there is always the situation in which two doctors vying for the third room must wait. But these circumstances are relatively rare and can be managed effectively with a solid operational model and educated, trained staff.

We have developed a workable and reliable program for flipping three surgeons into four rooms, a thought largely unheard of until this work. Using similar analytics to those described above, we can assess whether or not as many as three surgeons can share four ORs without delay. As the model predicts, it can work swimmingly if set up and staffed correctly. This saves as much as 4800 minutes per week of OR time, which can be used to cut staff requirements and/or expand surgical volume without expanding physical plant.

Example

In one client site, we implemented the SFR after rigorous testing of multiple pairing of physicians through simulation modeling. We found the exact pairings that would work best, and allowed them to be paired together in an SFR program. Over time, the predictions of the model were proven quite accurate, with performance made even better by the experience of a good board runner and a proactive OR manager. We were able to take their total joint volume up by over 100% without expanding the number of rooms available or pushing other physicians out of their OR/block times.

In Figure 10.9, the lowest of the four lines represents the finish time of an orthopedic surgeon *without* any ability to flip a room. Clearly, the surgeon is finishing the day later than in the other scenarios, as shown by the percentage of cases completed by a given HOD (on the x-axis). The other three lines represent three other modeled scenarios. The top line of the four shows the results of the use of a dedicated flip room, which offers the best performance, though it is negligibly better than the other two. The third and fourth lines, tightly packed together with the top line, show the results of two SFR scenarios. Clearly, these three tightly grouped lines indicate that all three

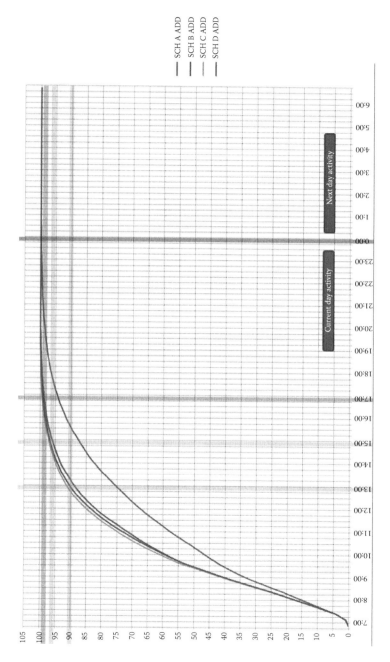

FIGURE 10.9   All-cases finish time for four-modeled scenarios for a given surgeon paired with another.

scenarios perform better than the no flip room scenario. But, the differences between the dedicated flip room and the shared room are negligible. Indeed, the long-term simulated analysis shows that there is a slight delay in finish total time over the course of a long period of time (several years), but only less than 1%–3% of the time does the surgeon's day become significantly delayed. This can commonly be mitigated with knowledgeable human interventions by the board manager and schedulers.

If you want to get the benefits of the SFR concept, you will need data, appropriately accurate simulation models, an OR manager capable of proactively managing these scenarios, and a strong executive leadership team to push these reforms through to recalcitrant physicians. We would *highly* recommend that you *avoid* trying this operational model without proper vetting, as it could result in poor outcomes and angry staff and surgeons.

EXTERNAL PROCESS CONTROL

You would also be wise to account for the processes and flow within the OR to effectively determine if the schedule will be constrained by the need for process improvement efforts. If, for instance, your pre-op processes call for patients to be moved from pre-op to a holding area, wherein they are seen by their anesthesiologist and/or physician prior to surgery, the location of this area needs to be accounted for in the analysis of the potential of TAT. If, as another example, your facility has ancillary space for induction prior to surgery, this can impact the speed with which patients are moved into the OR and prepped for surgery. Or, as another example, if your OR is aged, and storage is an issue, you may find that cases run longer than necessary due to the "scrambling" for supplies during cases which in turn delays case finish times and thus next case starts. Or, as yet another example, if Endo patients take up space in pre-op, you may find that your blended pre- and post-op areas become constrained to the point of delaying surgeries.

Importantly, as we have described elsewhere in this book, poor processes elsewhere in the facility can lead quickly to constraints "upstream" and "downstream" in surgery. For instance, if registration and pre-op create delays in patient flow, patients may not be ready for surgery when needed. Likewise, if the post-anesthesia care unit (PACU) is backed up due to constraints in the availability of inpatient beds, surgeries can be delayed as patients are held in the OR awaiting space in PACU.

Process optimization throughout your hospital is therefore paramount to the successful operation of all major departments. You *must* consider the entire system when evaluating and undertaking process improvement efforts, else you risk the "Whack-a-Mole" effect of chasing constraints throughout your hospital and never reaching true optimization.

For instance, if you move a significant portion of your orthopedic surgeries to Monday, you'll need to ensure that the ortho unit upstairs is big enough and staffed sufficiently so as to handle the ebbs and flows in daily volume. Failure to tee that up effectively will surely lead to surgeon frustration and even case cancelations due to lack of unit capacity.

When considering the "upstream" and "downstream" of your ORs, consider Figure 10.10. It is a good visualization of the complexities and interdependencies of

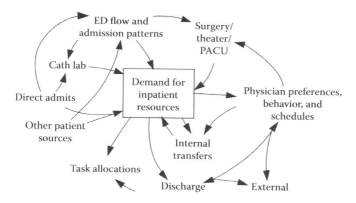

FIGURE 10.10   Visualization of the interdependencies hospital-wide capacity.

hospital-wide capacity and its many potential constraints. Thus, as you redesign your surgical schedule to offer your surgeons greater access to the OR and your hospital greater revenue potential, consider that the ED and direct admissions will need those inpatient beds as well!

GOVERNANCE

While you'd think that governing the hospital's own surgery area would be relatively simple, we all know otherwise. Without proper authority and control, some (sometimes many) surgeons will inevitably abuse the system, causing a quick deterioration in capacity, efficiency, and staff morale. Much of this governance must come from the physicians themselves, as they are best able to control the actions and inactions of colleagues. (We will cover the physician's role in capacity optimization in Chapter 12.)

While this book is not meant to cover every aspect of OR operations, a quick review of the necessary governance requirements seems reasonable here, because these can impact your ability to make a dramatic change in the OR. These include but are not limited to the following:

- *Block release time*: When blocks are to be unused, they should be released to other surgeons such that additional cases can be scheduled into the now-open time.
- *Block maintenance requirements*: What does it take to get and maintain block time? Generally, we recommend working at least 60% of the available weeks and working no less than 4 hours per week. These metrics, especially the latter, can vary widely depending on the demand for OR time, the availability of open time, and the competitiveness of the market. We would also add on-time start percentage (no less than 70%), with egregious delays considered more harshly, management of required paperwork and processes (e.g., H&Ps sent before the day of surgery), case paperwork completion, and other requirements as necessary for the function of the facility.

- *Block removal and reduction*: Removal and/or reduction of block time must be a very real possibility for the failure to comply with requirements. This can be a very touchy subject, especially with the busiest surgeons (who are well aware that they are the busiest surgeons and thereby bring the hospital the most revenues). Nonetheless, physicians must understand that compliance by everyone is required for the system to function, and thus bad behavior cannot be rewarded with passivity and tacit approval.
- *Disciplinary actions and adjudication*: Of course, there must be penalties for failure to comply with the mandates and rules, inclusive of loss of block time. This must be supported at the C-Suite level.

Proper and effective governance is key to the management of this complex system and the changes that the future will require.

CREATING THE NEW SCHEDULE

By now you should have utilization data on your ORs, your surgeons, and your existing and future blocks. You should also have the results of the SFR pairing simulations, and have explored any constraints to upstream and downstream patient flow *with the new schedule in mind*. You should also have the necessary governance structures in place, fully supporting your need for block release times, rules for maintenance and expansion of block allocation, and requirements for compliance. With this, you should have created a solid, data-backed case for the changes you need to make to the schedule. The last part is relatively quite simple … create the new surgical schedule!

I've seen schedules done on spreadsheets, powerpoint slides, and drawn on pieces of paper. It seems that just about anything will do. But, as long as the data backs it up, and your expectations are set forth, there is no one correct way to display a block schedule. Our only caveat is to suggest that it be in an electronic format that can be altered readily and transmitted easily.

We developed a simple tool called ORchestrate™ that allows for the quick and efficient entry of data into a table that then produces the outputs shown in Figure 10.11. It will allow for a quick, consistent, and reliable way to create, alter, and experiment with the existing, future, and potential surgical schedules.

Of course, your new schedule will need to be "sold" to physicians. This is where your senior leadership is so critical to success. Without good leadership within the C-Suite to help support the changes, your efforts may languish. But with the data you have in hand, and the analysis you will have done, selling it to physicians is infinitely easier and quicker.

REVIEW OF THE BLOCKING AND TACKLING OF BLOCK SCHEDULING

If you can't determine the following, you need to start right away. This is one situation in which I would highly recommend the services of external consultants if you do not have internal analytical capabilities with deep knowledge of your OR and its data, history, and operational model. Failure to effectively, deeply, and accurately

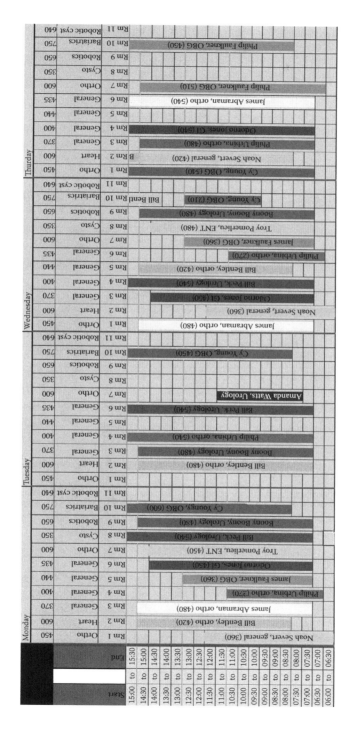

FIGURE 10.11 Screenshot of ORchestrate, our proprietary surgical scheduling tool. It is an easy-to-use tool that allows for an OR manager or scheduler to amend, alter, and play with the schedule on the fly, keeping outputs consistent and readily useful for physician and management discussions. Built-in functionality keeps the scheduling process easy, fast, and error proof.

analyze the following can lead to an inherent underutilization of surgical capacity, and a loss of potential growth at a critical phase of the transformation of healthcare. If you do go the consultant route, make sure that they have analytical capabilities and experience, even if those consultants are highly paid former nurse managers and executives. Titles mean nothing without good analytics!

- Surgeon, block, and OR utilization
- Case types
- Profitability of case mix and payor mix
- Volumes
- Case time versus peers
- Case starts
- Variance in weekly OR use over time
- Trending
- Forecasting and predictive analytics

SUMMARY

Surgical services is one of the most critical areas of the hospital, as it represents a great deal of the revenue, growth, and community loyalty opportunities. Furthermore, surgical services is one of those critical elements of community service that must be done well. Failure to manage this department correctly can lead to disastrous results in finances and community reputation. Alternatively, running this area well can mean great physician loyalty and community allegiance, both of which are very important as the new age of reimbursements nears.

There are a few things you have to do right in order to run this department well. The premier task is managing the OR schedule effectively, such that capacity, revenue, and community service are all optimized. There's more to running an OR than this, of course, but without an optimized surgical schedule, all other improvements put together won't make up the difference. You can have great OR turnover times, but if there isn't a to-follow case scheduled properly, it doesn't matter much. Thus, optimizing your schedule is the fastest and best way to start your facility toward a better operational standard. True optimization will encompass many elements, from staffing to efficient process flows to patient arrival times to revenue cycle management. But without an optimized schedule, you can never truly optimize your surgical capacity and your ability to serve your community.

11 Blocking and Tackling of Inpatient Capacity Management

Up until now, we've largely dealt with the "demand" side of the "Demand–Capacity Continuum." We have looked at the demand coming from the ED into the inpatient side, as well as the demand coming from surgical services. This demand commonly follows reasonably tight and predictable patterns, though there will inevitably be outliers when things either get very busy or very slow in the source departments.

As we learned, the volume and patterns of ED to inpatient demand is driven by the arrival patterns of patients into the ED and the workflow and workload of resources within the ED. We now understand that ED-to-inpatient demand is based on the communication streams between the ED and inpatient units and the process by which patients are admitted. We also learned that proper communication of inpatient bed need between the ED and inpatient units depends largely on how quickly and accurately ED clinicians can recognize possible admitted patients, how well historical inpatient demand patterns are known and understood, and how effectively known admission patterns are used to predict future admission behaviors.

From this, we learned that the concepts and "how to's" of eyeball disposition, scheduling admissions, and predictive analytics are critical for moving patients quickly to their appropriate care areas. These proactive steps help the ED and inpatient unit managers see into the future and use data to better manage their census, workloads, and workflows.

Likewise, we learned that surgical patients are admitted largely based on the output of the surgical schedule. The use of the schedule as a predictive tool to help inpatient units predict their workloads and workflows is critical to the availability of inpatient capacity on surgical units, the smoothness of inpatient operations and surgical admission processes. As the admission patterns of surgery patients are somewhat more predictable than that of ED patients (especially once patients are scheduled for surgery) it stands to reason that their admissions could and should be properly scheduled as well.

Thus much of the inpatient demand is both reliably and predictably known well in advance of the initial "bed request" call or data entry.

CAPACITY VARIANCE

However, just as there is variability in the demand patterns from our major sources of inpatient demand, so too is there variability in the capacity that is made available. This also commonly runs in patterns. Patterns for discharges (the source of most of inpatient capacity) are based largely on the operational models, attending physicians, nursing workflows, case managers, communication with and availability of families and transportation, and the general prioritization of discharges within the overall workflow. And because the workload varies depending on the number of discharges and, to a certain extent, the number of admissions, the patterns of capacity can vary from day to day. This means that it is not uncommon for the variance in capacity patterns to fluctuate throughout the week, thus making it more difficult to predict the availability of beds.

This can be particularly true when it seems that entire units clear out on certain days or within short periods. For instance, specialized surgical orthopedics units can nearly clear out completely on Thursday and Friday when patients from Monday's joint surgeries are ready to go to rehab or home. Or, short-stay units might see a tremendous turnover of patients on a given day, as high as over 100% turnover of beds in a single day.

This, of course, is one of the main reasons why the management of inpatient capacity is so important to the overall operational efficiency of the hospital. Without some semblance of consistency and predictability, even if variable, those who need beds for their patients in source departments become like children in the back seat of the car repeatedly asking, "Is there a bed yet?"

Any good, proactive unit manager must therefore understand the patterns of demand, how those demand patterns are generated, how they might be controlled, and how to best match them with capacity on their unit. This, then, is the subject of this chapter.

ESSENTIAL ELEMENTS

There are several key things that all good inpatient unit managers can and should do to better make necessary capacity available when it's needed. These are neither difficult nor burdensome … it simply requires preparation, diligence, communication, and thought.

UNDERSTAND THE DEMAND PATTERNS

This is as basic as ABCs. Unit managers must be very familiar with the volumes, patterns, and variability of the demand from *each source area* that sends them patients. Any data analyst can provide you with the necessary graphs and charts to show you the patterns each unit faces, from each source area of interest. Some of these patterns will look like that in Figure 11.1.

Notice that the average is shown with its concomitant variance. The variance shown here is the "80–20" range around the average (which is of course based on the concept of the Pareto principle).[*] That is, the upper line (called the UCI, or "Upper Control Interval") shows the volume below which occurred 80% of the time in the

---

[*] Bunkley, N. 2008. Joseph Juran, 103, pioneer in quality control, dies. *New York Times*. March 3. The Pareto principle (also known as the 80–20 rule, the law of the vital few, and the principle of factor sparsity) states that, for many events, roughly 80% of the effects come from 20% of the causes.

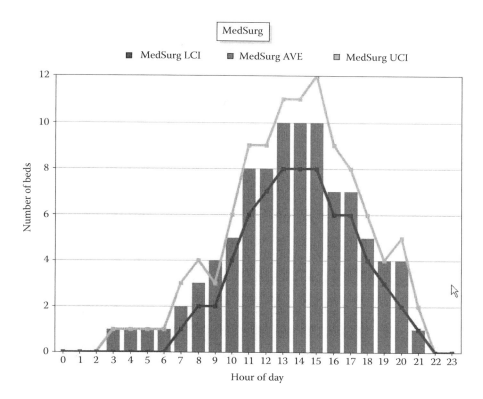

FIGURE 11.1 Sample demand pattern to an inpatient unit, by HOD.

data set. Similarly, the lower line (LCI, or "Lower Control Interval") shows the volume above which occurred 80% of the time in the data set. We show these to represent the "typical" (but not the average) day, as the range shown around the average encapsulates much of the typical daily variation. The "outliers" are those events that occur outside this range (either above or below the "typical" volume) and occur between 10% and 20% of the time. The statistical average is shown by the bars that end somewhere between the two lines. By showing the typical range, we immediately get an understanding of the most common occurrences and the volumes which constitute outliers, both on the high side and low side.

DEFINITION OF DEMAND

But let's first be very clear (though perhaps repetitive) on what we mean by "demand." Demand data is normally captured from historical data in your IT systems. However, your demand is NOT when patients have historically arrived onto the unit. This was the admission time, not the demand time. Indeed, that admission time might have been literally hours after patients were ready to be admitted. Their demand time, by contrast, is the time at which the patients were ready to be admitted from the source area in question. So, the demand time for ED patients would be shortly after the ED physician made his *final* disposition decision, which is commonly after all labs and x-rays are completed and reviewed, after all consults are completed and signed off, and all the other necessary steps taken. In a perfect world, an inpatient bed, a nurse, and a transporter are waiting and ready at the demand time.

Similarly, PACU has a demand versus an admission time. Demand time in PACU can be more difficult to ascertain in the short term, as patients react to anesthesia differently, resulting in different necessary lengths of stay. Overall however, many admitted surgical patients can be grouped into time segments based on their surgical procedures. Thus, their LOS should be relatively predictable, certainly to the point that one could peg a 30-minute window based off the surgical schedule. Units expected to take these patients could be readily notified days in advance, with an update delivered the evening prior or first thing in the morning as add-ons and cancellations are accounted for.

GRANULARITY OF DEMAND DATA

For the unit manager, this analysis should be constructed for each DOW. DOW matters, particularly for those units accepting surgical patients, as some surgeons can generate significant volumes to "preferred" and/or specialized units. DOW also matters because these demand volumes need to be understood within the context of the workload that will be expected for discharges. If discharges are known to be later in the day due to late-rounding physicians or poor process control, admissions may stack up from the ED and PACU, creating large boluses of activity that must be matched with appropriate resources (at least until the broken processes are repaired).

Second, you should create data for different seasons of year and seasonal volume changes (e.g., "flu season," winter in the south, summer in resort areas, etc.). Flu season can wreak havoc on inpatient capacity depending on the strain severity and impact on the local population. Although the exact timing or extent of flu season is often rather unpredictable, the volumes and workload can be compared against historical data when it becomes clear that a relatively sedate or bad flu season is about to erupt. If you happen to be a southern "snow bird" state in winter, your inpatient volume may increase with the population, or change as the case mix index is altered with the changing populations. Regardless of your situation, find a good data analyst or HSE (health systems engineer) to help you decipher your seasonal volume variations if you feel this is an issue for your unit/facility.

As mentioned above, the demand patterns must also be generated for each source area that sends patients to the unit. This is in part to understand the total volume for each DOW (which can, as we'll see later, be shown on a single chart) but also the associated workload. If, for instance, the ED is known to send patients who require more "settling in" than those coming from the OR, this extra work must be taken into account when planning staff workload distribution and task allocations. Likewise, surgical patients who are "wrapped in a bow" and ready for admission require less work. You will also want to compare the variances in DOW volumes from each area as they can shift throughout the week, with perhaps more ED patients coming on Mondays, more surgical patients on Tuesdays and Thursdays, etc.

What to Do with This Demand Data?

What can be done with this new wealth of information? For starters, you can start to see when your beds are actually being demanded, versus when they are typically made available. The variability in your data will show you what is a "typical" day/ HOD, and what constitutes a true "outlier." This will help you and the staff to understand more accurately what you should expect from day to day and hour to hour. As we'll see later, these patterns may allow you to allocate scheduled slots for certain high-volume source areas, such as the ED. You should study these patterns and check your current daily volumes and demand patterns against the historical data to help staff understand their relevance and importance. The data should present, in one snapshot, what volumes you should expect to see on any given day, when you should expect to see them, and what might happen under the one in 10 or so instances when things "go off the rails" on the down- or upside.

The patterns can also help you predict and manage workload and workflow. Recall that these are different terms, the former referring to the amount of work to be done and the latter referring to the way in which the work is completed. If you can predict admissions, a rather large element of the total workload on a given unit, you can start to understand how you might align resources, tasks, and other necessary work (such as discharges) with the work of admissions and thus manage the workload on the unit. For instance, you might consider task allocations to specific staff members, such as medication distribution or some of the admission work. You might reallocate staff dollars to use more techs and aids, freeing nurses to do more nursing-focused work while the supporting staff does the non-nursing duties around admissions and discharges.

Furthermore, you may want to reconsider your staffing patterns based on the demand for resources as shown in your analysis. Often, nurse staffing patterns have little to do with the actual work in the system and more to do with nurse preference, "the way we've always done things," and/or common shift length (e.g., 12 hours). Less common is to plan shifts based on the increases and decreases of arrivals of work into the unit and when resources are more and less required. I've worked on units wherein the shifts were significantly out of phase with the workload. Due to the toxic culture in this facility, this resulted in staff manipulation of the workload on the "day shift" so as to delay work until the "evening shift" came on, essentially dumping work on the next group of nurses. This, needless to say, did not lead to the kind of positive culture that Joe Tye describes in Chapter 4. But because the work was not aligned with the staffing and vice versa, there was a propensity to dump the excess onto the next shift.

To analyze staffing and match your staff to the workload, be sure to study how long each major task takes, and how many resources are engaged. If an admission takes between 25 and 45 minutes, and two staff including a nurse, study the volumes and allocate a certain number to each staff member so as to avoid overloading one or another. More times than I can count, I have seen nurse managers make excuses of delays in discharge processing while they allow multiple admissions and discharges to fall on one nurse, while others have easier work days. This obtuseness leads to numerous bad outcomes, not the least of which is nurse burnout and frustration.

It is likely not necessary to do "time-motion" studies here, but it is not unreasonable either. As part of your process improvement efforts, you might have your facility's HMEs come in to take a look at what nurses and staff do all day, how they do it, and how their work might be made more efficient. After all, basing total workload on bad processes within the system will inevitably lead to higher-than-necessary staffing. And by bringing in some process improvement help (if needed) you may find that you can change the "work breakdown structure" even further, reallocate tasks to less utilized resources, or refine your staffing grids.

Once you take a look at the workload (by hour or other limited time segment), decide how many of each resource type would be best to deploy for a given time period (though this might be heavily restricted in unionized environments). This should be based solely on the work to be done rather than your traditional shift patterns. Yes, it may take some time to adjust schedules, but the staff should find that their work is smoother and more efficient with a revised model.

Lastly, once you've used the "typical day" data to surmise your workload, workflow, and resource requirements, you'll want to look at your outliers. Outliers, those volumes that are outside your typical range, are an important consideration for management. Indeed, the management of outliers should eventually become your major focus, as you'll have set your systems up to handle the "typical" days without issue.

If the range of your typical demand (the aforementioned "80–20" range) on Monday afternoon goes from, say, six to nine patients from the ED, the outliers are 10 and above and five and below. (Commonly, of course, we don't stress too much about the latter slow days, though it may require the unit to call off staff and make the Chief Financial Officer [CFO] nervous.) The high end of the outlier range creates "one of those days" in which volumes and/or acuities overwhelm the inpatient units, and/or cause significant holds in the ED and other source areas. Certainly these days can cause a great deal of stress and significant work for staff.

Being able to predict these outlier days would be extremely beneficial to both unit managers and source department managers and staff were it possible. Unfortunately, accurately predicting these days is difficult if not almost impossible, as there are few or no external indicators that would allow us to predict them in advance.[*]

How to "Manage to" Demand Patterns

Can you change the patterns through which patients demand access to your unit? In many ways, yes! Of course, you cannot prevent or even stall ED arrivals or surgeries, nor should you ask PACU and the ED to hold patients until such time that an admission is convenient (they have patients too, but without a way to stop the next ones from arriving). But you can regulate the flow of patients to your unit through collaboration, communication, and predictive analytics.

---

[*] Nurses often say (mostly jokingly) that the full moon phase can result in weirdness and high volumes in the ED and ICU, but there's no scientific statistical evidence to show this. Halloween, local festivals, large concert events, Mardi Gras and other "party" holidays, and even Thanksgiving can result in unusual volumes. You should always examine your patterns to look for volume and acuity anomalies that can be tied to predictable events, cycles, and seasons.

Before you can alter the demand pattern, you need to thoroughly understand it, as we've described above. So if your ED is effectively using eyeball disposition (see Chapter 9), you should know about a probable admission as the patient is triaged, literally hours before the actual "bed call" is made. Furthermore, the unit managers should have had a chat with the OR scheduler before each day begins to learn about possible/probable admissions to their unit long before patients arrive in pre-op. Thus, one can plan many of the admissions before the patients ever hit the "front door" of the facility and the ED or OR by communicating with those source departments and planning discharge patterns and the availability of beds accordingly throughout the day.

Of course, you won't be able to predict and thereby manage all ED demand … just that within the range of the typical day. And you won't likely be able to manage all of that, as patients still arrive randomly even within the expected patterns. Furthermore, there will be "those days" in the OR when cases run late, physicians are late or behind schedule, patients don't show up, or emergencies preempt your expected admission case. Yet, you can nonetheless start to manage the flow to your floor via the knowledge of the demand patterns.

One way to achieve this is through the scheduling of admissions. Mentioned in Chapter 9, I demonstrated how a simulation model might be used to help you ascertain when and to what extent ED admissions might actually be scheduled. If you skipped that section or need a refresher, review the section on "Scheduling Admissions" in Chapter 9 before continuing.

MANAGING INPATIENT CAPACITY PATTERNS

Of course, one of the key roles of the inpatient unit manager is to manage the discharge patterns so as to best match the admission patterns. This allows the entire demand–capacity continuum to come into alignment and frees up the necessary capacity for true optimization. Knowing the demand patterns from key source areas, we must adjust the capacity patterns to match dynamically as shown in Figure 11.2.

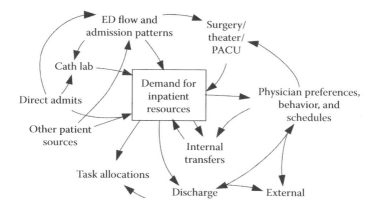

FIGURE 11.2 The interdependencies of hospital-wide capacity.

To do so, there are a number of tactics you can take, though I'll only cover a few in this book.

You will notice that the main theme of these recommendations revolves around proactive processing, preparation in advance of future work, and "getting out in front" of the discharge process. The more you can get out in front of the discharge process, the smoother and more efficient that discharge will be. See if you can count the number of times your nurses and staff have scrambled to process a discharge once a discharge order was finally placed by the attending physician, or how many times you see case managers wait until the last minute to order durable medical equipment (DME) or call families for rides. How many times have discharges been delayed in your hospital awaiting a consulting physician to round, or a hospitalist to write an order? How many times have staff waited on a transporter or a family member to move a ready and waiting patient? These are but a few examples of the many delays that can and do regularly occur when discharge processing is put off until the last minute.

Of course, there are numerous reasons why these delays are not seen and stopped. There's no need to go into detail on these here, except to say that a critical component of many delays is staff. Some staff might have a vested interest in delaying a discharge due to the workload associated both with it and the next admission that's sure to follow … better to pass that work on to the next shift. Another critical factor is physicians, both attendings/hospitalists and consultants. And still others include poor communication, lack of or poor IT systems, poor processes, and a general lack of interest in process control. Of course, all of these can show up in your logged delay reasons along with the usual fingers pointing at the various players.

Yet, there are ways to address each of these and other issues with the solutions herein. Done together, these make up a powerful and dynamic approach to an often intractable problem.

DISCHARGE UPON ADMISSION

Let's start with the general concept of getting out in front of the discharge as early as possible. Recall, we already know the demand pattern of many of our admissions, so it should be no surprise when the pattern holds and we see an expected admission. Indeed, we should be fully prepared for the imminent arrival of ED and surgery patients long before they ever hit the "front door." Thus, knowing that patients will arrive, there should be no issue with thinking about their discharge as they enter the unit. This is the concept of "Discharge upon Admission."

Simply put, the discharge process needs to begin as the patient arrives. This means immediately beginning the process of determining an estimated discharge day and working toward that throughout the patient visit. Within this concept, there are a few key elements that are important.

First, the attending physician should estimate a discharge date after the initial assessment. This should be communicated with the staff, written on the patient's white board in the room, discussed with family members, and generally made known. This sets a reasonable expectation of length of stay, and allows everyone involved in the care process to begin thinking about the discharge of the patient and the steps necessary to ensure a smooth transition to the next location. I cannot stress enough how important this concept is to the optimization of your capacity, and how much it means to timely discharge, LOS management, and patient satisfaction.

Why is this so important? It's all about expectations and planning. If the nursing staff, the patient, the patient's family, and the unit manager all have a good estimate of the LOS and a discharge day, the planning for discharge becomes much easier and smoother.

Let's say we have a patient who arrives on Tuesday afternoon and is assessed by both a nurse and an attending hospitalist. They agree that, based on the patient's condition, history, and mental status that a reasonable LOS is roughly 3 days. This is communicated to the family, who can begin to make plans for the next steps in the patient care. Can Johnny get off work on Friday to come get grandma and take her home? What is the condition of her house, and should someone conduct a needs assessment? Are there communal resources with which the family might form a care circle for grandma if she doesn't already have one? Has her church been notified that she is in the hospital?

For nursing, the date can allow for task planning and task allocation. For consulting physicians, it offers a date before which they should ask for and expect testing results, etc., and allows unit managers and attending physicians to legitimately push them. It also should pressure attending physicians to focus on the treatment for which the patient was admitted, and avoid the common inclination to treat the patient for everything possible while he/she is in the hospital, even if the ancillary conditions could and should be better managed through a PCP in an outpatient setting. This should help to limit the unnecessary referrals that extend LOS and drive up unnecessary costs, testing, and staff workload. Likewise, Case Managers can start working toward that discharge date, lining up discharge needs and communicating with the family about discharge-related issues.

Lastly and importantly, it allows unit managers a glimpse into the future capacity of the unit, allowing them to begin the process of communicating with source departments (e.g., the ED), planning for the pending demand (already largely known via historical data) and then planning specific discharge times for all the patients on the unit (more on this later).

The best place to relay this information is the patient's white board in their room. We aren't too bashful about writing, in public view, the name of the physicians, nurses, and techs caring for the patient, so why not offer specific information relating to their discharge? After all, that might be far more important to a patient than the name of the tech on shift. Doing so is a constant visual reminder to patients, families, and visitors that their length of stay has a limit, and that their length of stay will be expected to end on a certain date (barring unforeseen circumstances, of course). This helps everyone begin to prepare and manage expectations.

Indeed, it sounds easy, right? Well, that's because it is. Indeed, with surgery patients and many medical patients, it's quite easy. Certainly, case managers are quite good at it. Normally, a good case manager can do this in his sleep! Yet, sadly, many hospitalists and attendings commonly balk here. For a number of what I consider to be very weak excuses, they will often refuse to cooperate with this simple but important step. Here are just a few of the excuses they will toss out—just so you'll be prepared to hear them!

- "What if I'm wrong?" Well, guess what, doc? You're going to be wrong sometimes! That's why it's an ESTIMATE, and not written in a legally binding contract. This is perhaps the worst and weakest of excuses, hiding the real reasons of objections to the concept. When piloting this concept, hospitalists have complained that they received complaints from patients when their LOS was longer than first estimated. Of course, this is nothing more than proper expectations management. With the right message, patients will understand that their expected date is indeed an estimate. For patients with questionable medical conditions, that estimate can be made more "fluid," perhaps even erring to the "long end." But the estimates should always reflect an appropriate LOS for the patient's condition and should not be extended to allow for a "fudge factor."

  Importantly, patients who want to go home should be the ones most likely to object to an endless parade of consultants, tests, and other LOS-extending tactics.
- "It's not up to me." Some attendings/hospitalists will complain that it is the consultants and specialists who drive the LOS, not them. So they would be on the hook for an estimate that might not work out by no fault of their own. Again, a weak excuse. The attendings/hospitalists will say that if, for instance, cardiology only rounds once per day and decides at the last minute that more testing is needed, the care process is beholden to this and thus must abide by a longer LOS. Yet, as the person in charge of patient care, the attending/hospitalist has the responsibility to push back, suggest outpatient testing, and generally manage these belated requests. Indeed, attendings/hospitalists know their colleagues, and know which consultant typically wants what information for a given condition, who is very cautious and (overly) deliberative, who typically wants more testing rather than less, and who rounds when. With this historical and interpersonal knowledge an adept attending/hospitalist should manage the patient's consultants and their LOS, pushing back as needed, and helping the consultant by preemptively ordering the tests that the consultant is likely to require. Remember, we're all supposed to be doing the "collaborative" thing! Again, this is all about management of expectations, management of relationships, and management of information to achieve a better management of patient LOS.
- "I can't keep up with a Dry Erase marker." That one's a classic!
- "Families get angry because they don't want the patient to go home." Although perhaps a real circumstance, I have never witnessed it. When it does occur, it is most likely a situation for Case Management to take on. The attending/hospitalist needs to stay on task and on message, and prescribe the appropriate treatment and LOS to manage the patient's condition and allow them to leave.
- "I won't be here later this week, so, I won't be in charge of the patient's care. So, it's up to the next hospitalist to manage their length of stay." Another classic. As if, in most cases, there should be that much difference in the initial assessment of a patient's given medical condition. If there is debate, let that debate be had early in the patient visit, such that an LOS estimate can be generated.

All that said, let's be very clear! I am not naïve enough to believe that a patient's condition won't change. I am also not naïve enough to believe that complex medical patients can be medical mysteries, with days of testing required to determine a proper course of medical intervention. But these are your outliers, and they should be treated as such. For these two groups, it might be quite unreasonable indeed to estimate an LOS, perhaps even irresponsible. But that should not preclude a hospitalist from estimating an LOS for most patients based on assessment of the patient's condition upon admission.

You should not let your attendings/hospitalists use the outliers, or these and other excuses to refuse to take responsibility for care and LOS of patients in their stead. If they won't do it, perhaps they were not meant to work in a hospital setting in an attending role.

"DAY BEFORE DISCHARGE" PLANNING

If you have set forth the expectations of an expected discharge date as patients arrive onto your units, working toward discharge throughout the patient visit should be a natural next step. This is achieved through the existing nurse workflow augmented by the knowledge of the expected date of departure. By adding in the expected date of discharge, nursing, staff, and Case Management can plan the care and necessary processes to create a smoother discharge day. This includes

- Management of daily workload. On many units, the arrivals of patients are more numerous on specific days of the week. This can mean that discharges are also more numerous on certain days of week. This knowledge alone can assist the care teams in managing the workload of the heavier days, while working to smooth the workload between admission and discharge.
- Case Management engagement. As Case Management can play such a critical role in patient discharges, it is imperative that they engage early and often in the management of the discharge process. Indeed, in a very few facilities, unit Case Managers are placed in charge of managing the discharge process flow, as they can touch so many aspects of the discharge process. They work closely with nurses and physicians (attendings and consultants) to ensure the availability of timely information and the readiness for discharge. Importantly, they work closely with the families to ensure the decisions about future care plans and locations are made in a timely fashion, nursing home visits are made early in the patient visit, and transportation and at-home care is managed appropriately.
- Consultant orders and communications. (**Note:** State rules and regulations may play a role in the implementation of these concepts, so be sure to check to ensure that you won't run afoul of the laws of the land.)

     There should be little reason for the request of unanticipated additional testing on the day of discharge unless a patient's condition has changed. Patients can degrade on the last night of their visit, though statistically this isn't common on most units. Thus most, if not all, testing and orders that are needed to confirm a patient's readiness for discharge should be required to be written no later than the day before discharge. This should always include consultants' discharge orders or preliminary approval to discharge. These latter orders permit the speedy processing of discharges and elimination of last-minute steps and hassles for the staff and patients.

Nothing is more frustrating to conscientious staff, attendings/hospitalists, and nurses than having to chase down a discharge order from a consultant who rounded the day before but neglected to input even a preliminary "OK to discharge" order. The latter is simple and relieves the consultant of the need to round again on that patient and permits timely processing for the attending/hospitalist and unit manager (again, barring unexpected changes in status).

This simple "ask" should not cause consternation, especially if proper communications between unit staff and physicians can be established and maintained. Conversations with consultants as to how and when they wish to be contacted as test results are available should clear the way for smoother discharges. Importantly, it should help consultants to be more productive and reduce the hassles associated with communications, call-backs, and rounding.

Even with a patient at risk of degrading, or when testing or patient condition requires monitoring throughout the evening (e.g., did the patient keep dinner down, did their potassium level maintain, etc.), "preliminary discharge" or "preliminary 'OK to discharge'" should become the norm. These orders allow the consultant to specify "Discharge if ..." certain clinical milestones are achieved, testing shows appropriate/adequate results, and the patient has not degraded.

Yet, as we all know, many consultants still want to "lay hands" on the patient on the final day (in some cases due to reimbursements for that "service") and refuse to let patients leave earlier. This delay is, of course, why hospitalists were hired in the first place, therefore consultants who routinely delay discharges should be dealt with individually in the interest of the proper function of the unit. The worst-case scenario is that the patients of these poor team players are slotted to be discharged last, leaving unit managers to focus on other patients earlier in the day.

There are of course exceptions to this rule. For example, consultants who round very early in the morning can be allowed to see the patient, check test results, render decisions, and write discharge orders on the day of discharge. However, even here, these doctors and their process speed will be greatly enhanced if all the necessary orders and information are gathered throughout the day prior to discharge. This leaves them will little to do other than sign off, but still requires the habit of "Discharge if..." orders.

Sadly, in most cases, however, the concept of "preliminary orders" and managing the day before discharge is utterly alien to most physicians. This must be taught within the context of the benefits to physicians and their patients. Senior management must be engaged in this process, and must support this new operational model.

- Hospitalists and nurse practitioners (NPs). Likewise, there should be no reason that hospitalists should not begin writing preliminary discharge orders (those "Discharge if …" orders) to help unit managers promote effective capacity management. Hospitalists, for the same reasons as the aforementioned consultants, should make it their practice to communicate with nursing staff about patient conditions, testing requirements, necessary monitoring, and other discharge-related tasks on the day before discharge. Just as with the consultants, this approach encourages discharge management and helps set expectations for day of discharge. Assuming patient conditions do not change between an afternoon "huddle" (we recommend between 1500 and 1600, certainly before evening shift change) on the day before discharge and the next morning, nurses can plan their workload and workflow, manage the incoming admissions and outgoing discharges, spread work properly among the nursing staff, and generally go about their work to ensure the proper management of the "Demand–Capacity Continuum."

   NPs can be of tremendous help here, if employed/deployed by the hospitalists to aid with discharge and admission processing. For discharges, NPs can act as an extension of the hospitalist and discharge a patient based on the preliminary discharge orders from the day prior. This allows hospitalists to see more critical patients during early rounds while preventing delays in early discharge processing. NPs are expensive but may be well worth the money if your hospitalists tend to be overloaded and are in need of better task allocation and a streamlining of the workload and workflow.

   NPs can also aid hospitalists in rounding when there are more patients than hospitalists can see in a reasonable time. Given the importance of discharge, NPs can tag-team with hospitalists to ensure that discharge patients are seen early in the day, writing orders and communicating issues as needed. Problem patients, patients whose condition degraded overnight, or patients whose consultant added orders, tests, or additional workup can be prioritized if unit managers are aggressive about communications. This will still allow hospitalists to see critical patients who might have come in during the night, go to the ED to see about admission holds or observation patients, and generally do more of the diagnostics and treatment planning work they were hired to do.

   The key to the effective utilization of NPs is of course the use of preliminary discharge orders, efficient task allocation, and quick communications.
- Family communications and rules of engagement. If Case Management, nursing, and attendings/hospitalists have done their jobs, families should know well the expectations for day of discharge.
- Use of evening shift staff. One of the key roles that evening/night shift staff can play is to aggregate information for next-day discharges so that lab results and paperwork are completed and ready for the day shift staff. This can eliminate many of the last-minute surprises that might erupt on the morning of discharge that delay processing and cause upstream bottlenecks. Some hospitals have night-shift staff responsible for med reconciliation and

other "i-dotting" so as to make discharges the next morning as efficient and quick as possible. This also helps to find delay-causing issues, such as meds that don't match and consultant orders that have not been placed, so as to address them first thing rather than later in the day when things are more hectic. This, of course, is helped greatly by the use of preliminary discharge orders and "discharge if …" orders that help nursing expedite the work early in the day, long before the demand patterns start to emerge. This also helps to spread workload around, and even makes the use of a discharge nurse more palatable and effective, as the time for each discharge can be greatly diminished. This task distribution can truly benefit staff by allowing nurses do more of what they are supposed to do … care for patients!

- Scheduling discharges. Recall that in previous chapters, we discussed the concept of scheduling what seem to be random admissions to inpatient units from the ED. This concept continues to be proven valid as unit and department managers look objectively at their arrival pattern data and begin to use Eyeball Disposition to promote the management of ED and inpatient capacity.

    Well, if even the ED, with all its concomitant variability, complexity, and randomness, can schedule some of its admissions, surely inpatient units can schedule what should be a very plannable event … patient discharge. Indeed, if the aforementioned discharge planning steps are taken, a natural outcome should be an ongoing knowledge of the patients to be discharged on any given next day. Thus, if we have properly informed patients and families of the expected date of discharge upon the patient's arrival to the unit; if we have planned for the discharge throughout the patient's stay; if we have obtained consultant "OK to discharge" orders on a timely basis; and if our attendings/hospitalists are doing their jobs, using NPs, and writing preliminary discharge orders on the day before discharge; then scheduling the discharges throughout the day to better match the expected incoming demand should be relatively easy.

    This means that inpatient unit managers must look strategically at the next day, examining the expected demand patterns, the surgical schedule (as appropriate), the patients expected to be discharged, and the workload and workflow of the unit for the next day. From this, it becomes possible to develop a schedule for those discharges that both matches the demand patterns and smooths the workload among the nursing staff.

DAY OF DISCHARGE PROCESSING

OK, by now you've teed up your discharges by doing the following:

- Eyeball disposition in the ED has led to a quick notification of a probable admission to your bed control or inpatient unit staff.
- Constant communication between the ED staff and inpatient units has meant that to-be admitted patients are fully expected to arrive on the units, with expected arrival times already set forth.

- Scheduled admissions have been planned (to the extent possible and reasonable) and are anticipated by both ends of the admission process.
- Discharges have been well planned throughout the patient stays, and patients, families, and Care Circle and community resources have been kept abreast of the process and are now expecting a specific, scheduled discharge time.
- Consultants and attendings/hospitalists have written their preliminary and "discharge if …" orders on at least the day before discharge.
- Evening shift staff has gathered all relevant information, testing, and paperwork on patients, readying them to the extent possible for the day of discharge processing. Constraints to discharge have been highlighted in notes to unit managers so that they can be handled immediately.
- Unit managers have examined the day's historical demand patterns, planned for the day's expected discharges, and know about any potential constraints in the discharge process.
- Workload and workflow have been properly aligned to ensure that the expected discharge times can be managed by the available staff. Work breakdown structure has been aligned so as to allow nurses as much time as possible with their patients and prevent the overload of some nurses.

You are now ready for the day of discharge. We often recommend the use of white boards and other visual cues to show the plan for the day, by HOD. These boards should show both the expected admissions, any previously set scheduled admission slots, and the discharges for the day. The boards should include the staff responsible for each action, so as to help spread the workload among the staff and prevent unnecessary boluses of activity. These boards might also include names of physicians and any information or actions required of them, so that staff and physicians know what is required to complete discharges. This will communicate clearly and plainly the workload and workflow, the parties responsible for each necessary action, and list any constraints to the admission and discharge processes.

Will your well-laid plans go awry? Of course they will! It's inevitable that something will go wrong, some nurse will call out, some consultant will disappear into the ether, a family won't show up on time, a nursing home will suddenly fill up, some case manager will have forgotten to arrange for DME, and a patient or two will cause a huge stink about something. Maybe, just for kicks, Joint Commission on Accreditation of Healthcare Organization (JCAHO) will show up and the ED will suddenly be swamped with elderly severe flu patients.

But does that mean that all your planning is for naught? Of course not! Remember the infamous 80/20 rule. Eighty percent of your problems will come from 20% of your processes, staff, and patients. This is the whole point of planning, for if 80% of your admissions and discharges can run smoothly and as expected, you are freed to focus your full attention on the 20% that are causing problems. Managing the processes in advance means that more should run as expected, leaving the "outliers" of the process, those issues and circumstances that would normally bring your system to its knees, to now be managed more closely and with greater focus.

Indeed, expect that a few of your patients won't be able to find a way to leave, either because local nursing homes won't take them, behavioral health facilities are full, they don't have the right insurance coverage, families don't have the ability to properly house them, or they simply have nowhere to go given their physical or mental state. Families or patients will change their minds at the last minute, seemingly just as the ambulance rolls up to the front door. These things will happen. But if they happen with any degree of regularity, it may point to an internal issue with communications that can be addressed with case managers and nursing, or may require higher-level discussions and strategies with your local long-term care providers. Study these patients as part of the entire patient population the unit serves, and determine the regularity of these kinds of constraints. This may require some process or operational changes that the data will point you to.

Thus day of discharge is simply the culmination of several days of planning, collaboration, and communication for each patient, which should yield a better and easier overall process. You are simply following the past several days of planning to their ultimate conclusion ... a patient discharge.

To Lounge or Not to Lounge?

The use of discharge lounges (DCLs) has long been debated. Some like them, many hate them. Most of the DCLs I've seen have been ineffectively used, with vague guidelines and protocols for use and misaligned staffing. The problem is not that the DCLs themselves can't work, it's that there is no systematic program and planning for their use. This is largely because they are seen as a stop-gap, "Band-Aid" sort of a measure that is haphazardly used only when things "get crazy" on the units. This leads to poor implementation and the inevitable patient dissatisfaction.

If you are going to venture down the DCL path, you must first plan for its use. Random usage commonly leads to inefficient usage, staffing inefficiencies, and frustration from staff and patients. When randomly opened, patients and families are often surprised by the move to a "waiting area." Staff often have to pick up transportation and extra paperwork responsibilities, while staffing must be pulled or called in for the DCL itself. Depending on the volumes of patients, these DCL staff can be very underutilized, with a 1:2 or even 2:1 ratio developing throughout the day.

However, with proper analysis and utilization, DCLs can be an effective tool for decompressing much-needed inpatient space. The proper planning for use will still demand the use of effective discharge planning as described in this chapter, from the source areas through to discharge. Failure to plan will yield the kind of inefficiencies and underutilization for which DCLs are known. You will likely also want to invest in a good simulation study to properly assess spatial and staffing needs, by HOD and DOW.

Lastly, DCLs can be a good "back-up" plan for periods when inpatient volume peaks, such as flu season. Properly planned and used, they can be a lifesaver for staff throughout the facility. Here, a good simulation analysis can determine when and to what extent DCLs need to be used, and can lead the way to effective utilization and staffing levels. I've worked on several DCL simulation and optimization projects in which staff and management assumptions were blown away by the realities of the function of the proposed DCL. Modification of the original (pre-simulation and data study) plans yielded an effective and efficient unit, complete with usage protocols, staffing grids, and patient and staff communication tools.

Bottom line: if you're going to try it, plan appropriately and completely, and do it well.

SUMMARY

Much of the blocking and tackling of inpatient capacity is about using data and planning for the inevitable. Data will show you what to expect and the capacity you need to make available on a daily basis. Proper use of the data sets up communication streams, processes, and operational models that promote the smooth flow of patients to and from a given unit. Proper alignment with physician workloads and workflows allows the timely stream of effective communications among unit managers, staff, patients, and other physicians. Proper communication with patients tees up transportation when needed, and prevents the need for a discharge "lounge."

All this yields a dynamic management of capacity that allows for the effective matching of the demand as it comes from the various source departments. This demand–capacity continuum should be the "holy grail" of hospital managers, and should be sought as part of every performance improvement initiative and project. With the proper alignment of strategies and vision for new operational models, this can become a reality in any facility.

12 Physicians and Their Role in Optimization

What are the major constraints to process, capacity, throughput, and efficiency optimization in healthcare? That is, of the major player groups, which ones are the most resistant and intransigent? In my humble opinion, and though it varies depending on the environment, the rankings would go something like the following:

1. Nursing unions (if present)
2. Physicians
2. Nurses and nurse managers
2. Administrators
3. Other healthcare staff

Not to pick on them, but nursing unions are infamous for their resistance to optimization. Where they are present, nursing unions commonly play a role in fomenting dissatisfaction, combativeness, and mistrust among nurses and with management rather than working to instill a positive culture that would create a better working environment. Ironically, this is one of the best things they could do for their nurses.

As for the next three (all in the same ranking, as you'll note), each has a hand in the passion for the status quo and the resistance to change. Of course, for every environment in which there are difficult physicians, you can commonly find administrators, or a history of administrators, who have helped muck the waters and create or encourage some of the bad culture. And within nearly every combative and toxic nurse culture there lies an equally uncooperative and combative physician culture. I have worked in hospitals wherein ED nurses and physicians literally do not speak to one another, and others wherein admitting physicians were out of control, with no governance to manage their flagrant disregard for staff and operations. And in still others, management was so weak and uninformed that even the basics of care quality, patient safety, and proper patient flow were seemingly disregarded.

Thus, depending on the hospital, its culture, and the political and social environment, the aforementioned rankings might see a shift of administrators or nurses closer to the top for appearance sake, yet would still demonstrate the links between intransigent behaviors and attitudes among the various key groups. In other words, all hold some responsibility for the resistance to change.

Yet, there is no doubt that physicians play a large role in the advancement or rejection of operational efficiencies. Indeed, without the physicians on board, as a group and individually, much optimization work is doomed to failure and frustration. Sadly, their role is sometimes as the resistance to change, which often prevents the entire hospital or health system from moving forward. However, one must understand that this reaction is not necessarily a conscious choice physicians make.

Rather, it is sometimes a seemingly protective reaction against the many changes that are being foisted upon them in this era of "reform." Therefore, in some situations, they must react negatively to new processes and operational models that are seen to impact them, regardless of the potential positive results, in order to "stay alive" and keep moving forward in a somewhat familiar way.

Unfortunately, without their cooperation and assistance, many of the large-scale leaps in optimization are unattainable. That's why I believe it is necessary to rethink the physician relationship with the rest of the healthcare community and the way in which they are compensated. Indeed, we owe it to our physicians, those hardworking souls committed to the health of our communities, to rethink the work they do, the way they are paid, and the ways in which they are rewarded for their service.

For starters, let's be clear. Physicians should be paid for what they do, and paid well. There's no doubt in my mind about that. Simple economic theory tells us that a limited and valuable resource can and should demand higher compensation in the marketplace based on their relative value, the number of competitors, and the ability of the market to pay them. In the case of physicians, reduced compensation and higher job pressures are already impacting their numbers in the market. Thus, remuneration for their valuable work should be in keeping with a scale that will attract the best and brightest to the industry and away from often higher-paying careers in law and professional services. Certainly, I'd rather have a lot more physicians and a lot fewer lawyers chasing them! Compensation should steer the uniquely dedicated and passionate to the industry, though money should never be the reason for entrance to this difficult career path.

But as "reform" continues to evolve, and new ideas for compensation and incentivizing are tweaked, sometimes only slightly, we should consider how we might completely destroy the current payment models and develop new models for a new age. As things appear to be evolving, in order to be compensated, physicians are being asked to "care smarter," meaning do less to achieve the same results (e.g., fewer tests, fewer consultations); check boxes (e.g., ensure that all your male patients over the age of 45 receive annual exams for X disease); and comply with numerous quality metrics reporting demands.

For example, recent work in overuse and unnecessary care shows that the concept of an annual checkup for healthy adults is largely a waste. Yet, that's what PCPs do with some 40% of their time. This is, of course, what they have been urged to do and even trained to do over the years. Yet, it may not be the best use of their time and talents. Perhaps it would be better to spend twice or thrice as much time with an elderly chronic disease patient, helping him to navigate their care, self-manage, and promote reductions in unnecessary utilization of EDs and surgeries.

Perhaps, then, we should not get into the business of paying physicians to do everything that they should already be doing in the first place. While I could understand compensation for the time required to manage paperwork, paying a physician to speak with a patient about end-of-life care, or diet and exercise regimens, etc., is not reasonable. Physicians must do what physicians should do … and that is managing the care of patients, especially those with diseases and chronic conditions and the propensity thereto. And that should include all the elements of a holistic approach to health management, including the course of the disease and the expectations for the future of disease progression and possible impact on the patient's quality of life. And if that requires more time per patient, then we must determine ways to help physicians manage their patient loads and their time such that they can focus their attentions where it will do the most good ... in the management of patient conditions.

Thus we need to narrow down the expectations of what makes a good physician, and hold physicians accountable without daunting reporting requirements and unnecessary and unrealistic expectations using practical approaches to the management of population health. Thus, we should stress:

- Patient responsibility for their clinical outcomes (at least coresponsibility)
- Patient-focused reviews of physician behavior
- Development of realistic clinical outcomes based on the patients in the population
- Essentials of effective care provision and avoidance of box-checking waste
- Cost-effective use of their time and talents

Physicians therefore need to be retrained on the thinking of care management. Gone are the days of overmedicating, overtesting, and overcaring for our communities. Soon to be "in" are the days of reasonable approaches to prevention and disease management, patients vested in their own cost of care, and reasonable expectations of physician accountability and outcomes.

Importantly, "in" are the days of physician acceptance of change, integration, and collaboration. The latter two are overused and now tiresome jingoistic terms, but the message remains ... physicians must be an integral part of a new health system that is dramatically different from the one in which they were trained, and dramatically different from anything else in the world.

And, most importantly, they must learn to embrace and (to borrow a phrase) "be" the change that we need to see in the healthcare world. PCPs, in particular, must become the instigators of dramatic change rather than the hardened resistance to even piecemeal tweaks. All physicians must help create new models that will help advance the ideals of self-management and efficiency of healthcare resource utilization, accept the dissemination of non-physician tasks, and become leaders of large teams that include clinical and non-clinical communal resources. PCPs' reach must go from "home to hospice" with the help of a truly integrated "community of care" over which they exert advice and limited control.

The compensation system in this new world of healthcare should be based on a rewriting of the expectations of the "front lines" of healthcare provision, the PCP, and his supporting staff. Surgeons and specialists should be salaried as well, with their incentives being based on the integration with their "communities of care," the reasonable use of medical procedures, and partial responsibility for the quality of outcomes (along with patients). Thus we must consider standard salaries for all physicians, based more on the decisions they make for the care of patients and not on the volumes of procedures they perform, the tests they administer, or the check boxes they fill in.

Most importantly, we must necessarily abolish the FFS environment upon which so much waste and inefficiency has been built. As more and more physicians are salaried, aligning incentives to promote the health and well-being as well as the personal responsibility of the population will become easier and more widely accepted.

UNTIL THEN, WHAT NOW?

As Peter Wood describes in Chapter 13 on physician alignment strategies, there are working options for new models of care delivery and physician compensation. We should pursue these alternatives without delay, aligning payors as we create the business and reimbursement models that will support an entirely new system of care provision.

Until someone changes the compensation models and removes the perverse incentives that drive the waste and inefficiencies for which the U.S. system is famous, hospitals and communities can still work to create positive and productive work environments for their physicians. First, follow the lead of Joe Tye's chapter and work to create a positive culture throughout your health system. *Nothing* is more important to your optimization efforts than a "Culture of Ownership." Work with your physicians to create care and operational models like those described by Peter Wood in his chapter. Then, team with physicians to provide integrated "Care Circles," made up of communal and clinical resources from across the spectrum, and allow physicians to focus their attentions on those patients who need them the most while still paying their bills. Certainly, if your physicians are employed, create work models and resource assistance that allows them to do more with their training and experience and less with paperwork, checklists, and the tedium of reporting. Work with physician leaders to create proper accountability through mutual governance among peers to limit the power of legal actions. Promote self-management and personal responsibility among patients. And embrace physicians as an integral part of your overall optimization efforts, bringing each along the long learning path as individuals, leaving none behind. Make your physicians the catalysts of change rather than proponents of the status quo.

FINAL THOUGHTS: LEGAL PROTECTIONS

Lastly, we must create protections for physicians, other healthcare providers, and community volunteers against the kinds of frivolous litigation that make malpractice insurance such a large expenditure. These protections should include clear paths for patients to address grievances and poor quality, so as to offer patients a legitimate and viable alternative to legal action. Physicians must accept that their protections from frivolous litigation are not a license to harm, intentionally or carelessly. Rather, physicians must accept responsibility while not needing to fear legal action at every turn. Likewise, patients and their families must accept responsibility for their own self-management and the likelihood of less-than-perfect results. Proper physician governance, community involvement in the grievance process, and integrity of healthcare providers will clear the path to assurances that the necessary protections from litigation will harm only corrupt attorneys.

SUMMARY

Physicians can be catalysts or constraints, promoters of optimization, or detractors to improvement efforts. Perverse incentives, poor hospital relationships, bad nursing culture, and an FFS model that encourages waste and overuse, all encourage physicians to behave badly. Yet, as perhaps the most important group in the optimization effort, physicians must necessarily be brought on board with your work. Without them, your goals will likely never be met.

We must therefore strive to create positive work environments with the right incentives and work environments to allow physicians to perform the work for which they were trained, supporting them with the necessary resources, tools, and technologies. Doing so will yield you financial and operational viability in the future world of healthcare reform, in whatever form it takes.

13 Preparing for Coming Change

Forming a PHO, by Peter Wood

Peter Wood is another colleague for whom I have tremendous respect and admiration. I met Peter years ago when I lived in lovely southern Maine. Though he started as a prospect for business collaboration, Peter quickly took on the role of mentor and expert for me. His depth of knowledge of physician relationships seemed to know no bounds.

Peter spent the better part of a life working to make healthcare a better place. For many years, he quietly led innovations in care and reimbursement models from the small city of Portland, Maine. While others were boasting of new ideas for care models, Peter had already tried them. Indeed, Peter and the organization he worked with, the Maine Physician Hospital Organization (PHO), continued to thrive through innovation while other like organizations in other parts of the country failed. The impact of his innovative spirit now lives on as he settles into a new life of semi-retirement.

Peter's contribution is instrumental to the value of this book. Without a perspective on the challenges of working with new physician business and reimbursement models, this book would be sorely lacking in its breadth and meaningfulness. I am truly blessed to have Peter's expertise included in these pages, and was thrilled when he humbly accepted my request to pen this chapter. Indeed, some will no doubt agree with me that this chapter is one of the two most valuable in the entire book!

Many thanks to Peter for his work in healthcare and his generous contribution to this book!!

INTRODUCTION

Where are you today? In the healthcare or illness care business? Or, both? Do you believe reimbursement reform is going to happen, and you will have to move from fee for service to population health management/reimbursement?

If you believe you will need to function in a population health reimbursement world, how ready are you to answer these questions:

- Do you know what it means to assume financial risk for the cost and quality of the services you provide?
- Are your hospital and medical staff on board making changes in how they provide services?
- Do you have the infrastructure to support population health management?

- Do you know what you need?
- Do you have a governance and management structure that will support the change and provide sustainable leadership, with physicians in major leadership roles?

This chapter will address underlying issues, suggested structural ideas, and ways to move your organization into this new environment. A case model at the end will provide a view of a structure and operations of a PHO. Many of the suggestions will not be comfortable and will challenge (threaten?) existing norms.

First, what are the issues that are transforming the environment and structure to PHM? The cost of care and the challenge to demonstrate quality of care are the leading issues. Focusing on cost without quality is unacceptable. But likewise, focusing on quality without cost considerations is unsustainable. With the advent of the Accountable Care Act, access for a greater share of the population is a clear priority. The current FFS model does not support these expectations.

So, what is PHM? In simple terms, PHM is the assumption of responsibility for the health of a defined population. For example, patients can be grouped by disease category (diabetic patients), payer group (Medicare), community, etc. with the providers focusing on reducing the cost of care, improving the quality of the health of the population and improving the patient experience and outcome (IHI Triple Aim Initiative).

At the care delivery level, it is the value equation: Value equals quality divided by cost (better quality at lower cost equals higher value). For providers, it means taking ownership of the care they deliver as they must commit to delivering value. That means assuming responsibility (risk) for the cost and quality of care for a defined population at a defined global budget (a fixed budget for the negotiated services). Any financial savings is not just determined by coming in under budget (as in the old HMO financial risk-sharing model), but also meeting quality measures—so it's about providing the right care at the right time using the right resources to get the best possible outcome. To be successful, this requires providers working together to coordinate care, measuring performance for improvement, and taking ownership of the population's health: more than just one patient at a time; knowing the health status of the population. It is not one individual diabetic patient's HbA1c level; it is the level for the population of diabetic patients that the physician is treating that is also important.

When providers take on the ownership of a population, which often means the population/communities they serve, the responsibility takes on a broader meaning than the delivery of healthcare. Healthier employees and lower benefit costs improve productivity for local employers and create an inviting environment for development. It truly can become a community effort. But first, the provider community needs to take the lead and that requires changing its culture of delivery care.

CULTURE AND BEHAVIOR

Ask not what your country can do for you, ask what you can do for your country—John F. Kennedy

The change from FFS to PHM is not just about a change in how you get paid, it requires significant changes in the culture of healthcare, how it is provided and how it is consumed. It requires full engagement of providers, payers (insurers), purchasers (employers, government, etc.) and patients. Although new programs are coming out at the federal level with commercial insurers following suit (accountable care), the true success and ownership of population health needs to be led by the provider community at the local level. But this will mean focusing on keeping people healthy, even with underlying chronic illnesses, and getting paid for these services that are not currently covered in an illness-oriented system. As the current system is paid to treat illnesses and injury, this will mean some very fundamental changes in the landscape of illness care delivery.

Providers will need to take ownership of the process of PHM. This will mean active care coordination and timely management of financial and clinical performance information to support improvements in how care is provided. It is not about judgment; it is about improvement. It is not limited to how care is provided, the role of the hospitals and physicians will change.

For population healthcare to work, there will be significant changes for hospitals. The focus will be on outpatient services. Not just the hospital outpatient services, but also the physicians' offices, ancillary services (PT, OT, etc.), and non-traditional services such as community support groups, pharmacies, nutritionists, etc. What this means for the hospitals is almost the reverse of the current thinking: there should be fewer admissions and longer average lengths of stay as only the sickest, most badly injured will need to be admitted. An admission is a failure of managing the care of the population.

The challenge: How to structure the delivery system to make the transition and sustain the new model? How to maintain financial viability during the transition is a particularly vexing challenge as the organization has one foot in FFS and one in PHM. Each organization has to approach this challenge on its own terms; but there will be a need for capital infusion with a slow return on the investment.

Another change, which may be uncomfortable for some hospital executives, is opening up the "C-Suite" to physician leaders. Physicians are a critical component of successful PHM and they must be in true leadership positions from the very beginning of the development of the new structure. Open communications between hospital and physicians is fundamental to the new partnership which needs to exist. This is a two-way street: physicians must be open about their issues and accept constructive criticism, just as the hospital leadership must. They must accept constructive tension and see it as a means to the common objective. These partners and this openness are essential in successfully providing the best quality of care and utilizing the best and most appropriate resources.

For physicians, the culture change will basically be moving from seeing themselves (and having been trained) as autonomous, to being team players. Not necessarily team managers, owners, coaches, but as a team member, recognizing their role in the continuum of services available to meet the needs of their patients. This will include coordinating care with traditional and non-traditional healthcare resources and trusting them. It will mean optimizing the resources of their own office staffs; allowing individuals to provide services to the maximum of their licenses and recognizing the contribution every staff member can make to the practice. They need to learn to ask—they may be surprised by what they will learn. One practice was having problems with new office software. A medical assistant (MA) said she had an interest in programming and asked if she could work on it. The physician said yes—in a week, the program was running as it should. This would not have happened without this practice engaging in microsystems and recognizing the value of all team members to their overall success.

How patients consume healthcare will require a new level of ownership for the individuals' health. While there are arguments whether healthcare is a right of citizens; it is a two-sided coin, as was best stated by President Kennedy: "Ask not what your country can do for you, ask what you can do for your country." The point is that we as individuals and consumers of healthcare, must share in the management of our own health, and not rely on others to cure us; while we fail even the most fundamentals of reasonable diets and exercise. The purchasers (employers, etc.) of health insurance can influence how benefits are constructed to provide positive incentives for individual ownership and active participation. While this will be touched upon in the rest of the chapter, the focus will be more on what providers can do to influence and survive in the new healthcare world.

Why should providers lead these cultural and behavioral changes? Why should they take the risk and reinvent themselves and their profession? What is the threat, the burning platform? Why not wait and see what happens; let someone else go first. We can catch up, if we have to. Let someone else make the decisions and determine how we will practice and dictate how we will get reimbursed. Someone else can determine the "performance" measures upon which we will be judged and paid. Some things to consider. Change is already happening. Medicare and commercial payers are paying based on services and quality—miss on quality and get paid less. Commercial insurers are working with employers to create incentives for employees to look for better costs and better outcomes; and there is the explosion of information on the internet—correct or not, do you have time to track it and correct it? Perhaps a team approach is better than going it alone; especially if healthcare delivery systems (networks) are forming around you.

GETTING STARTED

"The secret of getting ahead, is getting started"—Mark Twain.

Whether it is the hospital leadership or physicians in the community who first realize the need to consider preparing for the move to PHM, they will quickly realize that to be successful, they will need partners with hospitals and physicians at the core. There are alternatives, but this brings together the key providers and their strengths. This partnership must be based on mutual trust, open communications, and commitment to a common vision. In support of these, it is helpful to mutually establish guiding principles and a "compact" outlining the roles and expectations each partner brings to the arrangement. A solid foundation will help address the challenging issues that will come up in the future.

The first step is the establishment of a steering committee consisting of hospital leadership (CEO, CFO, CIO, and CNO) and physician leaders (CMO/VPMA, president of the medical staff, etc.). Both primary care physicians and specialists should be represented. In addition to the formal physician leaders, there should also be informal leaders—physician leaders recognized by their peers, who don't hold any formal titles/positions. There should also be hospital employed and private practice physicians. Initially, the committee may be small, but should expect to expand to include other stakeholders, create subcommittees and advisory groups to help share two-way information sharing. The committee size should be big enough to make sure enough members can attend any given meeting, but not so big as to be hard to manage discussions. To be successful and properly address the changes that will be encountered, expect the process to be cumbersome, but that will result in a more sound foundation. The members will benefit from educational programs to provide them a framework for what they are creating, how it will be different, and the impact on existing organizations. It may be helpful to engage legal counsel early on as there are federal and possible state regulations to be aware of.

With some baseline education and the steering committee meeting, a first question is to determine what type of entity you want to create. A PHO is the most common structure. You then need to determine the legal structure: not for profit, for profit, or LLC. One thing that needs to be reinforced is that the financial success is in managing the care provided within the scope of the risk-sharing arrangements, not surplus or profit from operations. The PHO is the vehicle for supporting the work of the providers and has limited funding sources and should not be expected to make a profit/surplus from its operations. In addition to the PHO model, there are other provider structures as well as alternative PHO structures.

Model	Advantages	Disadvantages
PHO: hospital employed and private physicians	Physicians engaged and accountable; large network to meet payers needs; broader membership on committees for diverse input	Cumbersome decision making; must overcome distrust issues between P and H; and multiple EHR systems to coordinate data
PHO: hospital and its employed physicians	Easier to manage value performance, behavior is contractually defined; no limits on capitalizing/financing the organization	Limited network—may not meet population needs; lacks constructive diversity
Independent Practice Association (IPA): private physicians only	Physician ownership—more commitment; can selectively contract for hospital and other facility services	Lack of capital and human resources of PHO; may lack the ability to negotiate with payers; no investment by contracting providers

For purposes of this chapter, I will use the PHO with both hospital employed and private physicians as the vehicle.

It may prove helpful to begin to develop documents such as the vision, guiding principles, and compacts. These can always be changed as the process progresses and you find what works and doesn't work, but it will help the committee focus.

It makes the process real. Some of the questions to address include: Why do you want to form a PHO and share ownership of the healthcare delivery system? What is the common vision that you plan to achieve? What are the expectations and responsibilities of the partners and how do they align with the common vision?

Documents	Samples
Vision	*To be the leader in supporting value-based, integrated, and patient-centered healthcare (MMC PHO—Portland, Maine)*
Guiding Principles	Shared responsibility for risk and rewards; mutual commitment; improve the health of the community; assure access to care; work together to achieve the Triple Aim
Mutual Commitment/Compact	Pursue the goals of the PHO; work together in a honest and open manner; recognize the value of differences; and accept mutual accountability for improving health of the community
Physician Commitment/ Compact	Strive to provide the right care in the right place the first time; being patient focused; support the coordination of care with other providers; participate in the change process
Hospital Commitment/ Compact	Bring business expertise to the PHO; engage hospital staff in goals and activities of the PHO

With some grounding in place, the steering committee should begin to develop the governance structure. Who are the members? How many directors will be on the board and who are they (physician and hospital representation, not named individuals at this point)? Quorums and voting structures? Committees? Officers? Terms of office? Etc. This may go through a few (several?) iterations, but again it will begin to make the concept of the organization real.

Structure	Samples
Members/owners	Hospital(s); physicians (individually or in physician corporation); other providers (?)
Legal entity	Not for profit; for profit; LLC
Directors/terms	50/50—physicians/hospital or other than 50/50; Physicians should reflect components of physician membership (private, PCPs, specialists, urban/rural, etc.); majority of physicians should be PCPs. Staggered terms; term limits
Quorum	Majority of each class (hospital and physicians) of directors must be present
Voting	Supermajority issues; Member issues; etc.
Officers	Chair, Vice Chair, Secretary/Treasurer, and Executive Director (CEO)
Committees	Executive Committee; Payer Relations Committee; Quality/Value Committee

While the steering committee is developing the PHO, a communications plan should be under development. There should be updates provided to appropriate hospital and physician leadership. It is critical that the stakeholders have a voice in the development of the PHO from the earliest point and understand it. Ownership and trust in the PHO and its partners are the fundamental building blocks of the organization. One consideration is the creation of a physician advisory group to work with the physicians on the steering committee—a two-way communications channel. If not on the steering committee, skeptics should be included on the advisory committee—they must be part of the process. ("Keep your friends closer and your enemies closer."—Machiavelli)

As work is underway on the PHO structure, the committee needs to assess the physician community to determine both its makeup and who should be recruited to join the PHO. Which physicians are employed by the hospital and which are independent? What PCPs and specialists are on the staff? Are there others who need to be recruited? The PCPs are critical, but the specialists play an important role that is sometimes neglected to the detriment of the organization. There are basically two model structures: inclusive and exclusive. The former will offer membership to any physician who meets the professional and participation criteria. The latter limits the membership to physicians invited to be members. The inclusive model is the usual starting point, with ongoing physician membership based on performance. With the exclusive model, it may be harder to recruit members who were not "selected" the first time around.

Perhaps the biggest challenge in developing the organization is recruiting and engaging physicians—and this, while different at some levels, is a challenge with both employed and independent physicians. Doctors are concerned about how much autonomy and control they might be giving up. Again, this underscores the need for clear and trustworthy communications.

The development of trust and open communications as cited above are critical components for successful implementation. If the formal and informal physician leaders are not on board and effective ambassadors for the project, it cannot happen. They must be able to articulate the vision and the process in ways that are meaningful to their physician colleagues. It requires a physician to ultimately engage another physician. Non-physicians can lay some of the ground work, but only a physician can close the deal. When the PHO is up and running, the executive director or CEO must be able to gain the physicians' trust to be able to manage the organization.

There is a common adage that the first question a physician will ask when approached will be: "What is in it for me?" Below is a sample list of points that have been used:

Why be a member of a PHO?

1. Future reimbursement will be based on quality—the PHO will have the resources to help track the necessary data.
2. Care coordination will be expected among physicians—the PHO can facilitate the necessary communications.
3. The payers will determine reimbursement based on population health status, beyond what an individual physician can provide.
4. As a member of the PHO, there is the opportunity to share in any savings that are achieved, that will not be available to a non-network provider.
5. As a member of a PHO, the physician can have a voice in the direction of healthcare.

6. All physicians will be held accountable for quality and cost; the PHO will have the resources to support its members.
7. A non-member will still be expected to coordinate with a network or be excluded from referrals (there may not always be readily available specialists, but eventually the network will find one).
8. The world is changing—the PHO can help facilitate the change process for its members.
9. There are no guarantees that a physician will be successful in the future either way (in or out of the network), but chances are better in a network that can effectively negotiate and optimize opportunities.
10. Which is more likely to be effective in working with a payer to implement change: an unaffiliated physician practice or a network of providers?

The PHO should present itself as a vehicle for change, in which the physicians can play an active and meaningful role. There is also the need to recognize that change is not just going to affect providers: payers, purchasers, and patients will be approaching healthcare differently and that will impact what providers do and how they get paid for their services. The "baby boomers" are healthier and living longer than previous generations. They are bringing different needs and demands on the healthcare system.

But how do the providers get reimbursed under population management? What is this "risk sharing?" First, the PHO is not an insurer with the core competencies inherent in an insurer, so the risk sharing is reconciled at the end of the contract year, or "downstream." While it may not be the end of FFS payment at the individual provider level, it will not be your father's FFS payment structure. But first, where does the money come from? It still comes from the payers on behalf of the purchasers, but now there is an intermediary that manages the distribution of the payments: the PHO. The concept of financial risk-sharing by provider entities is not a new one. It had been around throughout the HMO days and even before with organizations such as Kaiser-Permanente. What is new, is that risk-sharing is based both on financial and quality performance—one could call it value-based risk-sharing. In simple terms, the PHO negotiates a financial budget and shares the gain or loss with the payer. But, unlike an HMO financial risk, the payout of the gain or recoupment of the loss is also determined by the PHO achieving negotiated or predetermined performance measures. Most organizations will want to limit the number of "targets" to those defined by the Medicare Shared Saving Program, currently 33, but changing as this is being written. A few of the current measures of the Medicare Shared Savings Program are shown in the table below.

Domain	Measure Title
Patient/Caregiver Experience	CAHPS (Consumer Assessment of Healthcare Providers and Systems): patients rating of doctor
Patient/Caregiver Experience	CAHPS: how well your doctors communicate
Care Coordination/Patient Safety	Medication reconciliation after discharge from an inpatient facility
Preventive Health	Influenza Immunization

The PHO has now been formed and the risk-sharing agreements are being negotiated. How is the PHO going to manage its performance to know how it is doing and where it needs to improve? As was said many years ago: "The future of healthcare is not bricks and mortar, it is data." The PHO needs access to claims (administrative) and clinical data. It will need its own data programmer/analyst and should not rely on the payers to manage the data/information. The PHO wants to own the data and be responsible for how the information is developed and used. The PHO needs to track financial activities and variations as well as the performance targets. Many PHOs have either developed or purchased a clinical registry program which is used by the PCPs to track key clinical indicators (such as the ones for diabetes) and which the PHO can use to identify opportunities for improvement.

Although the data analysis helps identify opportunities for improvement, it alone will not change provider and patient behavior. The PHO needs to implement support programs that will augment the existing provider services. The core program is referred to as "care coordination" throughout the "care continuum." The providers must be actively engaged, but have supporting resources to help them work differently from the past. Accountability for care does not end when the patient leaves the hospital or physician's office.

One of the first care coordination activities to consider is the development of compacts, or agreements, among the physicians and with the hospitals, which describe how they will interact with each other. These are more clinically oriented, unlike the PHO membership compacts cited above. For example, PCPs will commit to using guidelines when referring patients to specialists and specialists will agree to provide timely treatment reports to referring PCPs. These are "low-hanging fruit" actions that can have significant impact on the cost and quality of patient care. Another step can be the creation of a simple, common referral form that the PCPs and specialists agree to use. This can eliminate the complex array of forms that different specialty offices use now which is an unnecessary burden for the PCPs' offices. These are actions which enhance the ownership of the programs by the physicians.

Beyond these communications and relational activities, the PHO needs to provide support for the patient care services—both the physician offices and the facilities that lead to successful PHM. These can include the following:

Care managers: Usually RNs who work with the PCPs to provide support for chronically ill and high-risk patients. They are often trained in motivational interviewing and become advocates for the patients and their health.

Transition coaches: Again, usually RNs who work with patients prior to and for a month after discharge from an inpatient stay in a hospital. They conduct drug reconciliations, usually at the patient's home, home environmental assessments, ensure a timely visit to the PCP's office and the specialist's office if needed, and identify actions the patient needs to take to optimize his/her recovery. Besides the goal of the patient's recovery, the program helps reduce readmissions to the hospital. Dr. Eric Coleman's Care Transitions Program® is well recognized as the model program for these services.

Practice coaches: The changes that the practices are expected to make will require help and expertise in workflows, team engagement, and data use. Programs such as LEAN and Microsystems can be very helpful in the transformation of an office to the new environment.

Care coordinator: Usually an RN on the PHO staff who helps with the intersection of patient health stratification data and clinical application of care coordination services.

Community resources: Perhaps the most underutilized resource in supporting the health of a community or population is not part of the traditional healthcare system. These are resources such as disease-specific support groups, churches and church congregations, social workers, senior care communities and agencies, pharmacists, nutritionists, community centers such as YMCAs, libraries, etc. The care managers and the care coordinator need to be educated about and work with these community resources. They often have little or no cost to the patient, but can provide positive benefits.

Beyond the clinical support opportunities, the PHO should develop relationships with the major purchasers and government representatives in its service area. After all, these are the entities that are buying healthcare and have the most direct interest in the outcomes for their employees and constituents. The PHO wants to keep them informed about its activities and how it is performing. The successful PHO has a story to tell that is worth telling.

WHAT DOES THE OPERATIONAL STRUCTURE LOOK LIKE?

The staffing for the PHO will start modestly to get the programs started. More staffing will be needed as the activities become more complex. The hospital partner may have resources it can share. The staff it should include are shown in the table below.

Position	Job Summary/Candidates
Executive Director/CEO	Overall managerial responsibility; lead contact for negotiations and external parties; prior experience in HMOs, multispecialty group practices, or IPAs
Chief Medical Officer (CMO)	Key link with physician members and responsible for clinical/value performance; prior experience with an HMO or as a medical director for IPA
Data Programmer/Analyst	Manages all data sources and develops meaningful, actionable reports; trained in SAS or other report-writing programming
Care Coordinator/Population Health Manager	Translates the patient reports into action by care managers, transition coaches, etc.; nurse with data and management experience—home care is a good background
Care Managers	RNs based in PCP's offices who work with high risk and chronically ill patients to help them manage their conditions; nurses with motivational training
Practice Advisors	Support practices in redesigning work flows and understanding new data information to improve performance; background in operations with training in programs such as LEAN or Microsystems
Operational Staff (provider relations, administration support, etc.)	Support physician members with PHO and payer issues, provide effective communications through multiple channels; experience in provider relations or group practice management; administrative assistant who is able to work with projects on his/her own

FUNDING THE PHO OPERATIONS

There are several different ways to fund the PHO operations, with the operative word being "fund." These are not services sold outside the PHO as a marketed service, but rather the tools the PHO has to be successful in providing value to its members and patients. While it is good to have a profit or surplus from operations, this is not why the PHO operations exist. Below are some examples of funding mechanisms. The PHO should engage an accountant and attorney to review the methodologies the PHO plans to use.

Methodology	Source
Member Dues	The physician members pay a joining fee and annual dues to support operations. This is often matched by the hospital member, unless it can contribute more based on its legal structure.
Network Access Fees or Management Fees	Usually a per member per month fee charged to the payer for contracting with the PHO.
Performance Fees	A "bonus" or one-time (annually or quarterly) payment paid to the PHO for achieving specific performance standards independent of the risk arrangement, if one exists.
Share of Risk-Sharing surplus	If the PHO achieves a surplus from its risk-sharing agreement(s), the PHO board may vote to allocate some of the funds to operations before payment to the members.

PULLING IT ALL TOGETHER: A REAL CASE MODEL OF A PHO

The MMC PHO based in Portland, Maine was incorporated in 1994. The PHO was established as a not for profit but taxable entity that included Maine Medical Center and the Portland Community Physicians Organization as partners. (The Portland Community Physicians Organization is now the Community Physicians of Maine [CPM] and consists of hospital employed and independent physicians).

The Board of Directors has 14 members with seven physicians (four PCPs and three specialists) and seven hospital representatives. The PHO was initially established to contract with HMOs by taking financial risk. The operations were funded by a management fee charged to the commercial payers as part of the contract. The physicians also had a joining fee, which helped fund their operations, which were limited, as the PHO staff provided support to CPM. The PHO contracted with several commercial carriers and were at financial risk for the care of the defined population (patients in PHO PCP practices).

A withhold was retained from the physicians payments to cover their share if a loss was incurred. The PHO was able to return all or a portion of the withholding in every year and share some of the surplus in most years.

In 2003, the PHO began looking at how it could track and deliver value to its patients and the contracting payers and purchasers through direct contract with employers. It developed the Clinical Improvement Plan (CLIP) that initially consisted of nurse care managers, practice improvement advisors, a quality performance improvement recognition program, and a web-based clinical improvement registry.

The program has expanded to include care coordination support, transition coaches, provider compacts, and guidelines for referrals and treatment.

All of this was established before "accountable care" existed. It was done because it was the right thing to do and the PHO recognized that the future (now) would require the provision of value (quality/cost), not just FFS for reimbursement. The PHO now contracts with payers with risk for both financial and quality performance. It monitors performance through its committee structure, particularly the Value Improvement Committee. It is a participant in the Medicare Shared Saving Program where it has successfully completed the first 2 years of the program.

The MMC PHO now consists of several MaineHealth hospitals, MaineHealth itself, and CPM, which now includes physicians from all of the member and some of the affiliate hospitals of MaineHealth. In addition to its history of risk sharing for medical services, it has also managed and assumed risk for several mental health contracts with payers and employers. The PHO began with three staff, and now has over 60, with half being nurse care managers. It is still funded by management fees, and also performance recognition "bonuses."

What did it take to accomplish all of this? From the time the MMC PHO began its clinical improvement activities in 2003, it took about 3 years to have the basics operational and then build from there. But they had no blueprint to follow. Today, an organization starting a PHO or ACO, has outside pressures that will require having the basics in place, depending on when it is started, in 2 years or less. Three years may be a luxury. Now there is information to help an organization get started.

The MMC PHO was able to use savings from prior year risk contracts and negotiated performance "bonuses" to fund the start-up and ongoing accountable care operations, as cited above. The majority of the costs of the PHO operations is in staffing (approximately 75%). The costs will vary based on the size of the organization and the resources that may be provided, in kind, by the members. The impact of the transition to risk-sharing from traditional FFS may not be as significant for the PHO (other than capitalization) as it will be on the providers, particularly the hospitals. Successful risk-sharing will mean less was paid to someone (if done right, this is usually the hospital[s]) and the risk-sharing savings will not make up for the loss in traditional revenue. The members of the MMC PHO continue to work through this transition to the new population-based world, even with its years of experience.

IS THIS ALL FOR REAL? DOES IT EXIST ELSEWHERE?

Besides the MMC PHO, there are systems that have been very successful for years at managing the quality and cost of the services they provide. Intermountain Health System (UT) and Geisinger Clinic (PA) are two examples of integrated systems with employed physician staffs. Like the MMC PHO, St. Francis Health Care Partners (CT) has independent and hospital-employed physicians, though mostly independent.

When these organizations started the work of "accountable care" they did it because it made good business sense to them and it was the right thing to do. In today's world of healthcare with the emphasis on achieving healthy populations, it is essential for hospitals and physicians to move away from the past and embrace a more coordinated approach to care with goals such as the Triple Aim. This is still the right thing to do; and as a professional, it is what providers should expect of themselves.

14 Care Circle Networks
An Introduction

If you are a hospital trying to optimize your capacity to care, hold down costs, and prep for or introduce a new population health payment and business model, you should consider all the elements of care available within your community. Your community of care is far broader than the physician practices you've purchased or the post-acute care sites with which you have alliances. The potential community of care surrounding your facility encompasses old and new resources, including sources that you've passed every day on the way to work but never considered incorporating. These resources could make a huge difference in the lives of your community if they were only fully and effectively integrated into patient care strategies. They could do a great deal to expand your overall care capacity, improve your key metrics such as unnecessary readmissions, unnecessary ED visits, and post-acute morbidity. However, most care systems ignore these resources, as incorporating them doesn't add directly to the bottom line or expand volume or improve revenues. Yet, it may just be the right thing to do.

Thus, to truly optimize your total capacity to care, you'll want to go to the next level and tap into ALL the available communal resources. That's what the next sections of this book are all about.

BACKGROUND

Recall what Vince Lombardo once said about the basics of football, "Some people try to find things in this game that don't exist but football is only two things—blocking and tackling." Meaning that without the essential elements of the game for offense and defense, one cannot win. Likewise, I contend that there are essential elements in the management of our capacity to care and in the management of hospital capacity without which we cannot achieve optimization.

Now that we have thoroughly covered the blocking and tackling elements for the inpatient hospital side, we need to jump outside the four walls of the hospital to address the capacity available within the community. In the next several chapters, I will not focus on the capacity of current, standard resources in the community such as nursing homes, home health agencies, etc., though I would always include them in the grander scheme of system-wide capacity management. These institutions are familiar enough and will obviously be an integral part of any future healthcare systems. Furthermore, those who know these institutions better can use the principles within this book (e.g., predictive analytics for demand patterns, resource task optimization, etc.) to optimize their internal capacity. Rather, I will focus on a way to bring these resources to bear along with new and untapped resources to form a more holistic and effective "community of care" that will enable the Five Pillars and achieve a true optimization of community care capacity. The concepts of this section related to the "community of care" came from years of work in healthcare and research into the flaws of the current system.

ACHILLES' HEELS

One of the Achilles' heels of the current healthcare system is its reliance on an FFS reimbursement model that not only creates but also encourages siloed resources and separation of care into specific, disparate entities. Even in community facilities which are state or federally funded, collaboration with other communal resources is not well coordinated and encouraged. Though there is an inherent understanding that collaboration and cooperation will yield better care and outcomes, lower costs, increased efficiencies, and happier patients and care providers, we consistently fail in our efforts to bring collaboration into the system, largely due to the inherent requirements for funding of each individual component.

Interestingly, the Bible puts forth a message for our healthcare systems in 1 Corinthians 12: 15–26, where Paul described the need for synergy, inclusion, and cooperation among members of the Christian faith. The same calling, and the same message, applies to all those who work in the fields of health and wellness.

> [15]If the foot should say, "Because I am not a hand, I do not belong to the body," it would not for that reason cease to be part of the body. [16]And if the ear should say, "Because I am not an eye, I do not belong to the body," it would not for that reason cease to be part of the body. [17]If the whole body were an eye, where would the sense of hearing be? If the whole body were an ear, where would the sense of smell be? [18]But in fact God has arranged the parts in the body, every one of them, just as he wanted them to be. [19]If they were all one part, where would the body be? [20]As it is, there are many parts, but one body.
>
> [21]The eye cannot say to the hand, "I don't need you!" And the head cannot say to the feet, "I don't need you!" [22]On the contrary, those parts of the body that seem to be weaker are indispensable, [23]and the parts that we think are less honorable we treat with special honor. And the parts that are unpresentable are treated with special modesty, [24]while our presentable parts need no special treatment. But God combined the members of the body, and has given greater honor to the parts that lacked it, [25]so that there should be no division in the body, but that its parts should have equal concern for each other. [26]If one part suffers, every part suffers with it; if one part is honored, every part rejoices with it.[*]

So it is with the provision of care. Each part, each component of the system from PCPs to labs to EDs to community clinics to nursing homes to volunteers should all be part of a larger system of care, coordinated to efficiently direct the necessary resources to their appropriate tasks to achieve the optimal outcomes for each patient.

As you are likely painfully aware, we in the United States generally do a lousy job of "care coordination" even though it is the current buzz phrase in the business. We have not, in fact, collaborated and coordinated as we could and should, and thus there

---

[*] 1995. *The NIV (New International Version) Study Bible.* Zondervan Publishing House, Grand Rapids.

remain great inefficiencies in the care process and our care system. Furthermore, we routinely leave potentially vital communal resources out of our care planning and lose the potential impact of the tremendous available capacity. In other words, our current efforts towards "care coordination," though admirable, don't go far enough and leave out many potential resources that could greatly benefit the community of care.

One of the other important Achilles' heels of our current system is a current and pending dearth of critical resources. Or, put another way, the growing relative lack of clinical capacity. Depending on whose numbers you believe, we will either have a moderate or a severe shortage of clinical resources, from techs to nurses to surgical specialists. This dearth will lead to inevitable constraints in capacity and increased costs, the severity of which depends on the degrees of shortage in your community. Already, many hospitals fight for nurses and are constantly short staffed. To address these current and pending issues, we will need to both advance training efforts to bring more resources to bear and develop new resource pools that can enable greater capacity at the same or lower cost. These resources are actually widely available in our communities, if they were only tapped effectively. Indeed, many work now to help care for the patients in your community, yet they cannot collaborate with the clinical resources at physician's offices, clinics, and hospitals and thus work in many little siloes, all trying individually to do the right thing. This of course can lead to confusion, overlap of tasks, mass inefficiencies, and less than optimal scenarios for patients.

Cost is another heel of our system. Though I've written earlier about the foolishness of international comparisons of cost, the U.S. system is still quite expensive and not getting any cheaper. Coupled with the pressing need for more clinical resources, care will likely become more and not less expensive per encounter as wages are driven higher in a competitive marketplace. Hospitals and health systems may otherwise be forced into making difficult decisions based on increasingly difficult financial situations.

Alleviating this means making one or more of several changes, one of which is resource substitution. If one can substitute the role of a less-expensive resource for the role of a more expensive, often overqualified resource, the overall cost goes down. Likewise, if a task needs to be added to the list of care provision requirements and a less expensive or even free resource can be used, the total cost of care doesn't increase much if any. Therefore, finding less expensive and/or free resources and finding ways to substitute them for the tasks currently being performed by more expensive resources could be an easy and effective way to improve overall capacity (more work done by the newly freed-up expensive resources) while reducing or maintaining the total cost of care delivery. These resources are freely available, but mostly lie latent awaiting an opportunity to serve the health and well-being of the community in which they live.

And of course, the lack of health ownership in many parts of our society makes changing behaviors and ensuring patient compliance difficult. We simply do not ask, let alone demand, that patients "own" their health. Indeed, though we might suggest that smoking, drinking, overeating, and sedentary lifestyles are bad, we do little if anything to offer anything more than a suggestion of improvement. We might offer a few carrots here and there, but certainly no sticks.

This could also be helped with additional resources, but the resources we normally tap all cost money and are, in varying degrees, in relatively short supply.

SUMMARY

Simply put, if you are going to truly optimize your "capacity to care," you must necessarily embrace the many "non-clinical" resources available within your community and integrate them as fully as possible into the care of patients within your community. Furthermore, you must re-examine the use of your paid clinical resources to see how, when, and to what extent clinical and non-clinical tasks can be re-allocated to those communal resources awaiting opportunities to serve.

In nearly every city I've visited where this issue has been discussed, there is a wealth of resources available who already perform various roles in the care of our patients. These roles may be minor or major, small or large. Yet, each fills a certain vacuum within the care system that traditional resources and systems have left behind. This might be a meal to an elderly shut-in, a visit from a pastor or church member, a ride to the grocery store or physician appointment, or monitoring of medication and diet. Each task is vital yet is often disconnected from and unknown to the "official" care plans of our patients.

Resources within our communities span a wide spectrum, from EMTs to pharmacists to church congregants and general volunteers. They bring varying expertise and levels of passion and dedication to individuals and groups, in patient homes or myriad other care settings. If we were to put a true monetary value on their services, it would likely be in billions of dollars annually.

Yet, these resources are rarely tapped and integrated into our care systems. Commonly, they remain "outside" the care plans of patients, and are only involved to the extent that they can force themselves into the patient's world. If they are known anywhere, it is within Case Management where interactions are more common and the concerns for "external resources" more pronounced. Furthermore, in most cases, their direct involvement can only be "second-hand" since it is only through the patient that they can know the patient's needs and potential opportunities to assist.

Most importantly, these resources could provide tremendous additional capacity at a very low cost if they were effectively tapped. Indeed, they are already providing necessary services that healthcare providers mostly take for granted. But if they were truly "dialed in" and fully integrated into the "care strategies" of patients, their value could do nothing but increase! Think of a small and integrated army of volunteers all properly and fully directed and aimed at the core health problems of our communities. What value might they bring? What good could they do? This could relieve what we know to be a pending gap in clinical resource availability as an aging population requires more care than the current and predicted number of clinical resources can provide.

This "next level" of integration is the basis of the remainder of this book. In the subsequent chapters, I will outline a model I've written about in the past in order to bring to light the potential resource pool lying latent in most if not all of our local communities. By fully integrating these currently available but rarely tapped resources into coordinated, holistic "Care Strategies" we can augment the capacity of the healthcare system, encourage health ownership at all levels of society, manage costs and improve quality, outcomes, and patient and resource gratification. Doing this is paramount to the future of the U.S. economy and the viability and effectiveness of the U.S. healthcare system.

15 The Care Circle Network Concept

This chapter will offer a brief overview of the Care Circle concepts and its goals, some of the nomenclature, and the general requirements for implementation. As you read the later chapters in this book, these topics will be discussed in greater detail.

CCN DESCRIPTION

A CCN is an engineered, interconnected, community-engaging care "subsystem" that simultaneously addresses cost, quality, access, system capacity, and gratification in our communities, especially for the most problematic patients in the population: those with multiple chronic diseases or a single chronic disease with multiple comorbidities (a.k.a. "poly-chronics").

CCNs align patients, clinicians, and broad arrays of precisely coordinated communal resources to support physicians' care strategies for patients. CCNs go beyond "care managers" and "patient navigators" by directly integrating myriad communal resources, such as churches, families, FQHCs, YMCAs, friends, pharmacies, community groups, students, volunteers, etc., into organized "Care Circles" that provide ongoing assistance and personalized care to their patients. Care activities are coordinated and delegated with the guidance and oversight of physicians, while patient status and care activity updates are communicated back "upstream" to clinicians via a "social/clinical networking platform (SCN)," (which could be thought of as a "Facebook for chronic disease management"). Via the SCN, Care Circle resources can coordinate their activities, collaborate on patient needs, exchange ideas to improve care, interact with patients, and engage in an ongoing dialogue with their patient's clinicians. This extends physicians' "reach" into the lives of their patients; expands their "capacity to care" to more patients; increases the number and quality of patient "touches"; and promotes and improves ongoing monitoring, compliance, and lifestyle management. Patients thus receive the right assistance and care at the right time via the most cost-effective, convenient, and familiar local resources.

This holistic communal approach enables physicians to focus on what they do best, outcomes management and resource direction, while improving patient contact, compliance, and overall disease management, especially for the poor, frail elderly, and rural populations, through a more appropriate allocation of care tasks. The CCN thus expands the total clinical capacity of the system without taxing scarce current and future clinical resources, yielding a simultaneous impact on cost, quality, access, gratification, and capacity while encouraging new business and payment model innovation.

Potential patients or patient groups that might be appropriate for a CCN include (but certainly are not limited to):

- Poly-chronics
- Elderly living alone at home
- Elderly living with their low-income family
- Patients struggling with obesity, addictions, etc., in need of support
- Single mothers, especially young working mothers
- Immigrants struggling with language barriers, access to healthcare, and other constraints

Your community, or a community your service/civic group or church is serving, may have specific needs that a CCN-like system might help. When reading this book, keep a very open mind to the possibilities for extending the concept into your community and thereby enhancing your community's health, wellness, and health ownership.

Size and Scale

Remember as you read this and the next several chapters that CCNs do NOT come in a single size, shape, and form. The CCN is an approach to care management and not meant to be a restrictive program. They can be of any size, scale, and population imaginable. A CCN can be a single patient in a small church; a single elderly male living alone in poverty; a group of working single moms in need of health assistance and guidance for themselves and their children; or an ethnic neighborhood banded together to fight obesity. Likewise, an iteration of a CCN can include all the poly-chronics in a physician's or hospital's patient panel, or an entire city focused on preparing its citizenry for end-of-life care. The goals of the CCN will be roughly similar … to engage members of the community into Care Circles around patients or groups of patients with specific needs and goals. How you do this, and on what scale, is entirely up to you, the needs of the community, and the requirements for care assistance, guidance, and management.

Keep this in mind as you read this book, as herein I will focus mainly on a larger CCN with many members, many patients and physicians, and the necessary breadth of technologies. However, this is for example's sake only and is not meant to preclude even the smallest, single-patient iteration of the concept. Thus, I will toss in thoughts throughout this book aimed at the smaller iterations, so as to keep you thinking of the less-extensive options available using this model.

If you are like me, you know individuals who could use such help. So, whether you start small or large, grow bigger or shrink down, the CCN is meant to be adaptable to the needs of your specific patient population and your community.

"Poly-Chronics" and CCNs

Throughout these chapters, I have referred to several patient groupings, categorized in a number of ways. However, my previous works focused specifically on those "poly-chronics" in the population using a more narrowed derivative of the CCN, the "Poly-Chronic Disease Network (PCDN)."[*] Think of the PCDN as a specialized type of the CCN, much like an orthopedist is a specialized type of surgeon. The PCDN is narrower in focus, having a specific set of disease states to address. One reason for the narrower focus was that the CCN seemed overly broad and too all-encompassing to introduce as a brand new concept. Furthermore, cost control was a dominant driving factor in national discussions in 2012 when the PCDN work was first published, thus a system like the PCDN that could more quickly address cost seemed a more appropriate topic. After all, its focus is those patients with the highest cost and the highest care needs for which CCN resources might offer assistance.

After its publication, the PCDN concept won great praise from many in healthcare leadership circles and was applauded as an industry-changing concept whose time had yet to come. Now that the PCDN has received attention and had some trials in the marketplace, I reintroduce the CCN herein as a broader iteration of the originally published PCDN community care model and as an integral part of the systemic optimization puzzle. I am opening the potential of the CCN to its original, wider state rather than using the more-narrowed approaches of prior books so as to incorporate as many patients as possible into the solution. Indeed, the CCN concept obviously applies to many in our communities, especially the elderly living alone, those in poverty without solid familial or social resources on which to rely, and even middle- or higher-income patients for whom the demands of care are simply overwhelming. Yet, there is still a very clear mission for the PCDN in our healthcare system given what it can and should be capable of achieving in cost savings, capacity expansion, and quality and outcomes improvement. It is therefore important to keep in mind that though there is an overarching operational model here in the CCN, its more-focused iteration—the PCDN—is likely the one that will receive the most attention due to its pinpoint focus on the main issues facing our healthcare systems today. Thus, I will continue to focus attention on the "poly-chronics" and their greater care needs as part of the "grander scheme" of systemic optimization.

CCN AS A VISUAL

Take a look at the diagram in Figure 15.1, and keep it in mind as you read the remainder of this book. Visually, it represents the extent of the resource pool and technologies suggested for a typical CCN. This book by no means excludes other resource types, nor does it preclude the use of new technologies, infrastructure, and approaches as they arise and are tested. Though the CCN is by far the most integrated and sophisticated approach to be published thus far, I hope it is only the beginning of the discussion on dramatically new care model development.

---

[*] Story, P. 2012. *Developing a Poly-Chronic Disease Network: An Engineered, Community-Wide Approach to Disease Management.* CRC Press/Taylor & Francis, New York.

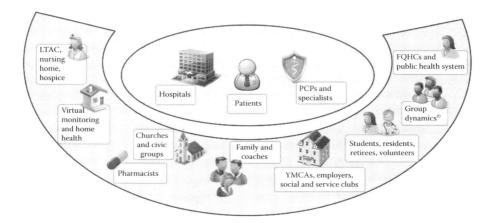

FIGURE 15.1   A visual representation of a single iteration of the CCN infrastructure.

APPLICATION OVERVIEW

As we already know, our healthcare system is broken and in desperate need of repair. Our system is at least somewhat incapable of managing the coming "gray wave" of an aging population, due to both a relative lack of resources and broken operational models. Think of the complexity associated with the management of the current poly-chronic population, then multiply that by severalfold as a relatively unhealthy population ages further. Furthermore, overeating, poor personal and diet choices, lack of exercise, and a general lack of health ownership will very likely lead the currently healthy to eventually become unhealthy, thus moving them from the least-expensive care group into more expensive categories. In other words, the 80 per-centers (who currently spend the least in dollars and resources) may end up being 5 percenters (who demand the most) if they do not manage their current health well. Thus it's clear that high resource costs and capacity limitations mean the current care models do not offer the ability to solve for society's growing healthcare needs in a cost-effective way, especially for those with complex chronic diseases, low access to care resources, and a lack of deep, local familial connections. Accessibility, capac-ity, quality, and provider and patient "gratification" and "ownership" for all patients, including those in the least expensive 80%, must be simultaneously managed if we are to truly and permanently fix the system.

The CCN is one way to help alleviate these problems. The CCN way of think-ing takes patients out of the old "cure" system in which episodic, longitudinally bounded care is the norm and places them into "Care Strategies" and resource pools specifically designed to address their complex care needs. Customized and resourced at the local level, the CCN is essentially a conceptual foundation upon which is built a customized care infrastructure, built for the community in which it is placed.

APPLICATIONS OF THE CCN MODEL TO POLY-CHRONICS

One of the core principles of the CCN and its narrowed relative, the PCDN, is quite simple: Patients with (single or multiple) chronic diseases (commonly those in the 5% of total costs) require a dramatically different care system because they themselves are very different. We already know that the "poly-chronics" are and will continue to be the locus of the real cost and capacity issues in healthcare. Their cost (some 70%–90% of total cost) is reflected in both actual care delivery costs as well as the costs of lost productivity and absenteeism. But the current system does a lousy job of meeting their needs. They need entirely different care streams and resource pools providing different services in different quantities than the 80 percenters. The 80 percenters don't commonly need ongoing, coordinated care from multiple disparate physicians and providers in order to try to maintain or improve health (except in instances of sudden injury or disease onset). Their care is simply not that complex. But for the poly-chronics, better care means developing an entirely new model of care delivery, one that literally blows up the existing systems and replaces, or at least augments, them with an entirely new look, feel, and functionality.

Thus, we essentially create a new care system (the PCDN) specifically for those who need it most, the poly-chronics, as we create new care systems for anyone else who might need it (the CCN). Both are iterations of the same model, one simply more focused on a smaller patient pool than the other.

THE CCN EVOLVING THE CURRENT SYSTEM FROM WITHIN

To be accepted, the CCN model must at least meet the same standards of quality, access, and resource accountability as existing systems. It must not only expand the capacity of the entire system via new resources but also assimilate all resources into a new care culture such that their individual capacities to support patients are greatly increased. Furthermore, the CCN requires not just care coordination but the "engineering" of these resources and their work in support of unifying "Care Strategies." This broader approach moves from a linear and disaggregated series of treatments, procedures, and care steps to an integrated, community-wide strategy for the general and long-term wellness of both the sickest of the population, from "home to hospice," and anyone else in the system in need of low-cost assistance.

The success of this unique approach to care delivery depends on a holistic implementation plan that includes some limited supporting technology; precise resource organization, utilization, and "assimilation"; training and ongoing mentoring, and patient and resource accountability. In order to achieve these lofty goals, the CCN requires specific but low-cost technologies and perhaps a few specialized, full-time support staff. Without its underlying infrastructure, the CCN could fall prey to the same systemic constraints, silos, and inefficiencies that plague the current models. However, there are a number of ways and speeds with which the CCN might be implemented, depending on the existing technology infrastructure (TI), community resources, physician engagement, and patient willingness. Commonly, there will be engagement with large physician groups and collaborative hospitals to develop mutually beneficial synergies for addressing populations that create unnecessary costs and burdens for clinicians, facilities, patients, and their communities. However, don't be surprised if your CCN has its roots in a church congregation or community service organization.

Though radical, the CCN has been universally praised. Recent efforts across the country show that community resources, such as pharmacies, YMCAs, and volunteers, are anxious to help save the system. Yet, they are stymied by lack of integration and clinical guidance. Coordinating these disparate and "siloed" resources into a functional, efficient, cohesive care continuum will allow dramatic change to take place at a low cost while improving outcomes, capacity, and quality.

AN ENGINEERED APPROACH

The CCN does not haphazardly throw resources, time, and materials at a problem. Indeed, one of the major issues I have with some of the initial efforts at care redesign is the seemingly careless use of expensive resources. Many of the current strategies are "resource intensive," making sustainability and dramatic cost savings difficult to attain without grants and stipends and ancillary payments.

Instead, nurses, techs, or any other expensive resource should only be used as they are appropriate to a given task. Furthermore, their utilization should be optimized within the context of the larger system, so as to prevent the misallocation of workload and the inevitable constraints that come with it. Cost overruns, overtaxed or underutilized resources, long waits for service, and frustrated customers/patients are a direct result of the failure to properly utilize the available resource pool. Just as a pilot of a commercial airline doesn't serve drinks mid-flight, a physician or nurse should not be required to do non-clinical tasks that might be better handled by another, more appropriately skilled and/or proximate resource. Indeed, misallocation of resources is quite common in non-engineered approaches to resource provision. We readily see the impact of inflexible and inefficient approaches to resource allocations in healthcare. You don't have to look much further than mandated patient–nurse ratios to see the negative impact of a bad approach to resource, task, and workforce management on efficiencies, cost, and capacity. These siloed and rigid work breakdown structures have always led to periodic over- and underutilization, higher costs, terrible inefficiencies, and increased risks to quality wherever they've been tried.

The only way to solve for a resource-constrained environment is to "engineer" the task allocations effectively such that all work is done by suitably trained and qualified resources at the appropriate time in the correct manner, maximizing the utilization of the resources and thereby sustainability of the model. The best way to do that is to use traditional "Industrial Engineering" principles, tools, and concepts. These have been used by industry for decades to squeeze out the kind of productivity that has made American business great and our economy strong. Data analytics and tools (such as simulation, as we'll discuss later), and structured deployment are all hallmarks of proper and effective work breakdown structures. Using these principles heavily in the planning and deployment phases of the CCN implementation almost guarantees a more optimal outcome. And by engineering a resource pool customized for the community and patients to be served, the CCN helps guarantee that there will be no constraints in service or resources, or lapses in care, access, capacity, and/or quality.

It should be noted that this "engineering" approach goes well beyond "Lean." Indeed, what is called Lean in healthcare is often referred to as "Industrial Engineering Lite" among the more sophisticated industrial engineers (IEs). Lean, though used widely by IEs and companies around the world, is not as sophisticated as an industrial engineering approach would normally be. In many companies, especially healthcare organizations, Lean is no longer Lean ... it has morphed into something more robust, complex, and useful. But because Lean is not a "dynamic" analytical system (as I described in one of my previous books*) it is largely incapable of the detailed and complete analysis of complex and dynamic systems. Though useful as a "process" improvement methodology, it is ineffective as a "systems" improvement methodology. Thus, we use DCAMM as our methodology of choice, as it is much more appropriate to the highly variable, interdependent, and ever-changing world of care provision.

Small CCN Notes: Even with the smallest of CCNs, you may need to consider task allocations if there is more than one communal resource. Of course, if there is only one, this gets very easy unless that single resource becomes overwhelmed with the tasks at hand, perhaps not initially realizing what is involved in the provision of services. Thus, it's always a good idea to sit down and map out, preferably with the patient and her physician, exactly what should be done, when, and how often. This will prevent confusion, dropped tasks, and patient and resource frustration.

CCN COMPONENTS

As we go through the subsequent chapters, we will delve more deeply into the following attributes of the CCN, and how they will be developed, implemented, and managed. For now, let's take a high-level pass at the concepts, principles, and requirements of the CCN model. Remember, as you read this and upcoming chapters, to think about the patients in your community who might be served by some iteration of this model. It is far more broadly applicable that you might first imagine!

RESOURCE POOL

Obviously, as seen in Figure 15.1, the pool of resources in a CCN can be quite broad and deep. It encompasses many of the existing resources that are common to communities, such as YMCAs, churches, and community colleges. It may include resources that are not as common and which might be listed in general categories like "volunteers" which might include parish nurses and pharmacy school residents. It may encompass existing communal resources such as Meals on Wheels, or largely untapped resources such as retired healthcare workers, EMTs, school nurses,

---

* Story, P. 2010. *Dynamic Capacity Management for Healthcare: Advanced Methods and Tools for Optimization.* CRC Press/Taylor & Francis, New York.

pre-med university students, and "promontores" in Hispanic communities. This pool, however constructed and populated, should encompass as many dedicated resources as are required to accomplish the tasks at hand. There is little doubt that a given resource pool will evolve and morph over time, as the circumstances, patient population, and resource availability change over time. Thus this resource pool may need to be augmented periodically as specific individuals or groups move in and out of availability. Recruitment and ongoing training will be required, as will monitoring and the occasional "weeding out."

That said, within every resource pool for every CCN currently imagined there must be a "core." This would include dedicated physicians, nurses, and other clinicians who will, of course, be augmented by the rest of the resource pool members. Without clinical oversight and direct clinician participation, the optimization of the CCN and the proper guidance of non-clinical resources are impossible. Likewise, without an expanded resource pool, even if small and limited, the CCN loses its value to the patients, the community, and the healthcare system as capacity and access continue to be constrained. The CCN thus requires an expanded resource pool to include core groups of clinicians as well as myriad non-clinical resources.

Fortunately, expanded resource allocations are becoming more and more common, as seen in the work of the state of Vermont, Cambridge Health Alliance, Gunderson Lutheran Medical Center, and others around the country. Care Coordinators, Patient Navigators, and other similar titles are popping up in physician offices and hospitals across the country as more and more see the advantages of the distribution of tasks, especially for the chronically ill. This demonstrates a growing sensitivity to capacity constraints and the special needs of specific patient types. But, while laudable, these models risk continued cost and capacity constraints, as the resource expansion is typically limited to highly compensated and often-specialized clinicians. These, of course, can and should be further augmented by the resources of the CCN model, which will advance their goals, expand their care capacity, and improve their "reach" into the lives and health of their sickest patients.

Key to the CCN resource pools are several specific roles we'll discuss in greater detail later.

- *Prime*: A Prime is the patient's choice as primary "care partner," and serves as the go-to resource for all non-clinical issues for all other resources in the patient's "Care Circle." The Prime is the "point person," and is normally designated by the patient as their advocate and the person responsible for ensuring communications and care strategy implementation are ongoing. (Primes may be assigned by the CCN rather than selected by the patient in situations of the lonely elderly, cognitively impaired, etc.)
- *Care Circle*: This is the group of communal and clinical resources aligned around an individual patient's care provision. These may be large or small, but will nearly always be directed by a physician, with day-to-day operational oversight usually offered by Care Managers, CCN Managers, and Primes. Care Circles will commonly use an SCN to communicate, coordinate, exchange, update, and support as they intervene in the lives of the patients they touch.

- *CCN Manager*: This role, whether housed in a local hospital, a community agency, or a physician office, will manage the communal resources and Care Circles, ensure task completion, handle issues and questions, promote new and current participation, and generally support the program.
- *CCN Trainer*: Resources, physician office staff, and others will need training on everything from the essentials of chronic disease management to the basics of the technologies to be used. Some or all of this training may require a specific resource to ensure continuity, ongoing mentoring and training, and the maintenance of information quality. So important is this role that it is one of only two possible full-time resources in a CCN implementation.

Small CCN Notes: Of course, a small CCN will not require many resources, and will likely not require Managers or Trainers. A single or few resources might act as co-managers, rely on the patient's physician's office for training, and be the Primes of the patient(s) in the small CCN. Even one resource with one patient works!

MANAGING COMMUNAL RESOURCES

Communal resources, even if passionate and enthusiastic, need to be properly coordinated and managed. Otherwise, they will remain as they are: caring, but disjointed and siloed. Therefore, the CCN is clinically directed by either PCP's or, in the case of the PCDN, clinicians whose interest and expertise lie in the management of chronic diseases. I call the latter, specialized resources "Chronicists." The Chronicist may be an Internist, Geriatrician, PCP, or other specialist. However, the Chronicist must have a passion for chronic diseases, as his career would now be dedicated solely to the care of the most complex of patients. Alternatively, as we'll see, PCPs are able to serve these same functions if their expertise is sufficient and their patient population warrants such focus. The PCP may have some 15 percenters and some 5 percenters in his population, thus requiring the work with both "poly-chronic" and less-severely ill patients, so the two terms are used somewhat interchangeably in this book.

The Chronicist or PCP sits at the "top of the pyramid," working with CCN Managers, Trainers, office- or hospital-based Care Managers, and the communal resources to direct and manage the care of the patients under their supervision. This "pyramid structure" is important for clinical, legal, logistical, and efficiency reasons, so it is unlikely to be altered unless there is a significant alteration in the structure of the CCN itself. This might occur in situations in which a given patient needs minimal clinical assistance that can be provided by a single communal resource or two, perhaps coming from a local church or synagogue.

These clinical leaders will, of course, need help from other clinical specialists in the care of poly-chronics, such as orthopedists, neurologists, and nephrologists. If the CCN is set up with the right technologies and infrastructure, help with poly-chronics can also come from outside via links to national and even international specialists in chronic disease management. This network of remote experts would be available (for a fee, no doubt) to assist in diagnostics, Care Strategy development, and general clinical advisement. Indeed, Mayo and other "famed" or highly specialized health systems already use remote conferencing and monitoring to aid disparate health systems in better managing patient care. This helps build a "body of knowledge of best practices" for these conditions, spreads the information throughout the country, and allows for communication of results and outcomes to specific care strategy regimens.

Operationally, the resources are coordinated and supported by a CCN Manager, as described above and later in the book. This resource will be the "go to" person in most iterations of the CCN concept, which will prevent structural and program breakdown and promote ongoing activity and accountability.

RESOURCE TRAINING

You might be jumping ahead and asking, "But how can communal resources care for patients without clinical expertise?!?" Fear not … this will be covered later in this book. But consider this: you needn't be fluent in a foreign language to get around, order a meal, or find a restroom in a foreign country. You need only to know the basics of the language, culture, and people to enjoy a visit and interact with the locals. Likewise, the myriad communal resources needn't become nurses or LPNs or physicians to assist in the care of patients.

Suffice it to say, for now, that communal resources will indeed require training and ongoing education in their roles, the patients they care for, and the diseases they will encounter. While they will not be expected to become clinical experts, communal resources will have the right knowledge to work with, engage, and assist in the clinical management of the patients in their Care Circle. Depending on the resource, their desired and expected role, and the needs of the patient, appropriately trained and vetted resources will be assigned so as to ensure high quality and patient gratification.

TECHNOLOGY INFRASTRUCTURE

One of the main reasons that the CCN is even possible is the technology that will lie "under the hood." In fact, such a concept would have been difficult, if not impossible, before the advent of web-based communication tools. There are several potential technologies which could be involved in the development, implementation, and sustenance of the CCN, though only a minimal amount is actually required. These technologies and a limited number of full-time staff support the resource utilization optimization, clinical information exchange, compliance monitoring, and patient engagement required to allow physicians to care for more patients at a lower cost while promoting more patient contact, better compliance, higher metrics, and optimal outcomes. The good news is that these are not exclusive or patented technologies. Even more significant, you may need only one or a few of those listed, depending on your particular situation. And, as this book is meant to give guidance on the necessary systems and implementation plans to develop your own CCN, any applicable technology, whether purchased or home grown, could suffice if it achieves your particular CCN-related goals.

The following technologies may be part of a CCN program. Some are more necessary than others, and at least one is critical to success.

1. *SCN*: The SCN is the only "required" technology of a CCN. Think of this as a private "Facebook for poly-chronics." The SCN provides patients, caregivers, and their specific communal resources with a means by which to communicate, share, exchange, and learn. The best example of the SCN (as currently developed by eTransX, Inc.*) is a web-based networking tool that allows for ongoing communication among the members of patient Care Circles and clinicians while ensuring the patient's privacy, personalization, and sharing preferences. The SCN can be used as a(n):

   a. Communication platform for private and open interactions among physicians, patients, and clinical and communal resources in and among the Care Circles.

   b. Private Social Network among patients with similar disease states and clinical conditions, and among communal resources within and outside their specific Care Circle(s).

   c. Extension of Group Dynamics™ through which patients can communicate with and support each other.

   d. Information dispersion system through which patients and resources can be kept informed on CCN news, relevant clinical research and treatment options, policy issues, and other important communal information.

   e. Means for scheduling patient interactions, visits, prescription refills, appointments, and other events among Care Circle members.

   f. General CCN information source, wherein CCNs from across the country can collect and disseminate information relevant to patients and providers.

   The SCN will give a personal and communal touch to the caregivers and their tasks; allow sharing of ideas, thoughts, comments, and suggestions among clinical and non-clinical Care Circle resources; empower the enthusiastic to share their successes; help patients better communicate with those with like clinical conditions; and support collaborative care by integrating both clinical, non-clinical, communal, and familial resources in a single online community environment.

2. *Process Simulation*: Because process simulation (hereinafter simply "simulation") is capable of the analysis and optimization of complex, variable, and interdependent systems like these, it can be a critical tool in the development, implementation, and ongoing improvement and optimization efforts of large CCNs. Depending upon how many tasks, resources, patients, and disease states there are in your CCN, simulation may be a

---

* eTransX is a data aggregation and analytics firm based in Brentwood, TN. They were the first and most aggressive in the development of the SCN concept and have done a truly remarkable job. Their software is second to none, and its capabilities for this application are simply outstanding. They have now added much-needed services to their offerings, which will enhance the applicability of the CCN concept (Note: The author has no financial interests in or with eTransX) www.etransx.com.

useful analytical and implementation assistance tool. Small implementations may not need the power of simulation, as the implementation logistics can more easily be worked out.

3. *Virtual Monitoring (VM)*: Technologies now exist, and more will be developed, that will aid the CCN in the ongoing and immediate monitoring of patient compliance and medical conditions. CCNs are in fact great support structures for the use of VM tools, as they can provide in-home assistance for elderly or "technology impaired" patients. Patients with VM systems can work with the Care Circle resource to ensure proper data collection and transmission, and even be onsite for "virtual appointments" with physicians to promote understanding and compliance with care directives.

4. *Population Modeling and Prediction (PP)*: PP helps you anticipate the health outcomes of future changes in the demographics and health characteristics of a community. Used commonly by insurers, PP allows for the prediction of population trends, down to the individual patient. By predicting the health outcomes of current and future health trends, PP can aid the CCN in better predicting the future need for space, resources, and even medical equipment and VM systems.

These technologies, however cleverly combined and utilized, will allow the kind of care transformation the CCN promises. Regardless of how yours is assembled, the goals of linking resources, clinical information, and patients together to form an efficient, truly integrated, and sustainable network is important to the longevity and functionality of the program. If properly implemented, the TI can morph as the CCN evolves, patient needs change, and the technologies develop.

Small CCN Notes: Obviously, a small CCN will not need all this technology. However, since the best SCN system currently on the market (eTransX) is available inexpensively on a per-user-per-month basis, this may be viable for even the smallest of programs. While you likely won't need simulation or population modeling in small CCNs, you will need some way to track tasks and communication securely with your patient(s) (keeping in mind that email is NOT a secure means to communicate!). You may want to work with your local hospital, or the patient's church or civic group to see about sponsorship of any necessary technologies like eTransX.

Regardless of what you choose to use, select the technology that will make it easiest and most efficient for both the resources and the CCN patient(s).

PALLIATIVE AND END-OF-LIFE CARE

If we are to create a truly holistic approach to the care of poly-chronics, palliative care and end-of-life care and planning must be a part. This is not, as some might suspect, strictly a cost and utilization issue. Yes, those are both impacted by these programs. But, more importantly, so are patient gratification and family comfort and compassion. As we'll see later, palliative and end-of-life care can and should be integral components of a patient's overall "Care Strategy," and should be part of a holistic engagement in a patient's spiritual, mental, and physical well-being.

Of course, these programs require unique and specially trained resources. However, these resources can be used as and when needed to add their small but important part to the Care Strategy, thus needn't be part of the individual Care Circles of all CCN patients.

ASSIMILATION AND PASSION

Resources must be passionate about the care they give. And in order to best channel that passion, resources will need to be properly assimilated into the CCN framework. This means more than just signing up for a few tasks. Assimilation is a status of engagement at a much higher level and intensity. Assimilated resources are therefore fully committed to the cause, the way some are committed to their politics, favorite sports teams, and hobbies. This is important because this will not be easy work. There will be setbacks and frustrations. And if your resources are merely "unpaid volunteers," the tendency might be to take a self-serving and easy way out: leave. Thus, it is important to work with your communal resources using techniques of "volunteer management" and deploy resources that are knowledgeable of their communities, patients, and fellow resources such that a high degree of loyalty, passion, and commitment exists.

CAPACITY AS STRATEGY

One of the key issues CCNs are meant to address is the capacity constraints that continue to face our healthcare systems. Too many very sick patients, with fewer and fewer financial resources, vie for too few care providers. As we saw in earlier chapters, the dearth of physicians, nurses, and other expertise will continue to grow worse over time, even with current increases in the number of enrollees of training programs. The capacity of the current model will be unable to meet the demand of the coming generation of retirees.

Furthermore, we face increasing financial constraints as the population ages with fewer and fewer taxpayers to foot the bill. As future demographic shifts take place, and fewer and fewer taxpayers support the full load of the system, the healthcare system will continue to feel the pains of financial constraints. These constraints are not expected to lessen in the foreseeable future, leaving us with harsh alternatives, from massive increases in taxation that will stifle the economy to the direct rationing of care.

Thus, either we dramatically ration care or we develop an entirely new delivery system that will expand the capacity of the scarcest of resources without expanding their workload. Thus a "capacity strategy" that accounts for the entire system is required.

The CCN encompasses all aspects of the patient's care, inclusive of their personal circumstances, community bonds, friends, self-respect, and self-worth. This is an important aspect of the expansion of capacity. As the CCN uses multiple resources in the community, including specialists, mental health workers, social workers, volunteers, etc., the workload is spread yet the care is ultimately coordinated and effectively guided. This allows the mission-critical resources, physicians and other caregivers, to do what they do best, what they are trained to do, and are paid to do ... manage and direct care provision. This capacity expansion helps the system to meet an ever-growing demand without demanding more resources at less pay or greater workloads.

Thus capacity becomes the ultimate strategy in the work to achieve a sustainable, effective, and efficient system.

OTHER IMPORTANT ATTRIBUTES OF THE CCN

The CCN should also include

1. An "outcomes" focus rather than a financial, activity, patient, or resource focus. By focusing on outcomes, the patient is automatically part of the equation.
2. Patient accountability and personal responsibility. (If healthcare is a right, it is also a responsibility!)
3. An "It's not about me!" mentality among all resources.
4. The promotion of health ownership.
5. Community learning and focus on chronic disease prevention and management.

The latter two should not be discounted. As the CCN takes hold in the community, and more and more communal resources become engaged in the care of complex patients, the understanding of and respect for chronic diseases will organically grow. This will be reflected in the way communal resources understand their own healthcare and that of those around them. Thus, through "osmotic learning," communities will become more and more self-aware of the need for lifestyle choices and preventative care that can reduce the likelihood of chronic disease onset, which in turn will promote health ownership throughout the community.

Small CCN Notes: The attributes of the CCN should be the same, regardless of the size and scale of the program. Health Ownership is always the goal, and the mentality of the resources is key to achieving it.

AN ADDITIVE SOLUTION

Is the CCN a better model? Based on the nearly unanimous accolades from experts I admire, I'd have to say "Yes!" Our current healthcare/"sick-care" system is not designed for the efficient, effective, and holistic treatment of poly-chronics. Just look at the state Medicaid programs and how they struggle with the cost of care provision for this group. And even while new concepts such as "Care Coordinators" and "Navigators" are being developed, and government agencies and private insurers tinker with the base business model, there has not been the kind of wholesale upheaval that will be required to truly save the system.

The CCN may be such a model. As a more holistic approach to care delivery, the CCN takes into account the sheer complexity of the care requirements, particularly for poly-chronics, and develops a more appropriate and broader resource pool with which to provide less costly, higher quality, and more accessible care. Furthermore, by engineering those resources into a truly integrated delivery system, optimized for the community served, the CCN helps ensure that the right care is always available and that the "bottlenecked" or constrained resources are always given as much capacity as possible. Lastly, by using technology appropriately, the CCN ensures its own longevity and sustainability for the long haul towards better care at a lower cost.

Note also that I've generally described the CCN as a "care subsystem." Meaning, the CCN doesn't require the current advancements in Patient-Centered Medical Homes (PCMHs), Care Navigators and Care Managers, etc., to be replaced. Rather, the CCN can and should be added to these important efforts, augmenting these care models with new care capacity and "reach" into the lives of patients. If implemented properly into even the most advanced of PCMHs, the CCN should offer its same benefits and help these advanced models do even more.

CCNs and ACOs

As they stand now, ACO models are collections of patients under "one roof." Though not particularly successful in lowering costs or improving quality, the ACO continues to be the U.S. government's business model of choice. Of course, regardless of the overarching business model, a small population of those patients does and will continue to drive most of the cost of any care system. Yet, the ACO does little, if anything, to help redesign the delivery of care of these patients other than "coordinate" their care under the auspices of the same constrained resources we have now. Thus the newer business models, like ACOs, will need some sort of CCN-type model within them to ultimately be successful in sustaining healthcare throughout the coming demographic changes and financial crises.

Thus, a CCN should be part of *any new larger business model if that model is to hit its targets of cost, quality, access, and gratification without breaking the bank or overloading clinical resources.* I am not suggesting that we blow up ACOs (though their time seems to be running short). Rather, if an ACO is your business model of choice, the CCN can and should fit within it as a "care subsystem" capable of aiding the reduction of risk, cost, and resource consumption among the poly-chronics. Thus integration of the CCN as a "subsystem" is expected and should be welcomed. (Indeed, full integration is required; else a health system might become a "Poly-Chronic Patient Centered Accountable Medical Home Care Network!")

CCNs and the Hospital at Home (H@H)®

This is a relatively new concept applying only to health systems aggressively pursuing cost reductions. Hospital at Home® (H@H) is a term originally coined in the mid-1990s at Johns Hopkins by Dr. John Burton. Dr. Burton and his colleagues did some of the original efficacy trials in the late 1990s, with other evaluations continuing today.

H@H is meant to deploy systems, technologies, resource pools, and operational models to provide more intense care of patients, particularly chronic disease patients, in their homes rather than in the ED or hospital inpatient units. Thus, the goal is to reduce hospital ED and clinic visits, inpatient admissions, and certainly unnecessary readmissions.

H@H normally starts with a target patient population, usually with a specific disease(s) or condition(s), such as COPD or other chronic conditions. Dr. Burton's original studies used the ED as the initiation point of patient interaction, though newer models are more aggressive about targeting patients prior to a clinical intervention need. Depending on the clinical needs of the patient, a list of tasks and associated resources is created, usually involving dedicated program nurses and physicians. Intense levels of care are offered in the patient's home, with daily visits from key resources such as nurses, until certain clinical milestones are met. Staff is normally made available 24/7. Most testing (e.g., EKGs, blood work, etc.) is done in the home, with more intense radiographic studies done on short, planned trips to the hospital.

In a more modern version of the original, one more in line with the Care Circle Network concept, the resource pool might be expanded to include local church members, family and neighbors, EMTs and firemen, volunteers, parish nurses, and social workers so as to provide longer term partners in the patient's health and promote Health Ownership.

Newer H@H/Care Circle models might also be based on geography or socioeconomic status such that a concentrated effort can impact many patients with similar issues in a given area using a given set of applied clinical and non-clinical resources.

These models are readily integrated into visionary community-wide care models in which the quality and cost of care overrides the need for revenues for providers. As such, these models should continue to hold promise as innovators seek new approaches to care provision.

A CAVEAT TO THE CONTENTS OF THIS BOOK

It is worth repeating that the CCN is meant to be a very flexible business and care model. Yours may be small or large, or broad or narrowly focused. You might start with a single iteration and develop an entirely new model later on. Your technology and governance structures may differ dramatically from that of another CCN across town. However, in order to offer as broad a view as possible, all the components of a CCN are described herein. You might need only a few, or only one of these components. Therefore, when reading this book, don't be alarmed if the need of your community would not support a massive technology and governance implementation. Likewise, you should not expect to have to deploy the entire infrastructure at once, nor will your participating population go from 0% to 100% overnight.

Take what you read here and, if you feel it is valid, apply the necessary components, small or large, to your program. As your CCN grows, expands, or contracts over time, "amend the blend" to account for the size, scale, scope, and population of your community and patients as they change over time.

Take what you need from what is offered, but don't think you have to have it all.

A MISSING ELEMENT

If you know this business well, you will quickly pick up on a major element missing in the discussions of this book: mental health.

A significant issue with the care of many patients, especially poly-chronics, is the prevalence of mental health issues. I understand and appreciate this conundrum, as it inherently makes the care of these patients more difficult. Indeed, additional work is now being done to configure the CCN with a mental health patient focus. This will be published in the coming years as these unique models are tested and vetted for effectiveness.

That said, while I recognize the importance of both this issue and the need for a holistic approach to patient care, this book will intentionally leave out deep references to this subpopulation of patients. This is for several reasons

1. Though mental health is significant among our overall population and poly-chronics, a large majority do not exhibit mental health issues. Thus, there is an opportunity to treat most of the latter patients using "standard and common" communal resources without additional mental health expertise in place.
2. Volunteer communal resources would need more significant training if they were to deal with patients with depression, bipolar disorder, etc. While not impossible or improbable, this training adds a level of complexity that some CCNs may be unwilling to take on. Indeed, some may feel that is it entirely inappropriate to use communal resources until a patient's mental health issues are under control and well managed. Furthermore, it generally adds to the complexity of the care required, which may put some patients out of the scope of a non-clinical resource mix.
3. Mental health patients may require specialized infrastructures, care tasks, and other elements that will not fit well with a generalized CCN model. Instead, you should seek to add mental health resources to the clinical resources, and use communal resources only insofar as they can aid in the care and management of these special patients.

Keep in mind, however, that though they are not explicitly mentioned in this book, mental health resources can be added to a CCN, or perhaps more appropriately a "sub-CCN," that focuses specifically on patients with these mental health issues. The structure, volumes, capacity, and resource requirements of such a specialized CCN might be very different from others, but the overall model and its goals and objectives can still be attained. Certainly, then, if there is a desire and willingness, and if proper training can be achieved such that these patients receive appropriate and truly holistic care, the CCN is an appropriate model to which to add poly-chronic mental health patients. And, of course you, the reader, can and will configure your CCN to your needs and desires, inclusive of mental health patients or not.

Therefore, do not read into this missing element a disregard for, or lack of interest in, patients with mental health issues. To the contrary, these patients are as important as any to the solutions for the healthcare system writ large. In this book, we will cover the non-mental health patients in the population, knowing well that mental health issues are important and all-too prevalent. We'll save the mental health CCNs for future, more specific publications.

SUMMARY

The CCN is a new and exciting concept. Though not "rocket science," it elegantly combines resources, technologies, and operational models as has never been done before to develop a powerful solution to the most difficult problems healthcare faces today. By using some combination of its attributes and some blend of its technologies, health systems can begin to close the enormous gap between cost and budgets while maintaining/improving quality, accessibility, gratification, and capacity for the sickest of our patients.

16 Assessing the Community and the Patient Population

As we look to create a new care subsystem for some of the patients in our community, we must first select a population of patients to care for, understand their care needs, and develop "Care Strategies" to be implemented to achieve the Five Pillars (defined in Chapter 5). This will lead us to the proper selection and allocation of the resource pool which will provide both the care and the necessary physical plant and technologies. We will then dynamically match the demand from the community we intend to serve with the capacity we create.

SELECTING PATIENTS

Let's start this discussion with the poly-chronics. Chronic conditions are, of course, closely linked to high expenditure levels. More than 75% of high-cost beneficiaries (the 25% of Medicare beneficiaries with the highest costs) had one or more of seven major chronic conditions, according to the Congressional Budget Office.[*] "The elderly and disabled, who constituted around 25% of the Medicaid population, accounted for about 70% of Medicaid spending on services in 2003. People with disabilities accounted for 43% of Medicaid spending and the elderly for 26%. The remaining 75% of the Medicaid population, who were not elderly or disabled, accounted for only 30% of spending."[†] This of course is due in part to several socioeconomic factors of the patients typically enrolled in Medicaid programs.

The patients in your poly-chronic population will likely come from both private payors and Medicare/Medicaid/Dual Eligibles. It might be surprising to find that the majority of poly-chronics are currently insured in the private market (65%)[‡] and not through purely government programs (31%).[§] Poly-chronics are typically 45-years old and older, and may or may not end up in government insurance programs later in life, depending on contractual agreements with unions and employers which currently sponsor their care. Of course, the sponsors of Medicare/Medicaid, i.e.,

---

[*] Congressional Budget Office. 2005. High-cost Medicare beneficiaries. A CBO Paper. Washington, DC. May. http://www.cbo.gov/showdoc.cfm?index=6332&sequence=0. Accessed February 1, 2010.

[†] The Kaiser Foundation, Kaiser Commission on Medicaid and the Uninsured. 2005. Medicaid: A Primer. Washington, DC. July. Accessed February 3, 2010.

[‡] Agency for HealthCare Research and Quality. 2010. The Concentration and Persistence in the Level of Health Expenditures over Time: Estimates for the U.S. Population, 2008–2009. January.

[§] *Ibid.*

taxpayers, are or should be quite interested in the reduction of costs for the poly-chronics as so many are cared for via these programs. Of the three groups (privately insured, Medicare, and Medicaid), Medicaid patients are by far the most costly. This is why you might find your Payors (State, Federal, and private) to be ready partners in your cost-reduction efforts.

Of course, your CCN may not serve any poly-chronics and might instead serve poor elderly, single working mothers, or homeless. Selecting the patients in the community to be served by the CCN could be based on several criteria, including (but not limited to):

- Underserved populations such as rural communities or poor urban areas.
- Pregnant teens and/or poor single mothers.
- Specific disease states such as chronic obstructive pulmonary disease (COPD) or diabetes, or other disease states with the highest prevalence.
- Highest-cost patients or those using the most expensive resources. These might be "frequent fliers" in local EDs.
- Communities known for low health scores, regardless of the disease states and populations within those communities (in other words, a small-scale population health effort).
- Immigrant communities/populations with substandard health statistics.
- Church, denominational, or other religious affiliation.

I do not recommend any of these as being a better choice than the others. However, I would suggest that the bolder and grander your vision for the population you'll serve, the better. Keep in mind that you may have a number of smaller "sub-CCN's" within a larger community or CCN infrastructure. This might occur due to

- Ethnic population or language mix
- Neighborhood or community ties
- Religious or congregational bonds and commitments
- Location and proximity to services and other CCN patients
- Physician or group service areas
- Location and proximity of resources

In some iterations, a large CCN infrastructure (meaning, the management team and structure, total resource pool, technologies, etc.) might serve several small CCNs within small subpopulations. Each smaller CCN might be different in focus and need than its brethren, depending on the population each one serves. For instance, one congregation-based CCN might service shut-ins within their community, while an employer-based CCN might only service the diabetics in its employed ranks and their families. Both might fall under the care of a single, large physician group practice and CCN infrastructure, which would serve as the locus of care management and clinical guidance. Management of the CCN would likely come under the physician group practice, as would the clinical responsibility and oversight. Although this adds some complexity, it is important to remember that the CCN concept is designed to accommodate just such a scenario, as it is flexible and dynamic enough to allow for this degree of customization.

SIZE, SCOPE, AND SCALE OF YOUR CCN

Important to the short- and long-term successful operation of the CCN is its size. How many patients should, can, and will it serve? Will its focus be broad or narrow, and thus its size be either relatively large or small? While this is a critical question to be answered, we can only address it as an estimate for the moment as we don't yet know how large and complete the resource pool will be or how many patients will opt in over time. The available resource pool may only have the capacity to serve a small percentage of the desired population. However, it is important to estimate the size, or at least the desired size, of the population to be served at this stage so as to allow for a more targeted resource assessment later. This will also help you develop your financial justifications, investment requirements, implementation timeframes, and potential clinical and financial outcomes. As the resource pool is further defined (after or during this community assessment phase), you can use simulation to test for care gaps between the demand and the capacity, and dynamically match the two.

The size of the population to be served will depend on more than just the number of patients in the community. There are a number of other factors that will influence the size of the CCNs you'll want to establish and manage in your community. In addition to those listed below, in the next chapter we'll see how the resource pool itself might limit or expand the CCNs capacity.

- *Proximity of space and resources*: This is especially true of rural communities, wherein there may be limited available clinical space. The rural CCN may rely more heavily on in-home technologies and "remote visitation" for distant patient contact (assuming connectivity is not an issue), and churches and community centers for space. Space is important not only for clinical care but also for group meetings, clinical coaching and instructions, and periodic wellness and health clinics. Space, like the resources in the community, should be openly considered for its possibilities such that not only community centers and health clinics but also local churches and even large residences would be considered opportunities for clinical and meeting locations.

    Of course, the proximity of resources is important as well. Taking the care to the patient, rather than the other way around, becomes more difficult and time consuming in rural and dispersed populations. If applicable resources remain distant, the CCN will need to reflect this in its capacity and resource utilization assumptions.

- *Physician participation*: Not all physicians in a community need to participate. Only a few offices, either solo or within a large group practice, or even a single physician can support a CCNs infrastructure with expertise and connectivity rather than demanding that all physicians in a community adopt the required technologies and care models. This means that the strategic selection of physicians and offices can improve the chances of successful impacts on your population. (We'll cover physician selection in much greater detail in Chapter 17.)

- *Technology constraints*: The availability of technology will have an obvious impact on the size and scale of the CCN and its capacity to care for patients. For instance, the lack of Internet, broadband, and/or wireless communications might make home monitoring more difficult and tedious and electronic personal health records more difficult to manage and maintain. Lack of technology will not only inhibit the patient in their home, but could limit access of communal resources to Care Strategies and clinical updates from physicians and other clinicians. This lack of electronic access may make the cost of delivery of care higher, as resources will need more face-to-face time to achieve the same goals, driving up cost of transportation and driving down utilization. Thus, the capacity of the system may be constrained by the technology infrastructure available.

  Additionally, the relative effective integration of various EMRs and paper records in both urban and rural areas may hinder the use of the CCNs recommended technologies. Many practices are only grudgingly entering the twenty-first century of medical management. For these practices, the addition of new technologies might be an unwelcomed strain.

  In urban areas, it is not uncommon to see multiple EMRs in use in a single geographic area. Fortunately, the CCN is flexible enough to manage even this as SCN can help manage connectivity even in the face of the worst or most limited EMR implementation.

- *Patient population chosen*: Depending on the patient population you've decided to impact, there may be inherent resource and capacity limitations due to their specific care needs. Some disease states may require more or less intense care or assistance. The higher the degree of acuity, the more intense the care requirements, and therefore the more intense the resource requirements will be. More or fewer clinical resources may be required for a given CCN population. Thus, it would not be uncommon to see the CCNs goals and affected populations altered if stubborn resource constraints emerge.

  Furthermore, choosing several disease states or a larger population of true poly-chronics from the population will mean more intense care and resource requirements than would a single-disease-state CCN or a small CCN with relatively healthy but still somewhat needy patients. Although this will not be understood until the care strategies are devised and resources assessed and aligned, it is worthwhile to consider the disease states the CCN is to attack as you consider the scale and scope of the effort as this will drive your population health results.

  There are, of course, several tacks the CCN could take from here. The CCN might focus on a single chronic disease rather than the full spectrum. For instance, it might only focus on diabetes, or all chronic diseases except cancer. A limited scale and scope might be wise in the initial stages of development, when resources and managers are unsure of the ground upon which they are about to walk, or if the resource pool is just developing and needs to "test the waters." The CCN might also take on a small group of "test" patients, such as the members of a single church congregation, or current poly-chronic members of the local Y.

As you scale your effort, keep the short- and long-term risks, costs, and opportunities in mind.

- *Community acceptance*: While this might seem an odd metric, one that cannot be effectively measured if even grasped, it is nonetheless important to the capacity of the CCN. Some communities and community members may be more or less inclined to accept the assistance from a CCN and its resources. There may be some reticence to accept the assistance of non-clinical resources, or even use non-clinical facilities as part of the CCN engagement. Shoving the CCN concept into a community and the lives of the impacted patients would more than likely fail. Thus the acceptance of the CCN concept within a given community or subpopulation is vital to its short- and long-term viability and sustainability because, in order for the CCN to work optimally, patients and resources must be fully engaged and committed. This commitment should go beyond mere willingness to be part of the CCN to being truly "assimilated" into the CCN concepts and culture of care. It is not enough for patients to merely go along for the ride, or accept care while not engaging in their own health and well-being themselves. They must instead fully accept the ideas of Health Ownership, the resource pool's goals and aspirations, and the requirements for the improvement of their health and the health of the other CCN patients.

  "Assimilation" should therefore be defined as a much stronger alignment than participation or engagement: a far more intense commitment to the CCN care processes and strategies, goals and outcomes, and population health of the patients served. Without true assimilation, patients will see the CCN much like a person who believes in God but never worships, goes to church, or reads the scriptures. He will not, in the end, commit to the requirements and will drop out at the first sign of hassle, failure, or frustration. Assimilation is therefore a requirement for all patients in the CCN. (At least for those, of course, who are mentally capable of understanding and making such commitments. For those unable, the caregivers and resources must have a similar level of commitment such that they will take responsibility for those unable to truly grasp the concepts).

"ASSIMILATION PROPENSITY"

In my years of working with communities and population health, I have come to realize that some communities are far more interested than others in promoting health and wellness. Some of this depends on the resources in the community, often notably a local hospital or widely used clinic. It may also depend on other social factors, not the least of which is community attitudes towards the environment, pollution, smoking, and other potentially causal attributes of healthy living; religious fervency; and the strength of communal ties. The willingness of both resources and patients to participate in the CCN is what I call its "Assimilation Propensity."

As you look to the willingness of the patients and community resources to assimilate, there are several factors you'll want to consider.

- How readily is technology already used, both for patient care and generally?
  - Is there solid accessibility to and use of broadband, wireless, and the Internet?
  - To what degree are local schools "wired" and computerized?
  - To what extent do local physicians use EMRs? Does the local hospital use an HIE or large-scale EMR within its physician network (assuming there is one)?
- Is the community known for its "greenness," recycling programs, and anti-smoking ordinances?
- How strong are churches in the community? Is it known as a solidly Christian or religious community, or do churches struggle to fill the pews?
- How prevalent is the Christian and religious outreach to the poor and indigent?
- How well/poorly and where are the homeless and indigent cared for?
- How strong are any ethnic or community ties? Is there a subpopulation of specific ethnic, religious, or language groups that are strongly bound together? Is language an obstacle to the dissemination of healthcare provision for this group(s)?
- Are local employers engaged in the wellness and health of employees?
  - How do employers engage with employees?
  - What programs are currently in place to encourage exercise, good diets, healthy lifestyles, smoking cessation, etc.?
  - Do large local employers have any degree of local "social commitment," such as sponsorship of health and wellness for the community?
- To what extent have local schools promoted wellness?
- What are the local community organizations, and how does their participation in the local community take shape? Are they merely private, social, or politically focused clubs or do they have a true community service mission (e.g., the Rotary, Lions, and Crusaders)?
- What public facilities exist? Is there a Y or public health facility readily accessible to the public? To what degree are chronic disease management programs available?
- What is the degree of participation of local hospitals and clinics in wellness programs and healthy living? Does the local healthcare provider community participate, or do they sit idly by? One way to tell this is to examine the calendar of events coming from the local hospital and healthcare providers. If there is no calendar of wellness events, or if there is little or no outreach, you'll find it more difficult to use this resource to unify participation.
- How prevalent is "dependency" versus "independence" in the mindset of the population?
- How strong are ties to extended families? Do the elderly of your community become "wards of the state" or are they more likely to be cared for by local and familial resources?

Answers to these and other questions will help you determine the likelihood that your community, or at least critical parts of it, will assimilate into the CCN framework. If you are developing multiple CCNs within a larger community or population, I would suggest you develop a scoring mechanism, by which you can gauge your various subcommunities according to the factors that most influence their Assimilation Propensity. This might be as simple as a spreadsheet with rankings of the variables, giving you a relative scoring and a means to gauge the relative ease of the various implementations.

CULTURAL BARRIERS

For some patients, simply preparing the foundations for participation will result in new-found motivation and willpower to join in. As Care Circles are formed and assimilation is promoted, communal resources will become intimately involved in all factors of a patient's life. Thus, the CCNs holistic approach to care provision can and should include a focus on those factors that often inhibit patients from self-management, whether they be housing or tendencies toward depression.

Therefore, in many ways, the CCN's communal resources must take up the slack for at least some of the patients in the population and promote and support their assimilation. This must be accounted for in the resource-planning phases of the implementation, as those patients who are least likely to engage may be the population most in need of care improvements.

On the other hand, employers will likely find that assimilation is a bit easier, as employees will have more of a vested interest in care enhancements, if for no other reason than employer pressure. After all, the cost of healthcare increasingly impacts workers' wages and benefits. For this reason, employers may have the best chance to start a localized and focused CCN and gain assimilation. Importantly, if the employer's CCN goes well, and aids in helping to improve the Five Pillars for the affected employees, it is likely that the CCN concept will spread further into the community. In fact, it may behoove the employer to encourage the dissemination of a successful implementation, because the productivity and absenteeism of employees are often impacted by relatives (parents, husbands and wives, etc.) who are poly-chronics.

BARRIERS TO ASSIMILATION

Keep in mind that patients and resources may need to break barriers in order to participate and assimilate. The sickest patients are often the least likely to be engaged in their own care. After all, some are as sick as they are because they've consistently made poor life choices. There may also be some reluctance to use new technology. Social constraints or inhibitions may also prevent full participation, much less assimilation, for some patients. These can include lack of local family members; availability of transportation; consistent access to food, medication, and treatments; safe living conditions; and proper housing and utilities.

Furthermore, patients whose mental health has impacted or will impact their physical health may be less likely to voluntarily engage in the network. These patients may require additional and specialized mental health and social workers who can help in breaking down participation barriers. As we've already discussed, a "sub-CCN" may be required for these less able populations.

SUMMARY

Assessing the community and selecting the patient population is a critical part of the short- and long-term strategic planning of your program. Carefully consider at least the elements related above, and wisely lay out a detailed plan for the initiation and roll-out of your CCN. Without careful consideration of all facets and attributes of the community and the patients to be served, your CCN may fail to achieve expectations and disappoint both sponsors and patients.

17 Building the Communal Resource Pool

OVERVIEW

Note: The details and "regimen" in this chapter will probably seem like overkill for small CCNs because they simply will not require this level of "sophistication." Nonetheless, I encourage you to take the principles of the following sections and apply them to your efforts, however seemingly small. All of these concepts are important, and knowing them will help you as you grow your single-patient CCN to a larger systemic effort throughout your community.

As mentioned in Chapter 16, in order to build a pool of CCN resources, you must first understand the community you wish to serve. This includes the disease state(s) you want to address, the population of patients to be managed, the Assimilation Propensity of the communities to be served, and the variation in the current demand and system operations.

To recap, without deciding which diseases and patients you want to treat (if not all of them) you will not be able to determine what each resource should do, when they should do it, and how many resources will be required to complete the necessary care tasks. Furthermore, you will not be able to effectively assess the needs of your CCN, thus you won't be able to accurately quantify the demand, either now or in the future. So, without understanding the total population to be served, you cannot properly identify and allocate resources and tasks from the pool. It is therefore important to assess the community as a first (or concurrent first) step. Once this is completed, you can move on to assessing and quantifying the possible available resources as a next step.

Commonly when we think of healthcare resources, we think of in terms of clinical resources. But this has traditionally caused us to miss opportunities in community-based organizations and denizens we wouldn't normally consider. Indeed, other efforts in PHM have shown a lack of clarity and vision around the resources that are and could be available within any given community. For example, the "Strategic Framework" for patients with multiple chronic conditions (herein "poly-chronics"), published by the U.S. Department of Health and Human Services, spells out generalities but offers few details as to the resources required to change the current care systems.[*] Though these and other publications offer similar concepts, none that I have encountered have offered the specificity and detail needed and that you see herein. Therefore, this chapter will assist you in broadening your horizons as

---

[*] U.S. Department of Health and Human Services. 2010. Multiple chronic conditions: A strategic framework: Optimum health and quality of life for individuals with multiple chronic conditions. December.

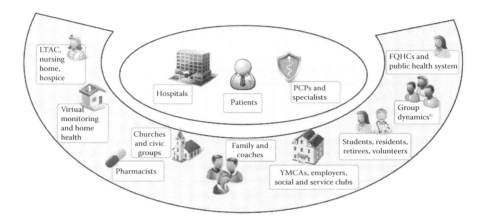

FIGURE 17.1   Sample CCN resource pool.

to what could be considered a "healthcare resource." See Figure 17.1 for a refresher of a sample of the CCN resource pool.

A key strategy for the CCN is to remember that not all resources will need to have letters behind their names (e.g., MD or RN). So rather than asking, "Is this clinical resource capable of providing the necessary care?" we should be asking, "What can this potential resource contribute to the overall health and well-being of the community of patients we want to serve?" This requires us to become more creative in the use of available resources. So rather than asking "Why would this person or group want to help?" or "Is this person qualified to help?" the better questions are "Why wouldn't they help?" and "How could they help?" and "What will cause them to be completely committed to helping?" This will help change your perspectives on the types and numbers of resources available in your communities.

Indeed, there are likely a number of readily available communal resources in plain sight. For instance, many small communities have firefighters who aren't always heavily utilized. Ditto for ambulance and EMS services and other similar resources with essential clinical knowledge. Have you considered retired healthcare workers, or local businesses with critical management and engineering talent? As you delve deeply into your communities, you may find there is a wealth of available resources awaiting an opportunity to make a significant difference in the lives and well-being of others, if only effectively directed, coordinated, and motivated. Indeed, volunteers may abound if properly motivated and incented to assist.

There may also be existing, successful programs through local hospitals, Y's, and health agencies designed to engage the community in healthier eating, exercise, and other beneficial activities. In rural communities, you may not find organized efforts, yet there may be a general awareness of the need for healthier living that may in turn lead to opportunities to engage patients through a variety of local civic groups and religious affiliations. Such information will not only help guide you to existing infrastructure and volunteers who might assist your efforts, but also assist you in understanding the degree of effort required to initiate and sustain a CCN. A disjointed and lackluster community with little guidance or concern for population health will likely find greater difficulty implementing a CCN (though such communities may be the most in need of its attributes and outcomes). In contrast, a community engaged and aware of population health issues may be quite willing to engage in low-cost, highly effective ways to care for patients.

RESOURCE AND CAPACITY VARIANCE

Before we dive into resource availability, we need to keep in mind that capacity, just like demand, is variable in most cases. Furthermore, resource availability and capacity is influenced by the systems in which they work. The actual capacity of a resource to complete a given task or set of tasks is dependent on a number of factors, all of which can constrain or expand the resource's capacity for workload. These include the variance in the number of tasks required, as shown in the previous chapter, as well as the interdependencies between tasks.

There are other ways in which the capacity of resources might be altered. These include

- Technologies that might increase or decrease a process (a.k.a takt) time
- Travel distances between patient homes
- Number of resources deployed to a specific series of tasks (e.g., care teams)
- Education, familiarity, and experience with the task
- Resource-specific attributes, such as age, health and strength, mental capacity, etc

All these factors mean that the average is once again a bad number to use when it comes to understanding resources and their capacity to care for patients. Failure to account for the cumulative impact of the variance in resource capacity will inevitably yield incorrect assumptions about the capacity of the entire system. Or, it will yield a recommended resource pool, that is, at least to some degree, incapable of caring for the population in question.

All this is said to restate the obvious: as you begin to consider resource allocations, especially the number of resources and the task load they are to take on, understand that variability can and likely will have a tremendous impact on their productivity and workload. This should not only be accounted for in your resource estimates, but also drilled into the brains of the resources used. As it is such a critical concept for the capacity of the CCN, all resources should have a thorough and complete understanding of the concept and its meaning.

Again, your local IE/ME can aid you with this and other similar analysis and planning.

Small CCN Notes: The smaller your CCN iteration, the less you'll need to concern yourself with variation in capacity, since you may only have one or a few resources to coordinate. Keep variation in mind as you lay out tasks for each resource in your CCN, however, as it may come into play at some point.

RESOURCE OPTIONS

Now you should be fully prepared to begin looking at resource options in your community. As you assess the available resources, consider at least the following:

- *Churches*: Already, congregations in the southeastern United States are banding together with local hospitals to help with patient care. Methodist Le Bonheur of Memphis, TN has created a Congregational Health Network to assist patients with transitions of care, disease management, and wellness. As another example, Inova Health of Virginia has created its own Congregational Health Partnership with similar aims and ambitions. Also, the African Methodist Episcopal (AME) church, the largest U.S. denomination of Christian blacks, and other traditionally black churches have a growing commitment to health as seen through their many health ministries. Churches are often ready-made for such assistance, as their members share a bond and are committed to one another through faith and friendship.
- *Pharmacies*: Hospital and local community pharmacies can lend a valuable hand in managing complex patient care through medication review and reconciliation. Even large retail chains such as CVS and Rite-Aid are committed to their communities and may be willing to commit resources. Pharmacists are a critical though constrained resource for the CCN, as they will aid in ensuring medication compliance and duplication avoidance. As they are constrained, like other clinical resources, wise and effective use of their time and attention is required. Keep this in mind as you lay out your swimlanes and task assignments, so as to avoid overload. Also, try using Pharmacy Techs and other similarly educated resources where available.
- *Service and civic groups*: These might include Rotary, Kiwanis, Lions, Knights of Columbus, etc. As some of these organizations struggle for purpose in an age of electronic communication and the breakdown of social structures, you may find they are ready to serve their communities in new ways.
- *Meals on Wheels*: MOW often has very regular and friendly contact with patients. Why not have them check on a few, specific clinical metrics as well, especially if the patient has some automated or easy-to-use virtual monitoring devices in their home?
- *Y's (aka YMCA's)*: Y's are already doing a great deal of work in helping communities get and stay healthy. This is particularly true of the elderly and youth populations. Y's are a good communal resource, already paid, and largely readily available in urban areas. Indeed, it is said that 80% of the U.S. population lives within three miles of a Y!
- *Hospital volunteers*: By tapping an existing group of committed volunteers, you may find additional resources come forth as the CCN grows in popularity. Hospital volunteers are often recent and healthy retirees, sometimes retired healthcare workers themselves. With their commitment to the community and the local healthcare system, it would be reasonable to assume that they would be quick to participate.

- *Retired or semiretired healthcare workers*: In many communities, retired healthcare workers are available for local volunteer work, including blood drives and education fairs. Again, as knowledgeable and committed resources, these retirees could serve as a tremendous addition to the existing, "full time" clinical capacity.
- *Community colleges and other schools*: Often a ready source of ambitious passion, students may be looking for a way to make an impact on the community while they study for a career. This would be particularly true of students working toward health-related careers and degrees.
- *Residency programs*: These would include pharmacy, nursing, physician, and others. Often clinical resources in training seek out opportunities to get involved in patient care, and could be readily used to augment clinical and non-clinical task allocations.
- *Existing fire, rescue, and police*: As mentioned above, many resources are relatively underutilized, though their presence is felt when needed. These resources are sometimes tapped to go to homes where elderly have minor issues (falls, etc.). These could turn into opportunities to help manage care and ensure safe home environments for home-bound patients.
- *Local business*: You will likely find that local businesses struggle in isolation with employee healthcare and the care of employees' extended families. Even a healthy, young group of workers has parents and relatives who require them to take hours and days off for healthcare-related reasons. Getting these issues under control is of great importance, particularly for small businesses with chronically ill employees and relatives. You may find willing assistance from small local businesses, even if it is only in the form of tech support!
- *Promontores*: These culturally specific resources in the Hispanic community have long been known to tie their communities to the healthcare (and other difficult-to-navigate) systems. Where there is a large Hispanic population, you will often find allies in these critical resources and their links within that community.
- *Industrial (and management) engineers*: One of the key resources I've already mentioned is an Industrial Engineer who can aid in the analysis, modeling, and set-up of the CCN. Engineers of all stripes can be found in small and large companies and even state and local government offices. Look for these as potential sources of assistance, especially for larger employers who might be willing to set up and support their own employee's CCN.
- *Clinics and FQHCs*: These will be mentioned later as a space resource, but deserve mention here as a potential pool of clinical resources. If properly tied to the CCN, clinical resources might aid in monitoring patients for medication compliance. Local "Doc in a Box" employees may be willing to see CCN patients to check key vital signs, weight, etc., on a volunteer or low-cost basis. They will typically have an IT infrastructure that will support these efforts.
- *Boys and girls clubs*: What better way to reach underprivileged kids than through the programs they rely upon! Special programs might be established

to reach children here and elsewhere as their parents are reached through other communal resources.

• *Other*: Of course, every community is different. Yours may have a nursing program at a nearby college or a tightly bound ethnic population that can lend assistance. It will not be uncommon to see multiple CCNs in a geographic zone, based on a "subcommunity" such as a large congregation or ethnic group, all tied to the same Chronicist.

As the scope, scale, and clinical challenge(s) of the CCN have now been decided and the potential resources mapped, you can move on to resource selection and/or detailed predictive analysis on population health. The latter is likely unnecessary for most CCNs, but could be a potential benefit when specific populations are targeted and/or are at risk.

Small CCN Notes: Of course, your smaller CCN may have only one of the aforementioned resources, or may need only access to one in order to achieve your patient's goals. A group of single working mothers may only need help from a local church for Christian mentoring and aid with obesity and diet management. Or, an elderly woman living alone may only need Meals on Wheels and someone to come by to ensure she is taking her meds and getting to the doctor for appointments. Indeed, your smaller CCN may have an easier time lining up resources, as smaller iterations demand less of a community organization's time and resources.

RESOURCE SELECTION

This should be a natural progression from the previous tasks. Based on the work identified in the swimlane maps and/or simulation, you should have a solid understanding of the task requirements and the options for resources. Now, all that is required is selecting the resources from the potential pool that you have now constructed. This may sound easy, yet there may still be several stumbling blocks in the way.

• Be sure to interview all the potential resources, and ensure that they understand the distinct differences between being part of the CCN and true assimilation. Ensure that they will have the same passion for the community's health as the CCN leaders, and that they understand both the infrastructure and the learning requirements. You will likely find that there will be people within cooperative organizations who either cannot or will not make the necessary commitments to the program to make it successful. These people will obviously need to be culled from the ranks. Though they may be convinced later, be sure that negative attitudes are not allowed to infect the more willing members.

• Be sure to keep the individual patients' interests in mind, and not just that of the CCN. Therefore, do not ignore potential resources which might only serve a very small number of patients, such as members of a small church congregation, or members of a single patient's family. These may be the best motivators yet they may only be able to touch a few lives in their work. These can be especially important for those non-chronically ill patients who only need support for diet and exercise regimens.

- Don't lose your creativity as you discover gaps and new opportunities. As you seek out resources, you might become myopic in your resource selection. Don't!! You'll need to constantly seek out new resources wherever they might present themselves.
- Don't assume all resources are created equal. Constantly analyze each resource's potential variance, as it is easy to assume that all resources from a given group (e.g., Y, church, or community service organization) are equally committed to the cause. Thus …
- Don't hesitate to cull resources, now and in the future, if their commitment, service quality, or capabilities fall short of expectations. I am not suggesting that there won't be issues with ongoing motivation, etc., nor that resources be "voted off the island" immediately upon any lapse. I am, however, suggesting that the importance of the goals and objectives of the CCN demand a certain level and quality of resource, and that this must be maintained at all times. Failure is not an option, regardless of the cause.

Small CCN Notes: Selecting resources for the CCN is important no matter if there are one or one hundred. If you, as the reader, are not personally involved in the life of the patients in the CCN, then it is up to the leadership of the CCN (in whatever form that takes) to ensure that CCN resources are properly selected, aligned, and managed. This could be as simple as a discussion with a local pastor or Civic Club in the selection of potential resource candidates. It is always a good idea to perform background checks on unknown individuals not tied and well-known to local organizations.

SELECTING PHYSICIANS

Physicians are perhaps the most critical component of a CCN, yet they are also the most constrained and the least likely to want to take on additional responsibilities, tasks, risk, and communications. Furthermore, as I've stated earlier, physicians are the number one constraint to capacity optimization in hospitals, clinics, and the system writ large. So, they will likely resist these efforts initially. While there may be solid rationale behind the reluctance to use non-clinical and external communal resources in the management of patient care, remember that the CCN was developed in part to support physicians and their efforts to provide the best care and service possible. Thus, once they hear of the advantages of the program and the benefits that will fall directly and quickly to them, physicians are quite likely to sign up.

Importantly, the CCN can be constructed in such a way as to support many physicians whose patients are primarily poly-chronics via a single communal resource pool. Thus, the issue of finding a single or a few physicians to act as "Chronicists" is lessened or eliminated. Lastly, physicians at the helm of the CCN needn't be masters of the entire domain. They only need to be cooperative members of the resource pool, which, in large-scale implementations, will be managed by the CCN Manager.

Therefore, in selecting the physicians for the CCNs, there are several keys to consider

- *Propensity to cooperate*: How willing are the physicians to allow a broader pool of care resources from the CCN to assist in the care of their patients?
- *Propensity to support*: How willing are they to *support the CCN resources?* This is a very important consideration, as *using and/or controlling* the CCN's resource pool is NOT the same as *supporting and enabling it*. The latter requires an entirely different mentality, personality, and approach. The former is not desired, and should be avoided at all cost.
- *Current poly-chronic population*: Some PCPs already run "chronic disease practices" by virtue of their location, patient population, or preferences. These should be tapped, if possible, as they may benefit most from the CCN's implementation.
- *Willingness to share, grow, and learn*: One of the key attributes of the CCN, called for in the HHS document on the "Strategic Framework" for poly-chronic management, is the enablement of a learning network to continue to expand the knowledge base of care providers. This will require a great deal of sharing, learning, and, to a certain extent, humility. Some of this will come naturally to some, not at all to others. An aversion to the admission of failure has sadly been built into our healthcare system by malpractice litigation and a free-roaming and politically connected trial-lawyers association. This makes finger-pointing infinitely easier and much less risky, making for a difficult work environment that unfortunately lessens cooperation and trust. Nonetheless, physicians must be willing to share, grow, and learn from both successes and failures if the body of general poly-chronic care is to expand.
- *Passion for change and new ideas*: There are some, perhaps many, in your community of physicians who not only accept change but seek and embrace it. These are not typical, mind you, but they will be important for your implementation efforts. Finding those who challenge the status quo and make new ideas the hallmark of their practices is thankfully not difficult. They tend to stand out and make themselves known, and should be corralled into the network to the extent possible and necessary.
- *Propensity to accept new technology*: Some see technology as a savior, others as a detriment to their practices and a waste of resources. While the latter are not necessarily totally incorrect, the judicious use of technology in the CCN is a requirement for its success. Thus, only physicians willing to take on and use the available technologies should apply.

Many PCPs will have incentives to participate in the CCN, especially if they are willing to give up their "difficult" patients for others who also might be easier and more readily cared for. This would mean a more profitable practice while keeping the overall control of their patients.

PCPs within large group practices may have added motivation to "release" patients into the care of the group's own CCN as the practice would not lose the patient revenue or long-term relationship. For this scenario, group practices may benefit from the concentration of patients into the care of a few, select Chronicists while others in the practice are free to add less resource-intense patients to their rosters. Similarly, some specialty group practices may find that a limited number of physicians can cover the poly-chronics of the selected community without disrupting the flow and care of other patients, allowing colleagues to add new patients and create non-poly-chronic CCNs as needed.

Lastly, the incentive programs put in place for both PCPs and specialists may entice some to participate who otherwise might have seen the CCN as too difficult or cumbersome to deal with.

Selecting physicians will therefore depend on a number of factors, not the least of which are the propensities and attributes listed above. Above all, remember to screen each one for passion and enthusiasm for the new business models of the future, and select only those physicians who will fully support the goals and objectives on the network.

Small CCN Notes: Needless to say, physicians are an important part of most iterations of the CCN. However, in small CCNs they needn't be intimately involved. They might simply be a resource for clinical information as needed, or a place to call when care needs of patients change. Physicians and their offices may want to be involved in small CCNs if their patients are engaged. However, the level of integration depends on the needs of the patients, their goals, and the requirements for clinical assistance.

So, a small ethnic group trying to manage weight and diet may require no physician involvement, unless and until drug or surgical therapy becomes necessary. However, a single elderly man living alone may need the involvement and interaction of his physician if clinical conditions are being continually monitored.

CREATING A CARE CIRCLE TEAM

If multiple resources are required for a given patient, it is vital for the CCN's functionality and long-term viability that a team environment be created. With this, there is risk that resources will drop or neglect their responsibilities, infighting and competition between resources will emerge, and a few resources will "take over" the entire system. To prevent this, it is imperative that the CCN be set up and managed as a communal, team approach to care delivery. No one resource should have the power or the desire to take over the system, nor should resources feel they are being dictated to, used, or manipulated by the CCN Managers and physicians. All must attain and retain a sense of a communal, "it's not about me" shared passion for the work being done. Neither physicians nor any other resource should assume their roles yield a fiefdom to be ruled.

However, neither should resources presume anything other than personal responsibility and accountability for their tasks. As the level of trust given can be enormous, the level of accountability should also be high. Governance structures are meant to ease the burden of the management of tasks, not hound resources into doing what they have volunteered to do. Resources should be self-motivated and supportive, while supporting others in the CCN who are likewise motivated to help both the patients and other CCN resources.

This team environment is one reason why the Core Action Values mentioned in the chapter by Joe Tye are so important. Joe Tye's approach promotes a true cooperative and passionate team work environment, and should be used to help develop the kind of camaraderie common mostly to military units and sports teams.

The CCN must therefore create a team environment of disparate resources while also creating a system of accountability, responsibility, and governance. Much like a team of remote programmers, all working on the same software from different areas of the world yet with a common goal, the CCN must utilize a wealth of resources while managing, motivating, and monitoring all simultaneously. This is even harder than it may sound, which is why the resource selection process is so critical to the long-term success of the program.

USING THE CARE STRATEGIES

If you used a swimlane or similar mapping approach to your community's CCN care requirements, you now have a detailed understanding of the "what, where, when, how, and how often" of your Care Strategies. What you need now is the "who." As you will likely have options as to the resources you choose for each task (assuming both clinical and non-clinical task assignments), it is wise to begin the resource assessment process by looking broadly within your community for resources to complete the tasks laid out in your CCN's Care Strategies.

For each task, you should have an understanding of some of the attributes of the resources to be used. These will include minimal clinical requirements (e.g., RN, LPN, etc.), task groups into which the tasks will commonly be placed, time and travel requirements for each task and task grouping, number of tasks to be performed in a given period, etc. Don't forget to include patient preferences. These qualifiers will help you gauge the requirements of each task and task grouping, into which you can plug the appropriate resource.

If necessary, there may be an additional step if you feel you have not thoroughly pondered the resource possibilities, or if new tasks arise during the life of the CCN. Either now, or after you've assessed your communal resources for options, go back to the swimlane maps and brainstorm ideas for possible resource options. Start asking "What if?" questions about the tasks and resources in your swimlanes, such as

- Could that particular home visit be handled via an interactive web platform and distance monitoring? Could a process be accomplished by a mobile LPN, or does it need to be performed in an office environment?
- Can a nurse pass off that task group to a non-clinical resource if follow-up is direct and specific enough?
- Could that patient's goals (e.g., diet and obesity management) be attained through the use of group sessions and interactions, rather than individual visits from CCN resources?
- Might there be a technology solution for this task? If so, does it eliminate or assist in the task, or merely automate inefficiency? How much would the technology cost and is there a definitive benefit?
- Might this task group be better managed via group meetings?

Asking these questions will then drive you to the next questions, including "What non-clinical or clinical resource would best handle those tasks?" or "If a nurse is too expensive to use for that, what other clinical resource has similar qualifications, enough to manage that specific task?" or "Assuming physician interaction and sign-off of this step, does a nurse have to perform it or could a trained non-clinical resource manage it just as effectively and less expensively?"

Now that we have the framework for a resource search, let's look for options within our community.

PERSONALIZING THE RESOURCE POOL

As explained below, each patient may require (or sometimes demand) a slightly different mix of resources. Without knowing which resources can do which tasks, or the impact of adding the personalization into the overall system, it may be difficult, if not impossible, to gauge the CCN's functionality within the personalized system. Furthermore, as you seek to assign different resource mixes to individual patients, based on their preferences or other requirements, you may find that your total system and individual resource capacity becomes an unknown. Furthermore, keeping up with task assignments, accountability, and other management duties might become very difficult and largely chaotic. This can be helped by the use of simulation and/or a deep understanding of the capacity of each resource type in the pool you are managing.

To avoid potential issues, you can analyze the personalization of the resource pool by completing the following steps:

1. Develop a "baseline" resource pool for the patient types in the population you've chosen to serve, based on the community analysis of the previous chapter. This baseline pool is a standardized resource allocation, developed using either a simulation model or other simpler means and based on the community's available resources, which is sufficient to care for the patients in the CCN. Let's say, for the sake of this discussion that it includes one nurse, two LPNs, three church members, and two EMTs.

   Small CCN Notes: Of course, in a small iteration of a CCN, you won't need this degree of sophistication. Your "baseline" might be one volunteer acting to help one or a few patients. The customization of the resource pool outlined below is therefore simply a matter of working with your patient(s) and determining the best approach to managing their goals.

2. Examine variances. Let's take the following as an example. After discussions with the patients in the CCN, you discover that one patient is particularly opposed to the use of church members in their care and refuses to allow the church volunteers into her home. You would then look to the other resources to see which might be able to effectively, and hopefully for the same cost, take on the volunteer's tasks *for only that patient.* Let's assume that the church volunteers would normally conduct one task group per week for this patient, which now must be done by another resource. Let's assume

that the EMTs agree to split the task group between them, increasing their workloads by two task groups per month. A simulation model will allow you to reallocate the specific tasks for a specific patient in the population, or you can use simple math to increase the workload for the EMTs and decrease the workload for the volunteers by four task groups per month. Either way, the output of the analysis would depict the new time requirements for all resources in the resource pool, including the new demand for EMTs in the community. It should also depict the new additional capacity for the church volunteers, which might lead to another task allocation that would use the newly available time.

As another example, let's assume that one patient has a recently discovered issue with depression. This might require the CCN Manager to seek out a new mental health resource to be part of the resource pool, even if for only this patient. Failure to account for this patient as an "outlier within the outliers" may lead to poor outcomes, additional strain on untrained resources, and potential capacity variance that might impact other patients in the CCN.

As a final example, some patients will take readily to a group environment like a Y, while others will demand in-home care and more personalized attention. Thus, knowing the individual patients in your CCN population is critical to both the successful use of community resources and the overall clinical outcomes of the CCN. Much of this information comes from the patients' physicians, Primes, and other connected communal resources.

3. Push back as necessary. Develop variance from the CCN baseline resource pool for each patient's requirements while pushing back as necessary on unreasonable or impossible requests. So, for instance, let's assume that a patient demands that only a physician see them for any medical intervention, and that no other resource type will do. This would, of course, not match the goals and objectives of the CCN and thus would have to be addressed through patient education and assimilation rather than resource and task allocation.

Therefore, a manageable variation should be allowed, such that patients have legitimate choices without creating resource allocation issues. However, variance in the clinical roles should be avoided. For instance, physicians will necessarily be at the top of the care system in most cases, so as to avoid confusion over care strategy development and implementation. However, non-clinical task allocation can be more loosely assigned, especially where patient goals are limited to diet and exercise regimens.

Importantly, there is a difference between varying who performs the tasks and varying the tasks themselves. Tasks should not vary, no matter which resource is used. For instance, the Primes might vary. One patient's Prime might be a church member, another's a social worker. In either case, the tasks of each resource classification (in this case the Prime) should be identical. Too much variation in the tasks within a CCN for a specific population will lead to a less predictable outcome. Thus the CCN construct cannot and should not allow for customization to overtake the need for consistency in quality, outcomes, and reliability. Indeed, one can make one's system too customized, cause it to lose effectiveness and reliability and lean more towards chaos than efficiency.

4. Constantly examine the capacity to care. With the new, total task allocation you can now test the resource pool's new capacity, looking for significant gaps or excess in resource capacity. "What if?" scenarios with the model will then help you to match the capacity of the resources and care system with the personalized demand patterns of the patient population.

Fortunately, simulation, swimlane maps, and/or even simple math can work for the kind of capacity optimization analysis needed to ensure that quality care is provided on a personalized basis to each patient, depending on their needs, desires, and requirements. Keep in mind that the baseline resource pool should be based on physician guidance, the patients in the population, as well as the resources available in the pool. Great degrees of variance should be avoided, as any degree of variance away from the standard inherently increases the complexity of the care system and the risk that tasks may fail to be completed.

RESOURCE ASSIMILATION

As we saw in the previous chapter, attitudes and motivation can have a tremendous impact on the expected outcomes of the CCN. If patients refuse to comply with Care Strategies, you may find that no volume or intensity of services will assist in moving their metrics. In that chapter, I suggested several considerations for evaluating the community's "Assimilation Propensity." As part of this analysis, you will want to consider the community's commitment to and attitude towards population health.

Resources, like patients, will need to be "Assimilated." We have already defined "Assimilation" as a much stronger and far more intense commitment to the CCN care processes and strategies, goals and outcomes, and population health of the patients and community served. Once selected, assimilating the resources of the CCN will require education on the concepts, principles, goals, and objectives of the CCN. Assimilation will require a new standard of commitment to quality, excellence, and service rarely attained heretofore in our society. These resources must be committed at a deep and intrinsic level, willing to do what is necessary to see the success of the CCN and the betterment of their patients and their community. Not all resources will muster this level of commitment, of course.

Furthermore, do not be surprised if the initial excitement wanes over time, as frustrations, time commitments, personal interests and circumstances, and other life changes take precedence over the focus on patients. Therefore, do not be surprised by an ebb and flow of resources into and out of the service of the CCN and the community. What might seem like a frustrating "revolving door" of short-term resources is actually a common, healthy occurrence in volunteer organizations. Resources, especially those who volunteer their time, are prone to moving in and out of interest and commitment over time. This constant change is one reason the management infrastructure suggested herein is so critical to the overall sustainability of the CCN in your community. However, this is not to imply that assimilation into the CCN is not required. Even short-term resources who pledge their time during specific and limited periods of their lives or the lives of those they are committed to care for must be assimilated into the "culture" of the CCN and its principles. Without an infrastructure much like the one recommended herein, your CCN risks become a flash in a disposable pan.

Resource assimilation is therefore based on a few key elements, all of which must be in place in order for the CCN to be sustainable in the long-term. These are detailed in the pages to follow.

RESOURCES FOR THE RESOURCES

In addition to the bodies of knowledge already mentioned, there is a wealth of clinical information available to both the patients and the resources of the CCN. This includes government-sponsored agencies and organizations that continuously crank out new research and perspectives, such as the Center for Disease Control and the Department of Health and Human Services. There are myriad state and local government agencies involved in care enhancement, management, and research. University-based research programs study everything from behavioral sciences to new medications for stubborn chronic conditions. Volunteer organizations, such as the National Cancer Society or the Alzheimer's Institute, are excellent sources of information. All this could be valuable to your local CCN resources and patients. Coordinating this information into a meaningful and helpful format for non-clinical resources will be, in part, the role of the CCN Management Team, CCN resources, the PCPs and Chronicists, and other clinicians. This information can be disseminated through the Social/Clinical Networking Platform or other appropriate means.

There should be no limit to the learning opportunities available to CCN resources, whether professional clinicians or community volunteers. The better educated the resources are about the conditions, diseases and patients they treat, the better and more effective the CCN will be. It is therefore recommended that the CCN Management Team develop a regular and accountable method for disseminating important care information to the CCN resources, such that the knowledge base is fully utilized.

On the flip-side, the CCN can and should be the source of ongoing "research" into patient care. Much is still unknown about the care patterns and systems necessary to yield the best possible clinical and wellness outcomes for our populations. It is not unreasonable to think, therefore, that your CCN would collaborate with others around the country to develop new strategies and approaches based on the successes and advances you encounter. Because the technologies envisioned are powerful yet flexible, it should be possible to extend them well beyond your local communities to create broad "networks of networks," through which CCNs can collaborate, share, and exchange. To this end, as is possible with your existing technology, I recommend that clinical resources in your CCN connect with the best and brightest of clinicians across the country to aid them in advancing the state-of-the-art in care delivery, medication management, and outcomes optimization. This is possible through either the Health Information Exchange (HIE) platform, services and connective technologies provided by large health systems such as Mayo or the Cleveland Clinic, and/or other Clinical Networking systems. I also recommend that your patients and their families utilize the SCN systems to better disseminate ideas and strategies as well as to encourage mutual support and friendship among people with similar healthcare interests.

RESOURCE EDUCATION FOR ASSIMILATION

Resources in the community must be educated on the following topics:

- CCN concept and the reason for its existence
- Shared and personal responsibility on the part of both patients and resources
- "It's not about me!" mentality as a requirement to service
- Their part of the system as an integral part of the greater whole

Additionally, they'll need to be trained in the following areas for their roles in the CCN:

- Technology education, such as the SCN and any virtual monitoring equipment they would deal with
- Understanding the impact of variability and interdependencies with other resources in the care continuum
- Care Strategies (conceptually)
- Organizational structure of the CCN, and the chain of reporting and responsibility
- Any aspects of incentives built into the CCN
- Essential responsibilities, duties, and tasks required
- How to deal with this patient population

And lastly, they'll need to be supported with necessary clinical information and task education, as well as with constantly updated patient and disease management education. This would include

- Individual Care Strategies (specific to their roles in the CCNs)
- Changes in clinical protocols, instructions, or patient care guidelines
- Specific tasks relevant to their patients/populations

This shouldn't seem onerous or frightening to either resources or those who will conduct this training. Indeed, most if not all of this training is helpful if not essential to anyone who might want to simply better care for a loved one, friend, or family member. These topics are not difficult to teach, and should be seen as opportunities to advance population health within the communities via the resources in the pool.

Furthermore, resources should see this as an opportunity to learn how to better serve the community as well as their own families and friends. As the education will be free for the taking (and indeed required as part of participation) it should be seen as a way to expand one's value in the community while learning something new about healthier living. In the end, it all promotes Health Ownership!

Small CCN Notes: Assimilation and education are largely unnecessary in small CCNs unless they are part of a larger system of CCNs. For instance, your CCN for a small group of overweight women living in a large apartment complex may work alone or as part of a hospital-based network of CCNs that provide management and training assistance. Once you graduate to multiple resources, whether caring for one patient or a few or many, assimilation and education become important since they will need to fully understand the overall goals and strategies of the larger CCN, and be familiar with its management objectives and available infrastructure.

SETTING UP EDUCATIONAL PROGRAMS

Once the patient population and the resource pool are chosen, the heavy lifting of coordination and education begins in earnest. For this, there are a number of steps which each resource must go through, and in which the CCN Management Team must be intimately involved. Under ideal circumstances, a CCN Trainer will be used to provide most if not all of the necessary training. This resource is one of only two recommended as full time for larger iterations of the CCN (or PCDN). However, note that each element listed below has an associated parenthetical training resource, which includes other members of the CCN Management Team. These resources can be used as Trainers if there is no full-time Trainer, or if the Trainer's role is limited by scope, task constraints, or knowledge. Also note that training resources are not set in stone, and can be flexible except where clinical resources are required. Therefore, as long as you provide at least the following elements in some way, the resources you use will be up to you.

The following are the training elements important to a successful CCN:

- *CCN concepts and infrastructure (CCN Manager)*: The CCN will be explained, its goals and objectives will be clearly defined and quantified for all participants. This is critical to the assimilation so necessary for the long-term success of the network.
- *Resource review and explanation (CCN Manager)*: An overview of all the resources in the pool and the infrastructure that will support the Care Strategies the resources will implement.
- *Resource roles and responsibilities (PCD Manager)*: Each resource must thoroughly understand his role in the Care Strategy, as it is related to the other resources, tasks, and outcomes. Thus training on the various roles and responsibilities is critical to an understanding of the system.
- *Essentials of processes and systems (CCN Manager or IE)*: This training, again for all resources in the CCN, includes simple explanations of the working of systems, the impacts of variability and interdependencies, and the roles of each resource within the broader Care Strategies of the CCN. You will likely be able to find simple explanations of these concepts, some of which were explained in a separate publication by this same author.
- *Technology (CCN IT or technology resources such as vendor reps, etc.)*: Obviously, to use the CCN's technology, training must accompany any resource use. This training should include hands-on experience and real-life

usage scenarios in order to prevent technology from becoming an inhibitor of the network's implementation.

- *Risks and legalities (CCN Manager, or local volunteer legal counsel)*: Clearly, there are some limited risks to the CCN and its sponsors if sentinel events happen specifically due to the care provided by the CCN resources. This is highly unlikely, even nearly impossible, given the infrastructure and the specificity of the task assignments. Nonetheless, each resource must thoroughly understand not only her role in the care processes but what *not* to do as well. Overstepping boundaries is a serious but altogether preventable error if proper training and certifications are provided.
- *Clinically relevant information (PCP, Chronicist, or clinical equivalent)*: This information would likely be limited to those directly involved in the clinical care of the poly-chronics, but might include the non-clinical but "clinically curious." Indeed, it might include all the resources should the CCN Management Team decide that clinical understanding by all is important to attaining the goals and objectives of the network. This training would include the specifics of the Care Strategies, the patient flow, clinical and non-clinical tasks, and goals of the patient's care. Although this might be routinely revisited and personalized for a particular patient, an essential "base" understanding by all is critical to the synergies of the effort and the assimilation process.
- *Core Action Values (Certified Values Coach)*: Based on the aforementioned Joe Tye's work, these Core Action Values will help your resources in their roles in the CCN as well as in their day-to-day lives. These will easily and readily match to values taught in most local Christian churches.

Other training will be ongoing, and there may be elements within your CCN that require additional special consideration. These might include

- *Religious considerations*: This might include specific requirements for working with patients of religions different from those of the volunteers. Such training would include how to speak with patients, what questions and issues are considered taboo, restrictions on male–female interactions, dietary requirements, etc.
- *Dependencies and mental health*: Drug and alcohol dependency, depression, and other mental health issues are not uncommon among the poly-chronic population. Therefore, it will be common for resources to encounter these conditions as they deal with and care for their patients. Special considerations for language and verbiage, signs and indicators of conditions, etc., will be important for resources to know well, as they may develop relationships that will allow influence over behavior. Resources must be trained to take care not to overstep their bounds and inadvertently cause harm while trying to do good. This training should be taught by professionals knowledgeable in the science of substance abuse and mental health treatments. Indeed, "sub-CCNs" may need to be created to deal with patients with these complicating conditions, as they might be outside the realm of possibilities of general CCNs and their resources.

- *Prison work*: Not all poly-chronics live in our local neighborhoods. Some live in prisons and mental health institutions, but nonetheless can benefit from the work of a CCN. If your CCN desires to take on the poly-chronics of a local prison, special training and background clearance will no doubt be required from the institution's administrators. Training on personal safety, prison procedures and policies, and issue avoidance will be critical to the success of such programs.
- *Youth*: The youth of America face unique health and wellness issues. A frighteningly fast rise in obesity and associated chronic illness, coupled with a stubborn and steady percentage of smokers and illicit drug users bodes poorly for the next generation of Americans. As chronic diseases often "run in the family," obese and chronically ill parents may yield offspring with similar issues. Thus, it may behoove a community to set up a special CCN through local schools and churches specifically for youth with and at risk of chronic diseases.

   Youth will likely require special training for the resources in the pool. Thus, trainers specializing in the management and improvement of youth health and wellness should be used for those resources that will interact with young patients and their families.
- *Immigrant populations*: Of course, language and culture can play a huge role in the effectiveness of your CCN among immigrants, particularly those whose English skills are limited.

If there is no CCN Trainer involved, resource training will require organizational efforts on the part of the CCN Management Team so as to ensure quality and positive outcomes, reduction of risk, and ongoing participation. Furthermore, it will behoove the CCN to provide ongoing clinical and non-clinical training, refreshers, and opportunities to learn and grow for its resources. Doing so will require a vision of the needs of the CCN patients as it relates to the requirements for resource knowledge.

Some of this training can be done online, some requires in-person interactions, and some might even require some degree of certification and documentation of capabilities and knowledge. This, too, must be considered as part of the management of the CCN.

LEADERSHIP AND CORE VALUES

Assimilation can be driven by the motivation, passion, and commitment of the leadership for the goals and objectives of the CCN. The CCN Management Team will be responsible for the dissemination of the principles and values of the CCN into the resources and community at large. This leadership must be more than direction and authority. It must engender a set of core values and principles that will not only ensure the successful direction of the CCN, but will assist individual resources and patients in their own progress towards a "better self," their own leadership qualities, and Health Ownership.

The leadership of the CCN will also come, in part, from the clinicians involved as they will be the inevitable "go to" resources for important clinical decision-making. They, too, will need to instill the values and principles of your CCN. However, leadership should permeate the CCN and all the resources, as they will have direct and influential contact with the patients. As leaders in their communities, the CCN resources will have the best opportunity to instill the motivation, faith, and perseverance needed to help patients battle their diseases and come to a better state of physical, mental, spiritual, and emotional wellness.

Of course, many of the CCN resources will be volunteers, unresponsive to the powers of authority common to the workplace. Volunteers commonly require a different set of motivators, benefits, and guidance mechanisms. Therefore, the CCN leadership may need training on how to lead volunteers, as this can be much different than leading employees.

Your CCN will therefore need a set of core, intrinsic values from which decisions are made and goals are set. Without these, you may find that your CCN is overtaken by internal, often selfish agendas of key players and participants. And this would inhibit if not doom your CCN to a troublesome and frustrating future.

I will therefore make a shameless plug for Joe Tye and his Twelve Core Action Values. These can be found on Joe's website, www.joetye.com. Joe is the author of several books, including *the Florence Prescription: From Accountability to Ownership,*[*] *All Hands on Deck,*[†] and a chapter of this book. Joe's philosophy, teaching, and approach could and should serve as an example if not a core component of leadership, service, and commitment principles for your CCN.

Small CCN Notes: The Core Action Values are important to every one of us, whether as resources, patients, or just human beings. I would recommend them to anyone struggling with life objectives and goals or those for whom life needs more meaning and substance.

GROUP DYNAMICS™ FOR RESOURCES

"Group Dynamics" is a key supporting concept for the CCN and its patients. Group interactions, support, and motivation may also be critical for the resources in the pool.

I've worked from a "home office" for much of my career as a consultant, and only once worked in a busy office of cubicles and coworkers. While this has its advantages, there are a number of disadvantages as well. One is the lack of a feeling of "connectedness" with others in the office. Even though one might be connected electronically via email or, in the case of the CCN, through Social–Clinical Networking technologies, there may still be a disconnect among the resources.

To solve for this, it is recommended that the resources in the CCN gather periodically. These gatherings needn't necessarily include all the CCN resources, as this might prove difficult. However, there should be group meetings for a variety of resources on a variety of schedules. These meetings may be "task focused," such as

- Meetings with clinicians to go over Care Strategies.
- Group discussions regarding specific patients, whose metrics or attitudes or general health needs additional focus. These patients may have become

---

[*] Tye, J. 2010. *The Florence Prescription: From Accountability to Ownership.* John Wiley & Sons Publishing.
[†] Tye, J. 2010. *All Hands on Deck.* John Wiley & Sons Publishing.

a frustration to the resources to whom they are assigned, and open face-to-face (FTF) meetings are the best way to work out solutions.
• Generation of new ideas and strategies for the care of the CCN's patients.

Meetings may also be more "resource focused," such as

• *Motivational and personal growth*: Even the best of resources need to be re-energized periodically. This is difficult to achieve remotely or even via interactive technologies such as WebEx. This is best accomplished via FTF meetings. Such meetings might include "success stories," assistance with frustrations, promoting ideas for better patient engagement and care, and general sharing of patient improvements.
• *Ongoing education*: It should not be unreasonable to expect that CCN resources should become "health evangelists" in the community, dispersing health-related information in their full time jobs, with friends and neighbors, and the non-CCN members of their communities. This, of course, requires ongoing education of these resources, which will help them help both their patients and their communities in living better and healthier lives. But this will also help promote Health Ownership in each interaction.
    This education might include both clinical and non-clinical information, including how to help identify the warning signs of depression, how to manage a difficult patient, how to interpret particular clinical readings from virtual monitoring devices, or managing physician orders and recommendations.
• *Resource expansion*: These group meetings might be used as a means to recruit new resources into the CCN, when and where needed. Nothing is more motivating to an outsider than seeing the enthusiasm and passion of a group working on a project like this. Inviting outsiders to see what is happening and how the projects are impacting the lives of patients and the health of the community can drive new enthusiasm into the CCN through new resource recruits. Success begets more success which begets more resources for you to tap into.

By using the same group support methodologies and concepts common to group therapies throughout healthcare, it is expected that the resources can and will be aided, motivated, and lifted up as they care for the most complex patients in the population.

These meetings can happen in a variety of settings, depending on the community's physical space and the needs of the resources themselves. Whether in the local hospital or a resource's home, the resource Group Dynamics meetings should always be considered a unique and special opportunity to engage, encourage, and perfect the resource pool, providing a level of support heretofore unheard of in healthcare or community service.

OUTCOMES AND INCENTIVES

First and foremost, some of the patients in this population are, for the most part, unlikely to be "cured" of their ailments. These would certainly include some of the poly-chronics. Their Care Strategies involve mitigation of future deterioration, improvement in existing conditions, maximizing the potential to lead meaningful and pleasant lives, and reduction in the overall cost of care delivery without compromising quality, access, or gratification. This does not equal "cured." Indeed, many will eventually die of the diseases they have contracted. It is how this inevitable decline takes place that makes up the driving objectives for the CCN. Thus a holistic and long-term approach that includes everything from disease management to end-of-life planning is required if the needs of these patients are to be addressed. Because of this longer-term approach, and the holistic nature of its care and service delivery, the goals of the CCN and its Care Strategies simply do not blend well with an FFS payment model in which short-term volume drives the motivation for patient care delivery.

For instance, patient weight or hemoglobin levels must be measured and gradually improved over the course of months and years. The payment system should reflect this longer term focus, with the goals and any related "shared savings" programs and incentives aligned with long-term, outcomes-focused Care Strategies rather than a number of visits or tests in a given cycle.

Secondly, the new care systems currently being considered must approach these patients holistically rather than as isolated users of individual services. Indeed, for the most complex patients, there is no other reasonable and effective way to approach their care and develop the plans by which they will be treated. Physicians and every other caregiver in the community must therefore lower their territorial walls and focus on the patient rather than their individual financial and related self-interests. This will require the "It's not about me!" mentality mentioned earlier in this book, as well as a payment system that rewards the long-term and the holistic while creating disincentives for the isolated treatments of the past.

Given the dollars to be saved, there should be ready access to incentive-driven monies. These payouts should be carefully crafted to enable a system that is more about rewarding quality than throughput; outstanding service rather than the volume served; and extraordinary care rather than filling out forms and checking the correct boxes. While volume is a factor and should remain as a metric in our systems, it should never be the only factor determining relative success or failure. However, "quality" and financial returns to the payors (particularly CMS) should not be the sole focus either. "Quality" for this patient population is a relative measure, and might prove difficult to quantify. Quality metrics should therefore be included but, again, carefully constructed to match the long-term nature of the diseases being treated.

And certainly all savings to the payors (and taxpayers) is not derived equally. Simply reducing the amount of care provided is not the goal of the CCN. Rather, cost reduction could be thought of as a by-product of the efficiency rather than an explicit goal of the system. Thus, "shared savings" from the optimization of care provision should be rewarded based on attainment of a number of key milestones for most, if not all, patients in the CCN population. Those milestones should include everything from health improvement or maintenance, to cost reduction for each patient, to new patient enrollment, and overall "community engagement" in health promotion and CCN participation.

Of course, as mentioned earlier in this book, we are creating a business model for which there is no payment model. However, as this and other business model concepts are already catching on, it won't be long until there are new ideas in payment and incentive models to help save the system. I predict that we are on the verge of a great degree of energy and motivation for new care and business models both here and abroad.

CHALLENGES AND OBSTACLES

A number of challenges face the CCN and its developers and managers. Here are the main ones worthy of consideration.

LEGAL HURDLES

If the government is serious about healthcare reform in the coming decades, legal air cover must be given to organizations willing to challenge the status quo. This includes the initial CCNs that will rely on resources across a community to care for patients in a new way. Without legal protection, resources and the CCN Management may become skittish about the use of non-clinical resources, caring for patients using volunteers, etc.

Legal protections can come in several forms in the existing environment. However, I would recommend that you consult with your organization's legal counsel to ensure that resources are adequately covered against liability for the care they provide. Regardless of your state's laws and legal precedence, it is likely that education, certification, governance and accountability, and strict adherence to resource roles will be important to ensure a smooth and litigation-free existence. However, understand that there are lawyers who constantly seek enrichment from any source, however good and honorable its intentions. The "trial lawyers" may try to prey upon both the CCN organization and its resources if they are not given the correct legal cover via documentation, written agreements with patients and families, and proper infrastructure.

Small CCN Notes: Legal considerations are always necessary when interacting with patients and their physicians. I would recommend that you seek legal counsel even if you are only serving one patient, especially if that patient is not part of a local church, civil club, or other group of which you are a part.

TOO MANY COOKS?

The integration of many resources might dilute responsibility rather than promote it if the resources are not properly managed and led. Too many resources, tossed at a problem willy-nilly, will likely lead to a scenario in which chaos is overly prevalent, tasks are not completed, resources and patients are frustrated and unhappy, and quality and consistency suffer as care is placed at risk. Keeping this, as well as territoriality and infighting, out is like keeping blackspot fungus out of your rose garden. It requires constant vigilance, preventative measures, and the assumption that bad events and circumstances lie unseen and waiting for an opportunity to disrupt the beauty you've worked so hard to create.

Thus, again, there is the need for team accountability, Group Dynamics meetings, knowledge of and respect for the infrastructure, Core Values training, and a distinct "It's not about me" mentality. All this must be ingrained in each and every resource in the pool in order to avoid the potential chaos of many resources being thrown at a very big problem haphazardly. Even the best of fire departments would fail to effectively douse a fire if they just showed up and started squirting water. Organization, regimen, and accountability are all vital to the CCN's success.

FINANCIAL INCENTIVES AND DISINCENTIVES

As is obvious by the current FFS reimbursement system of U.S. healthcare, financial incentives can drive behavior, sometimes even self-destructive and counterproductive behavior. For example, while PCPs and experienced nurses often try to do a good job of seeing "the whole patient," the rest of the medical community is less holistic in its approach to care delivery. This is largely due to the government-imposed and industry-supported FFS payment structure which has so blinded providers and patients to both the actual cost of care delivery as well as long-term outcomes of care delivery. Clearly, for this or any other business model innovation to become reality, there needs to be wholesale removal of the old habits, thinking, and payment systems. The CCN, as at least one of the ways in which the healthcare system might be salvaged, has a vested interest in the successful improvement of population health. Saving the few will aid the many. But this becomes difficult if not impossible in the long-term without changing the incentives of care provision.

Thus in order for the CCN to ultimately work effectively and universally and obtain its expected results, the entire resource pool will have to change focus away from financially-focused FFS mentalities and a myopic, task-oriented approach to care provision. Doing so will require an entirely different approach to care delivery and resource support, one which supports the CCN, is enabled and supported by the CCN technologies and infrastructure, and is paid for (to the extent cost is generated) with a new payment and incentive model. Thus, for a number of reasons, this means a gradual shift towards the idea of "capitation," "bundled payments," and "population health reimbursement" and away from FFS.

Of course, the CCN can be initiated and run without new payment models in place. But, as the new payment models evolve, they will no doubt support the CCN and its infrastructure more completely.

SUMMARY

Resources in the CCN, whether clinical or volunteers, are the lifeblood of the system. Without enough of the right resources, the provision of care still suffers and your CCN will fail from lack of support. Understanding what and how many you need, as well as where and when is critical to success. The "engineered" approach to the CCN's resource and task allocations help to ensure the right resource mix for your patient population. By using the above guidelines to develop your own resource pool, and training them well in the "art and science" of CCN care management, your network will be assured of the best chances for success.

18 CCNs, Palliative Care, and End-of-Life Planning

If a truly holistic approach to care provision for chronic disease patients is to solve for quality, cost, and patient gratification, we must necessarily address some of the most costly and difficult periods of a patient's life as well as the entire disease progression process. This includes the EOL and the pain and suffering that occurs throughout the disease episode. Often confused for one another, palliative care and EOL care are two concepts born of the same general principle: caring for patients as they wish in a dignified and personalized way, while providing relief from pain and the distress of symptoms. If we are to address holistic and truly compassionate care within the context of the CCN, we must necessarily integrate EOL and palliative care into our program strategy. (The best news on this front is the recent willingness of CMS to begin paying for physician discussions of EOL with patients as early as 2016.)

Palliative care and EOL planning and care are important for a number of very different reasons. EOL care is most commonly noted due to the costs and inpatient capacity associated with the dying process, particularly for Medicaid and Medicare patients, and specifically poly-chronics. As we'll see below, EOL care can unnecessarily use tremendous resources while often offering little in the way of substantive outcomes or patient and family relief. Furthermore, EOL care is often associated with difficult familial decisions for patients who have left few, if any, legally and morally binding instructions for their care. Alternatively, proper EOL planning and care implementation has been shown to greatly improve gratification and even quality outcomes.

Similarly, palliative care has grown in popularity due to its profound impact on patients, which is the result of its holistic focus on the patient's condition as advanced diseases progress. Both are important to the overall health and well-being of the poly-chronic patient population. And fortunately both can be readily integrated into the CCN care model.

In this chapter, we'll address the need for these concepts in the overall schema of healthcare delivery for poly-chronics, and describe the process by which integration into your CCN could take place. Keep in mind, of course, that the CCN model remains flexible and can accommodate a number of different configurations, and can therefore be structured so as to handle a variety of EOL and palliative models and resource allocations.

PALLIATIVE CARE: DEFINITION AND HISTORY

For those who are not familiar with palliative care, it is one of the fastest growing components of healthcare systems across the globe. Since it was adopted from the United Kingdom in the 1980s, millions of U.S. patients have used palliative care as part of their disease management regimen and/or EOL treatment. The word "palliative" is taken from the Latin word "palliare," which means "to cloak." Palliative care focuses generally on relieving and preventing the suffering of patients, whether physical, emotional, or even spiritual. Medications and treatments are said to have a palliative effect if they relieve symptoms without having a curative effect on the underlying disease or cause, and thus can be a vital part of the palliative program. This can include treating nausea related to chemotherapy or using morphine to treat a broken leg or ibuprofen to treat aching related to a flu infection. Unlike hospice care, which focuses specifically on care of the terminally ill, palliative medicine is appropriate for patients in all disease stages, including those undergoing treatment for curable illnesses and those living with chronic diseases, as well as for those patients who are nearing the EOL. Though commonly associated with patients having acute or chronic diseases, any patient with significant pain and suffering, mental anguish, and other symptoms would be a candidate for its use. Palliative care is also a broader care process than hospice or EOL care that can begin with the knowledge of a disease and extend throughout the curative process all the way to death and bereavement. Still, as you'll see in generally accepted definitions and models below, it remains commonly associated with EOL care and the very sick.

As its roots are in the United Kingdom, let's look at the UK definition of palliative care, taken from the United Kingdom's National Institute for Clinical Excellence (NICE).

> Palliative care is the active holistic care of patients with advanced progressive illness. Management of pain and other symptoms and provision of psychological, social and spiritual support is paramount. The goal of palliative care is achievement of the best quality of life for patients and their families. Many aspects of palliative care are also applicable earlier in the course of the illness in conjunction with other treatments.
>
> Palliative care aims to
>
> * Affirm life and regard dying as a normal process
> * Provide relief from pain and other distressing symptoms
> * Integrate the psychological and spiritual aspects of patient care
> * Offer a support system to help patients live as actively as possible until death
> * Offer a support system to help the family cope during the patient's illness and in their own bereavement.

By way of contrast, a World Health Organization (WHO) statement describes palliative care as

> An approach that improves the quality of life of patients and their families facing the problems associated with life-threatening illness, through the prevention and relief of suffering by means of early identification and impeccable assessment and treatment of pain and other problems, physical, psychosocial and spiritual.[*]

Most palliative care occurs in the acute hospital setting in part due to the equipment, medication, and monitoring requirements. The prevalence of palliative care teams in U.S. hospitals shows steady growth and indicates a rapidly rising trend. According to the most recent data analysis, 1568 or 63%, of U.S. hospitals with more than 50 beds have a palliative care team—an increase of 138.3% since 2000. Eighty percent of hospitals with more than 300 beds have palliative teams.[*]

Palliative medicine typically utilizes a multidisciplinary approach to patient care, relying on input from physicians, pharmacists, nurses, chaplains, social workers, psychologists, and other allied health professionals in formulating a plan of care to relieve suffering in all areas of a patient's life. This multidisciplinary approach allows the palliative care team to address physical, emotional, spiritual, and social concerns that arise with advanced illness.

THE ORIGINS OF PALLIATIVE CARE

The concepts of palliative and hospice care originated in the United Kingdom in the 1960s, with slow adoption to other parts of the industrialized world. Led by Dame Cicely Saunders, it began with research at St. Joseph's Hospice, where Dame Cicely was allowed to experiment by giving regular dosages of drugs to four patients. This apparently simple practice was a novel approach at the time, and was even observed with some skepticism. However, skepticism soon turned to interest as the results showed a marked improvement in the quality of these patients' lives. By the time Dame Cicely left St. Joseph's, she had observed and documented over 1000 cases of patients dying of cancer. Her scrupulous records provide the basis of this fundamental area of research.[†]

Dame Cicely's pioneering work was soon followed by others. In 1963, Professor John Hinton recognized the physical and mental distress of dying in the ward of a London teaching hospital.[‡] He later authored groundbreaking work on the progression of the awareness and acceptance of dying over time—one of the few longitudinal studies conducted with terminally ill patients and their families.[§] His research revealed different patterns of progression, influential factors such as depression and anxiety, and the relationship between patients and their relatives' awareness and acceptance.

In the early 1970s, palliative care in the United Kingdom saw its first large-scale epidemiological survey, led by Professor Ann Cartwright and her team. Drawing from a random sample of deaths in 1969, she reported the experiences of 785 patients and their families in the last year of life, which would later be compared

---

[*] *FY2002–2009 AHA Annual Survey Databases.* American Hospital Association, Chicago, IL. Published in Health Forum, an American Hospital Association affiliate, 2010.

[†] Cicely Saunders International, www.cicelysaundersfoundation.org/about-palliative-care. Accessed originally March 2010.

[‡] Hinton, J. 1963. The physical and mental distress of the dying. *Quarterly Journal of Medicine.* 32:1–21.

[§] Hinton, J. 1999. The progress of awareness and acceptance of dying assessed in cancer patients and their caring relatives. *Palliative Medicine.* 13(1):19–35.

with those of 639 patients in 1987.* In this comparative study, several changes were recognized: "... increasingly people were dying alone, older and with prolonged and unpleasant symptoms, in institutional and hospital settings, with improved home help though with fewer home visits, and with a greater awareness of the disease and dying."†

Palliative, hospice, and EOL care utilization is growing rapidly across the globe, as caregivers and patients realize the benefits and health systems see the results on key metrics, including cost and quality. In the United States, groundbreaking work was being done in the later 1980s and early 1990s, and is moving rapidly forward.

RESOURCES FOR PALLIATIVE CARE

In any business model, including the CCN, palliative care will require additional, trained, and specialized resources. However, these resources should meld well into the overall CCN infrastructure such that the communal resources are included and used as needed, and the entire resource pool is supportive and engaged in the palliative care model of delivery. The number and type of resources depends on the goals of the program, the locations of palliative care delivery (hospital or elsewhere), and the availability and use of any available communal resources. As palliative care is such a unique service, its complexity should not be taken lightly. Thus, any communal resources added to your palliative program should be specially trained, even if only used in a volunteer and/or temporary capacity.

From the information above, we can see that a number of potential palliative resources might be required. Fortunately, these include many resources already expected to be part of the CCN, which is testament to the ease of integration of various models. Pharmacists, nurses, chaplains/clergy, social workers, and psychologists, some specializing in palliative care, are added to the list of CCN clinical and non-clinical resources. As these resources might operate within the hospital rather than the community, proper integration into the CCN will require additional effort and collaboration. In this case, CCN Managers and Trainers will need to create an atmosphere and camaraderie with hospital staff that is conducive to "external participation" by CCN communal and clinical resources. If, however, palliative care programs extend beyond the walls of the hospital, CCN resources might be substituted and used as part of an integrated palliative–CCN approach.

EOL PLANNING AND CARE

If you were asked, "How would you prefer to pass on ... hooked to a machine in an ICU, or at home surrounded by family and friends?" Few, I'd guess, would take the first option. Yet, one of every three people who died in 2007 in the United States was in the hospital for treatment at the time of death. The cost of their hospital stays was

---

* Cartwright, A. 1991. Changes in life and care in the year before death 1969–1987. *Journal of Public Health Medicine*. 13(2):81–7.
† Cicely Saunders International, www.cicelysaundersfoundation.org/about-palliative-care. Accessed originally 3/2010.

about $20 billion, which was significantly more than that of discharged patients.* According to the same ARHQ research, the following statistics represent the patients who die while hospitalized:

- Thirty-two percent of all deaths in the United States in 2007 were inpatient hospital deaths.
- The inpatient death rate in 2007 was 1.9%. However, these hospital stays ending in death were responsible for 5.1% ($17.6 billion) of all hospital inpatient costs.
- Average hospital costs for a stay ending in death were $23,000, about 2.7 times higher than for a patient discharged alive.
- Medicaid had the highest costs for a hospital stay ending in death, $35,000, nearly 5.5 times higher than for a Medicaid patient discharged alive. However, Medicaid had the lowest death rate among payors, 0.8%.
- Medicare had 67% of all inpatient deaths, with a total cost of over $10 billion, which accounted for 6.9% of all Medicare inpatient costs.
- Twelve percent of all inpatient deaths were for elective admissions, with a death rate of 0.9%.
- The leading principal diagnosis for inpatient death cases was septicemia, which was the principal diagnosis for 15% of all deaths; 17% of patients with septicemia died in the hospital. Other leading causes of inpatient death included stroke, pneumonia, myocardial infarction, congestive heart failure (CHF), and malignancies.

Some patients die in hospitals simply because their medical conditions leave them with nowhere else to safely go. Others die there because they have given no other explicit instructions about EOL preferences, or because familial wishes cause extended stays and extensive treatments. Some even pass on there because there is no coordinated way to move them to a different care setting for a more peaceful departure. Regardless of the reasons, it is clear that the full one-third of Americans who die in hospitals do not need to, or would not want to, die there. If given a choice well in advance, and if properly consulted about their conditions and the options for passing on, patients routinely opt for a much different fate.

Yet, EOL care is a highly sensitive subject. Discussions are not easily or lightly had, especially with the poly-chronics whose mortality daily stares them in the face. Physicians, whom one might think of as a good source of feedback and advice, often prefer to be at arm's length from these discussions. Theirs is to heal, not to discuss the failure to heal. Patients are thus often left without an effective means by which to effectively plan for their own desires to be carried out in the event of their demise. This can lead to someone else making what are sometimes emotionally charged decisions.

There are a number of potential ways that patients can communicate their wishes to caregivers, ranging from "Do Not Resuscitate" agreements dealing with specific

---

* Zhao, Y. and Encinosa, W. 2010. *The Costs of End-of-Life Hospitalizations, 2007.* AHRQ Publications, November 2009, revised April 2010.

and singular points of care, to legal "Advance Directives" and more broad and sweeping "Advance Care Planning (ACP)." In some states, such as Oregon and West Virginia, POLST documents ("Physician Orders for Life-Sustaining Treatment") are used.* All have their uses and nuances. For instance, Advance Directives is an often long legal document, full of typical legalese, and may only partially cover the specificity of a patient's long-term care goals and wishes. In contrast, ACP is more comprehensive, and may deal with many aspects of care as a patient lives through many stages of disease progression. And POLST documents accompany the patient's medical record and augment the ACPs.

In order to effectively establish attention to EOL care, you should first consult with your attorney on the specific state laws and regulations that govern your patients and the expression of their wishes, as state laws can differ significantly. Once you have done this and understand fully what can and cannot be achieved in the advanced planning of patient care, you should strive to use both palliative and EOL planning as part of the CCN program. This planning should be as comprehensive as possible, using trained facilitators to lead both patients and caregivers through the EOL planning process.

Example: Gunderson

Perhaps the best example of a long-term and successful program in the United States lies in Wisconsin at Gunderson Lutheran Medical Center in La Crosse.† Gunderson has two related programs, one of which is known as "Respecting Choices," which began in 1993 as a community-engaging effort to reduce the frustration, angst, and fear of planning for one's own death. Programs copied from Gunderson's model have shown up in other states like Minnesota and countries like Singapore.

Gunderson's goals for its ACP programs are

- To provide qualified assistance to individuals in making informed health-care choices appropriate to their stage of illness and their goals, values, and beliefs
- To create plans that will be effective in providing personalized care—plans that ensure that individuals receive *all* the treatment and *only* the treatment they desire
- To develop strategies to communicate these choices to those who need to know (e.g., healthcare agent, family, Physician, and other healthcare providers)

---

* An excellent legal summary of the history of advanced care planning, POLST, and other tools can be found at the U.S. Health and Human Services website: Sabatino, C. 2007. *Advance Directives and Advance Care Planning: Legal and Policy Issues.* Office of Disability, Aging and Long-Term Care Policy, Washington, DC, October. http://aspe.hhs.gov/daltcp/reports/2007/adacplpi.pdf. First accessed in 3/2010.
† An overview of the Gunderson program can be found in: Hammes, B. 2012. *Having Your Own Say: Getting the Right Care When It Matters Most.* Center for Health Transformation Press, Atlanta, GA.

Gunderson learned all along the journey to its currently successful and ongoing program. As Gunderson's community worked through the education processes, they discovered many of the issues related to the implementation process. These include educating both Physicians and patients in the development of realistic and "doable" ACPs in order for patients and families to be happy and clinicians comfortable in the ACP execution. For example, a patient's home or living situation may not allow for the kind of EOL scenario a patient might prefer. She may have unrealistic expectations of caregivers or resources, desire outcomes that are unattainable, or even request services that are considered immoral or illegal (e.g., euthanasia or Physician-assisted suicide). Or, facilities and resources may simply not exist to execute the patient's wishes exactly as they would like. For instance, patient may want to receive all his EOL care in his home, yet his disease state may require hospitalization as his disease progresses but before he is ready to pass peacefully on. Thus a sort of ACP coordination and regimen is required to ensure that the processes that a patient desires can be implemented effectively and according to her wishes. And lastly, whenever possible, families should be intimately involved in the ACP planning process.

Importantly, patients must have records that can follow them throughout their care interventions. At Gunderson, this meant modifying the EMR to allow for the ACPs to be included. (Gunderson also adopted the aforementioned POLST paradigm, which records the legal preferences of the patient.) This allowed patient wishes to be followed anywhere in the Gunderson County area.

To compensate for a need for resources to work with patients (and relieve Physicians of the responsibility), Gunderson created "ACP Facilitators." Their responsibility is to engage patients, families, Physicians, and other community resources in the necessities of proper planning, and ensure that realistic and reasonable "Advance Care Plans" are developed such that Physicians and families can comply. These are part of both their palliative care model and an EOL care model. Other resources in the patient's care continuum are part of the ACP discussion, such that a communal knowledge and appreciation for the importance of patient wishes is obtained and sustained.

Data on the ACP and POLST programs shows great success. As per a study of 2007–2008 patient deaths, 90% of adults who passed on in local Gunderson County facilities had an ACP in place; 99% had a care plan in an accessible medical record; and those care plans were followed as prescribed 99% of the time.[*] While not the specific goal of the program, the ancillary benefits of reduced cost (via reductions in unnecessary or unwanted treatments) and improved patient experience are beginning to show up in the analysis.

INTEGRATING EOL AND PALLIATIVE CARE INTO THE CCN MODEL

In order to integrate EOL and palliative care into the CCN framework, there will need to be a commitment on the part of Physicians and other clinicians, hospital management, and the affected patients and families. Although the communal

---

[*] *Ibid*, p.16.

resources may be of lesser value to patients in the hospital (where they are already receiving ongoing care and constant supervision), the CCN Care Circles can still support and encourage their patients. The CCN Care Circle can also become immediately engaged as patients leave the hospital and move to other care settings, such as home, hospice, or nursing facilities. Furthermore, the CCN communal resources can remain the "patient's advocates" and ensure that the goals of the Care Strategies align with and are promoted by the EOL and palliative care process. Indeed, the EOL and palliative care processes should be part of a patient's Care Strategy once the need for those services is recognized (more on this later). Lastly and importantly, the CCN can offer a smooth transition to alternate care settings, expanding the reach of these services beyond the traditional hospital and hospice settings. Thus, the CCN should serve as an extension to palliative services, offering greater resource support, care, spiritual, and monitoring assistance, and flexibility in care settings.

The Gunderson example demonstrates several key points relevant to the CCN integration discussion. First, it demonstrates the power of the community to come together around a singular, important, albeit painful, subject. It also demonstrates that even players who might be hurt by change (e.g., Physicians who offer fewer expensive treatments and procedures) can come together to support the "greater good" of a program like Respecting Choices, or the CCN.

How does palliative/EOL care fit into the CCN concept? The CCN can

- Bring together families and others into the care process.
- Allow for broader discussion of the patient's health over a longer period of time.
- Allow for more spiritual and holistic interventions from familiar, communal resources, and organizations.
- Promote the discussion of care preferences through the ongoing relationship with poly-chronic patients, so as to promote early decision making in EOL matters.
- Reduce the need for government intervention and mandates by promoting self-management, self-determination, and freedom of choices.

To implement a palliative program within your CCN, you will need to refer back to the Care Strategies mapping sessions discussed earlier in this book. Using tools similar to those already in use, such as swimlane maps and even simulations, and incorporating representatives of all the resources involved in palliative and EOL care, you can map the palliative and EOL care process flows, the tasks of proper care, number and type of patient interactions and interventions, and the resources required for each process step. From this, you can begin to determine which resources from the communal pool are available and capable of handling various specialized tasks. You can use a small simulation or flow mapping software to experiment and tweak your care processes and resource allocations to match resource availability, patient preferences, care locations, and even legal requirements.

Using your newly found expertise in task optimization, develops workable and fully integrated programs that maximize the utilization of all available resources and optimize the cost and quality of care delivery.

Importantly, you will want to ensure that any and all resources utilized are properly trained in palliative and EOL care concepts, such that their support is made most effective. If you intend to use CCN communal resources for these tasks, you may need additional training staff beyond the CCN trainer if he is not an expert in palliative care, and/or special training programs.

Lastly, you will want to consider the legal ramifications of your programs. Consult with the hospital's attorney(s) or independent counsel on any state regulations or "witches behind the trees" of your program and the involvement of communal resources. This is particularly important in the management of information related to patient wishes within the Care Circles. Ensure that your processes have been vetted by legal counsel so as to protect all participants from legal issues and opportunism.

CCN PROCESS EVOLUTION AND PALLIATIVE AND EOL CARE

In the previous book on Dynamic Capacity Management, I spoke of "evolution" in the context of process change over time. Therein, I described how processes are altered over time, either through our own efforts or through changes to external variables. So, for instance, our efforts to reduce some process cycle time may result in a long-term change to the system as it "evolves" toward a more optimal state. Similarly, patient acuities in the ED will change over time, impacting key metrics like LOS. If these changes negatively impact our system performance, the system will also need to change in order to maintain improvements and/or continue towards optimization. Evolution thus requires our processes to be under constant evaluation as the internal and external variables impact our systems. Similarly, our poly-chronics in our CCNs will change over time. Volumes of participating patients and Physicians will change (hopefully growing due to the great successes we see!), and patients' health will change as they improve, age, or deteriorate over time.

Thus, the CCN and the Care Circles will need to evolve as patients enter the end of life phase and need palliative services during specific phases of their disease progression. Care Circles may evolve to include more clergy and a wider group of friends as patients near the end of life. Alternatively, Care Circles may begin to tighten as families of patients near their end of life find that they prefer a smaller and less-integrated group. End of life can also bring the need for privacy, intimacy, and greater or newfound spirituality, all of which should be respected.

Similarly, as patients enter into particularly difficult periods of their disease progressions, additional palliative resources may need to be brought forward into the Care Circles, such that the proper resources are involved in the CCN and not left to siloed and unsupported activities. This, in turn, requires three major activities of the CCN Management Team

- Constant updates to patient preferences and wishes
- Constant evaluation of the CCN, its resource allocations, and organizational and operational structures
- Ongoing infrastructure alterations as the needs of the community evolve over time

The CCN Managers and Primes must all be willing to allow for the changes to the Care Circles as the needs and focuses of the patients change over time. For instance, some patients who have not involved clergy in the Care Circle may suddenly have a spiritual need as their mortality becomes more evident through increased pain or suffering from disease progression. Likewise, non-hospital palliative services may require the alteration of Care Circle resource task requirements, or even changes to the structure of the Care Circle of a given patient. These alterations are part of the CCN evolution and should be welcomed, not resisted. Otherwise, the CCN will fail to serve the patients as desired, or silos of care may develop that exclude important elements of the CCN's value.

The Management Team therefore must be willing to allow for the changes within the community to reflect in the resource allocations and infrastructure of the CCN and its offerings, including "blowing up and starting from scratch" when the existing structure cannot meet communal requirements, or when the focus of the CCN is altered significantly.

Evolution *will* happen in your community, particularly if your CCN includes palliative and EOL care, so welcome it as much as you plan for it.

THE PAYOR ROLE

Cost is a very touchy subject when it comes to EOL care. Discussions of medical expenses can seem insensitive and cold blooded when the elderly, poor, and dying are involved. Yet payors do and will continue to play a large role in the financial implications of care during these difficult periods of life. Care should be taken to account for patient preferences as well as the patient's condition when analyzing and evaluating the costs of advanced treatments, palliative, and EOL care.

Though some, including famed lecturers at Dartmouth, have cited regional variances in care costs, the study of the cost of EOL care should be taken with a great deal of consideration of the patient condition in mind. Neuberg comments on Dartmouth's 2008 Atlas and its authors when he states, "Wennberg et al. did not measure or adjust for severity, as they believe their model involves measures of provider efficiency and performance that minimize the chance that variations in the care can be explained by differences in the severity of patients' illnesses." They further state that "by looking at care delivered during fixed intervals of time before death, we can say with assurance that the prognosis of all the patients in the cohort is identical—all were dead after the interval of observation." From a clinical perspective, this retrospective logic misrepresents the prognostic and therapeutic uncertainty that we must contend with in real time. What matters in providing care are the apparent severity and treatability of illness at the time of patient evaluation, not at the time of death.

Thus, the fairest way to assess treatment efficacy and efficiency is to assemble cohorts with comparable disease burdens at time zero, and then track subsequent outcome and resource utilization in survivors and decedents. In contrast, looking back at fixed intervals before death identifies patients whose condition at time zero varies markedly, more so for longer intervals, and this alone could explain substantial variation in resource allocation. Furthermore, EOL spending does not reveal whether a provider's efforts effectively saved, extended, or improved any lives. For example, EOL costs cannot distinguish a patient who lives 24 months (on whatever treatment) from a sicker patient who would have lived 12 months on the same regimen, but instead survives 24 months with more aggressive care. From the look-back perspective, care is viewed not a means to improve health, but as an accumulation of expenses that failed to prevent an inevitable death.

EOL spending would be a more straightforward indicator of provider performance if diseases progressed and presented in a uniform fashion, but this is not the case. In patients with fatal CHF, at least one-third die unexpectedly, whereas most others experience progressive CHF requiring episodic hospital treatment before their demise. By the (Dartmouth Atlas) authors' method, if my practice randomly sees a greater proportion of inexpensive sudden deaths, we will be rated undeservedly as more efficient than others who see a higher rate of costly progressive CHF. However, if we prevent sudden deaths by implanting more defibrillators, we will see and treat more progressive CHF (because of the competing risks of these outcomes), and our efficiency rating will decline. If we offer such patients greater access to life-extending procedures like biventricular pacing or cardiac transplantation, our rating will plummet further, because they are sick enough that some will not survive beyond the measured interval after the costly treatment, regardless of how appropriately or expeditiously it was provided.*

This tells us that the generalization of patient needs and care requirements cannot be treated lightly. If for no other reason than the complexity of their illnesses, polychronics are very different from one another, each requiring their own Care Strategy. So, just as one Care Strategy is only appropriate for one patient, so too one EOL ACP is appropriate for only one patient. Although clinical decisions can be regimented to a certain degree, based on "best practices," it would be a folly to assume that EOL care can be equally regimented. Patients will have their own wishes and desires for the end of their lives, and those wishes may change over time as their disease progresses (or doesn't), or other life-changing events occur. To assume that a patient's ACP will be the same before and after the death of a life-long spouse would be as risky as saying that one's attitude about life will be the same before and after a diagnosis of terminal cancer.

Therefore, payors will need to develop flexibility in the acceptance of ACP and EOL planning and the decisions made by patients and their families. Respecting Choice is not just a name of the infamous Gunderson program … it should be a mantra for our attitude about EOL decisions. This should be especially true for government payors, as they will deal with more of the EOL patients than any other. Without flexibility and respect for choices, patients and their caregivers will push back on the reasonable use of the very delivery systems that can best control costs, quality, and system capacity. Government payors should therefore strive to stay away from regimentation of rules and payment structures for this very sensitive period of a citizen's life.

---

* Neuberg, G. 2009. The cost of end-of-life care: A new efficiency measure falls short of AHA/ACC standards. *Circular of Cardiovascular Quality Outcomes.* 2:127–33.

GOVERNMENT AND EOL PLANNING

This of course brings us to the issue of government interventions in these decisions. As Michael Leavitt, former secretary of the Department of Health and Human Services puts it, "despite the mounting cost of Medicare, the treatment decisions of patients need to be left to these patients, their families, and the health professionals who provide the care rather than to the government … My worry is that if too few of us make the decisions voluntarily, someday government officials, with their backs to the financial wall, will feel that they have no alternative but to begin making decisions about the care that people with advanced illness will and will not receive. It happens in other countries now."[*]

The heated discussions over "death panels" within "Obamacare" demonstrate how passionately people feel about government intrusion in the most personal and private of decisions. But most would likely agree that, if given the choice, they would prefer to make EOL and ACP decisions themselves, with their own dignity, personal preferences, and health status in mind.

Government's role should instead be in the legal and cultural protection of the parties involved in the CCN and the critical decisions of EOL and palliative care. The risk is not in the following of patient orders, but the legalities of those orders and the threats to those who follow them. For every well-intentioned care decision, there is at least one trial lawyer quite willing to "cash in" on an unfortunate situation. Thus if it is to have a role, government should shield the CCN and its resources from liability in the care of patients willing to participate, including those making critical decisions for how they want their lives to end. I firmly believe that responsible, informed people can make responsible decisions most of the time. There will always be those situations wherein families, patients, and/or lawyers prove unreasonable and obstinate. And for these scenarios, protections need to be granted to those genuinely trying to help the community and its patients.

Fortunately, CMS will begin reimbursement to PCPs for conversations on EOL care with patients. This is a huge advancement toward bringing this issue to the forefront (though I still debate the value of paying physicians extra to do what they are supposed to be doing anyway). Hopefully, this will help drive more EOL conversations and community-wide efforts in the very near future.

SUMMARY

The CCN fits easily into the palliative, hospice, EOL, and ACP care models (and vice versa). Indeed, the Care Circle concept works well with the notion of a "coordinated" approach to care delivery for patients in the latter stages of earthly life. With proper training and education, each patient could and should direct their own EOL care in cooperation with their Physicians and caregivers, close family, and clergy. With this as part of the CCN's overall holistic strategy towards attaining higher quality and patient gratification at a lower cost, ACP and EOL planning and care will become integrated into the longitudinal Care Strategies for all patients, especially our poly-chronics.

---

[*] Hammes, B. 2012. *Having Your Own Say: Getting the Right Care When It Matters Most.* Center for Health Transformation Press, Atlanta, GA. p. xxv–xxviii.

19 Final Thoughts

As the writing of this book comes to a close in late 2015, here in the United States, the PPACA (a.k.a. Obamacare) is already beginning to unravel only a few short years after its implementation. Most of us who read it back when it was first introduced knew that it would not achieve the critical and necessary goals for our care system, namely cost, quality, and access, or other concepts in this book, such as Health Ownership. Alas, it was and remains unpopular. The lack of appealing options in the government insurance exchanges means that only those desperate for care insurance have signed up, leaving roughly 75% of the original uninsured population still uninsured. This number is not expected to decrease anytime soon, leaving the purpose of this expensive and onerous effort in question. The uninsured simply aren't buying the need for high-cost, high-risk plans. And as so many stay away, the actuarial accounting looks bleak for those companies and organizations offering health insurance policies. (Of course, those in the "private markets" whose employers offer insurance have already seen their insurance bills steadily climb as with PPACA passage insurance providers prepped for the new mandated coverages by increasing premiums, reducing coverage, and removing employee spouses from company plans. Many have seen triple-digit percentage increases in out-of-pocket costs in only 3 years.)

This has led to the financial deterioration of the PPACA insurance cooperatives and the rapid and drastic increases in out-of-pocket costs for those who have exchange-based policies. These massive, yet utterly predictable, cost increases are impacting the very people the system was designed to help. And thus comes the potential downward spiral in which actuarial costs create the need for high premiums, narrower policies, and higher deductibles, which are in turn increasingly unattractive to the very people the program was supposed to entice.

For our purposes here, many of the issues we face in the optimization of our capacity to care lie in the very payment and relationship models that government and payors have collaboratively created over the years, most of which were untouched in the PPACA. For instance, the common inability to discharge patients from the hospital on a timely basis resulted, in part, from a reimbursement model that pays attending/primary care physicians for each day that a patient is in the hospital. Indeed, an entire class of medical resource, the Hospitalist, was created, in part, to deal with this issue. Likewise, readmission penalties and other recent machinations to prevent excess cost have led to gaming of diagnoses, inappropriate placement of patients within our facilities, and misguided care guidelines. All these efforts, while no doubt well-meaning, fail to address the key issues and the core constraints within the payment systems, relationships and protected silos, and decades of toxic culture.

In the meantime and in the face of daunting challenges and enormous obstacles, innovation in the "private sector" must continue. We must think towards the future of healthcare delivery and payment models while still working within the confines of an outdated and dilapidated reimbursement system, stifling silos of care, and a workplace culture that is often counterproductive. Even as these and other shackles constrain us, we must innovate for the future of the viability of the delivery system and our population's health and well-being. Clearly, we cannot look to our national leaders for the ideas that will propel us to a better system.

Thus what I attempted to present in this book is one answer to the question, "How can we care for as much of our community as possible with the most cost-effective resources, the lowest cost, and the best outcomes possible?" I put forth a holistic and comprehensive view of our local healthcare systems, inclusive of hospitals and other "official" clinical care locations plus all the relevant non-clinical resources we have within our communities. This holistic view drives the need for truer integration and collaboration at a wider and far grander scale than is commonly currently considered or used, going beyond the confines of the physician–hospital–patient triangle that has limited our capacity to care in the past. While some models attempt to make gains here, such as the ACO, these commonly remain too limited in scope, constrained in the use of potential care resources, and forgetful of the critical importance of Health Ownership. Thus what I have attempted to put forth is an alternative approach, on a broader and grander scale as seen in Figure 19.1.

My approach herein is relatively simple. Start at a "micro" level, within the key departments of hospital operations, work outward into the entire hospital, then widen out into the broader community of care and integrate as many resources as is feasible and beneficial. This approach allows the reader to engage at multiple levels while keeping eyes on a broader vision of a larger and more comprehensive system.

As we examine our systems for opportunities, we must ensure that our capacity to care is optimized throughout. Thus starting with the hospital department level, I offered some of the basic elements of Capacity Management for areas critical to care provision, the ED and Surgical Services. Each is interconnected with the other and with other components of the hospital, such as laboratory, environmental services,

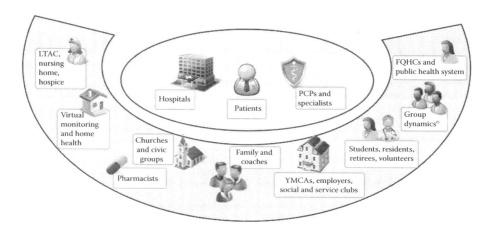

FIGURE 19.1   The community of care.

radiology, community physicians, etc. Each influences its upstream or downstream partners and neighbors, like cogs in a giant, dynamic, and ever-changing machine.

For the ED, we saw that what appeared to be chaos is actually part of discernable patterns that can be used for the improvement of resource utilization, care provision, and hospital-wide capacity improvement. I demonstrated several key processes and operational models that every hospital should be using, but which few even consider or understand. These are the basics of Capacity Management for the ED that must be accomplished before any other attempts at optimization are started. Without these, no amount of money or external consulting will help. Indeed, many of those high-dollar consultants offer less than these as solutions, leaving their hospital clients wanting and needing far more. Yet, these Blocking and Tackling elements are easy to grasp and require only some collaboration with inpatient units and open-minded physicians and staff for successful implementation.

Likewise, Surgical Services has its own elements of the "Blocking and Tackling of Capacity Management." Though Surgical Services has unique analytical require-ments, the proper use of Management/Industrial Engineers and data analysts will allow for quick and effective progress. Just as the key for the ED was shown to be the arrival patterns of patients, the key for Surgical Services and the OR is its surgical schedule. The optimization of the surgical schedule yields the optimization of capac-ity, and in turn allows for the optimization of any downstream inpatient capacity and a proper collaboration with other "source" areas of inpatient capacity demand, such as the ED and Direct Admissions.

As the patient moves from these "source" areas to the "inpatient side," inpatient units have their own "Blocking and Tackling" elements presented herein. By work-ing with the source areas of demand for their resources and care, inpatient units can better predict the workload and workflow required to maintain an effective amount of available capacity when it is needed, and manage the flow of patients into and out of their beds. These units must in turn get good collaboration from local physi-cians, both attendings and consultants/specialists, in order to maintain a level of control necessary to optimize their systems. Furthermore, these units can and must be highly proactive in the management of the patient discharge processes so as to eliminate delays and frustration, improve available capacity, and prevent upstream constraints. And to achieve this, of course, hospitals must collaborate effectively with external resources, from patient families to nursing homes to ambulance pro-viders in order to ensure that patients have a place to go when it is time to leave and return to the community.

This brings the book to a vision for a "next big thing": the CCN and a com-munity-wide model for care. As was described in my previous work, the CCN is an engineered, interconnected, and community-engaging care "subsystem" that simultaneously addresses cost, quality, access, system capacity, and gratification in our communities. CCNs align patients, clinicians, and broad arrays of precisely coordinated communal resources to support physicians' care strategies for patients. CCNs go beyond "care managers" and "patient navigators" by directly integrating myriad communal resources, such as churches, families, FQHCs, YMCAs, friends, pharmacies, community groups, students, volunteers, etc., into organized "Care Circles" that provide ongoing assistance and personalized care to their patients.

Care activities are coordinated and delegated with the guidance and oversight of physicians, while patient status and care activity updates are communicated back "upstream" to clinicians via an " SCN," (which could be thought of as a "Facebook for care management"). Via the SCN, Care Circle resources can coordinate their activities, collaborate on patient needs, exchange ideas to improve care, interact with patients, and engage in an ongoing dialogue with their patient's clinicians. This extends physicians' "reach" into the lives of their patients; expands their "capacity to care" to more patients; increases the number and quality of patient "touches"; and promotes and improves ongoing monitoring, compliance, and lifestyle management. Patients thus receive the right assistance and care at the right time via the most cost-effective, convenient, and familiar local resources.

As the CCN is integrated into the care strategies of patients coming out of the hospital and back into the community, our opportunities for Health Ownership, patient engagement, and reduced cost and resource demand are created. By fully and completely integrating more communal resources into the care of patients within the community, we expand our capacity to care and create an environment in which each member of the community becomes a potential care resource and an integral part of the community's health and wellness. This, in turn, promotes Health Ownership and aids in the long-term optimization of Population Health.

All this, of course, requires the right kind and amount of data. Data is the windshield that lets us see where we are going as well as the GPS navigator that tells us where to go next and how far is our destination. Data doesn't have to be complex or onerous. It only needs to be as informative as the task or job requires. Thus, data for the care of an elderly widow patient alone in her home may require little more than physician instructions for diet and a pill sorter. Of course, as electronic systems collect more and more patient-related clinical and demographic information, more data is available that might allow us to predict the likelihood of that elderly widow living alone having a heart attack in the next 3 years. Thus, as more data is made available and useful for the care of patients, we can do more as communities of care to further optimize outcomes and well-being.

Of course, there are other obstacles that will need to be addressed, such as the ever-present threat of trial lawyers and litigation against those resources aligned to help patients. We also have entrenched interests who might be protective of the work they do and the money they make, even if it doesn't match well with the future of our care delivery systems. And lastly we have a society that is not as cohesive as it once was, with communities divided along new and often strange lines. Yet, these other obstacles to optimization are merely hills to climb from which we can see vistas of a better future. Don't let these slow down your passion for innovation and creativity, else you will lose the chance to do something great for the patients and communities you serve.

SUMMARY

Bringing this all together … the hospital departments, the hospital's various inpatient units and ancillary services, external services and resources, data and the community of care writ large … is a seemingly onerous task, especially given that there are no real payment models to support it. Yet, even without a payment model completely appropriate for this communal care model, we can still begin to develop the infrastructure that will yield benefits now. And that is why this book was divided into the sections as it was.

Of course, ideally, we could step smoothly out of our current reality and into a business, operational, social, and reimbursement world that would allow for such systemic optimization to readily take place. More specifically, we might use a population health reimbursement model that localizes payment within a community or communities so as to allow for the kind of integration of services, collaboration of care, and payment for the human, technology, and physical plant resources required for the specific needs of a given subpopulation. Having no such model in place here in the United States (the ACO is only a step in this direction), we will need to imagine both what can be done within the current environment while thinking ahead to the next phases of care delivery. Don't let the reimbursement system or legal threats or community apathy stop you from innovating while the markets move slowly toward the inevitable. Change is coming. You might as well get out in front of it. Failing to do so may mean you get run over by it.

Take what I have given you here and do with it what you can and will. It may not solve all your problems, but it is my sincere hope that it will help you along your way.

Keep an open mind, a bold mission, and a positive attitude! I wish you all the best in your journey to optimized capacity to care in your community. May God bless your efforts!

Index